Fastrack Business Management

The Minute MBA

Fastrack Business Management
The Minute MBA

Charles Krause

Calumet Publishing
Milwaukee, Wisconsin

Editor: David K. Wright

Project Coordinator: Janice Hoffman

Graphic production: Montgomery Media, Inc.
Book design: Jennifer Zehren
Jacket design: Karyn Young, Karyn Young Designs

Printer: BookCrafters
Printed in the United States of America

Library of Congress Catalog Card Number
94-74605

ISBN 0-9644251-0-6

*To my wonderful clients who have provided rich experiences,
great learning, business challenges and a lot of fun along the way.
This is your book.*

Contents

Section III: Planning

Section IV: Financing the Business

Section V: Governance

Foreword

by Robert W. Lear

Way back, 10 or 15 years ago, it was possible to manage a business without having a lot of complicated problems.

You called on your customers and did as much as you could to keep them satisfied and paying their bills. When you needed more supplies, you ordered them from one of the salespeople who called on you. You bargained with your unions, groused about taxes, and periodically thought about putting together a strategic plan.

You knew and kept up fairly well with the technology of your industry. You read trade magazines, went to association meetings, and regularly sent your key people to training programs. You knew who your competitors were and where they were and what they were probably up to.

Gradually, and then with startling rapidity, things began to go faster and spread further and get more technical. New competition appeared from companies and even countries you had never heard of before. The computer, the mobile phone, the fax machine changed the way you obtained and arranged your information and the way you managed your people. Your people no longer wanted to stand in line and receive orders, they wanted to participate in all kinds of decisions.

The whole language of your business changed as you added Total Quality Improvement programs, Just-In-Time inventory management, Discounted Cash Flow procedures, foreign sourcing, empowerment, telemarketing, and PC's everywhere.

You surprised yourself by going to Korea, India, Brazil, and Portugal to seek out customers, alliances, suppliers. You found entirely new financing relationships and techniques for borrowing money. You began to hire different kinds of people who knew a lot about software programming, quantitative analysis, and Computer Assisted Design.

What happened to the orderly world of Peter Drucker and Laurence J. Peter and Tom Peters who advised us to work hard, avoid over-promoting our supervisors, put in a "skunk works" and we would be okay? Well, things changed and they changed faster than IBM and General Motors and

Pan Am and Russia did. And a lot of CEOs were left wondering where they should go for advice and help.

Fortunately, Charlie Krause is here with a calm, level-headed packet of sensible advice for business managers who are confused by the squadrons of new mentors with new toys and slogans.

Krause is a believer in the basic principles of running a business—hire good people, keep your costs down, know your customers, hold on to reliable suppliers, watch your cash, and keep looking around to see what's going on in the world you live in. But Krause also believes in adapting all of the modern tools available to make things better, faster, easier, cheaper. Above all, he is a devout believer in practical planning. Tritely, but sagely, he says over and over, "Plan your work and work your plan."

As a result, the advice he offers to business executives in this book is a distillation of what he has learned in more than 35 years on the Midwestern business scene. He has been a CEO of his own company, a director of several others, and, most importantly, a high-level consultant to over 100 diversified heartland businesses. Moreover, he is a student and a reader of business books and publications; he not only reads them, he thinks about what is said and how it applies to the many managerial situations he encounters in his daily work.

Quite properly, I believe, as Krause emphasizes the need for sustained planning and constant training in order to become and remain globally competitive, he recognizes the costs of such programs and tells how to derive tangible value from the time and money invested.

He is at his best, I think, when he offers examples of specific programs that have been put in and are working for people like Carl Just, manager of a Gehl Company plant in Lebanon, Pennsylvania, a plant that makes manure spreaders; and Robert Berger, CEO of the Johnsonville Sausage Company in Sheboygan, Wisconsin. What comes out is not academic theory; it is hands-on, practical stuff.

This is not a book for my MBAs at Columbia Business School. There is too much here about "boring" things like supervising a plant, training salespeople, putting in a cost-accounting system, and setting up a board of directors.

This is not a book to be picked up and read like a novel, either. It is effectively organized so that it can be digested a chapter at a time and revisited as a reference book.

I enjoyed reading it because it is *not* academic and *not* pedantic. I also liked it because it makes so much sense.

Robert W. Lear is Executive-in-Residence, Columbia School of Business; Former Chairman and CEO, F. & M. Schaefer Brewing Co.; Director, Crane Company, Cambrex Corporation, Medusa Corporation, Scudder Institutional Funds, Korea Fund, WICAT Systems, and Welsh, Carson, Anderson, Stowe Venture Capital Co. Recent Books: *Pressure Points* and *How to Turn an MBA into a CEO.* Regular Columnist: *Chief Executive Officer* magazine.

Introduction

If you are like most business executives, you want fast answers: "Give me the bottom line." *Fastrack Business Management* works hard to do just that without asking the reader to wade through hundreds of pages to capture the essence of an important concept.

This book's focus is on the new management skills and practices necessary for success in today's and tomorrow's challenging environment. It introduces several new concepts that are currently working for companies. You can choose to read the entire book sequentially or select first those areas that are the most interesting and relevant to you.

I tried to make this a practical, how-to-manage-a-business book with valuable, insightful information applicable to organizations of all sizes. This material results from 15 years of management consulting and 25 years of experience in corporate leadership positions. It covers all aspects of the management process. Each chapter incorporates case studies, quotations from key executives, and a nontechnical style of writing. The ideas presented are neither academic nor pedantic, but focus on what you as an executive can do to deliver results. The purpose is to enable you to quickly translate a concept into a profit-enhancing activity. There are no fancy sounding slogans or quick-fix approaches, but rather specific ideas that will make a difference for you—today and in the future.

My intention is not to provide an in-depth analysis of specific business issues, but rather to give directions, guidance, and thought-provoking ideas related to a wide range of business topics. Individual chapters will not provide all the answers but may inspire a reader to look with a new perspective at a problem or an area that needs improvement or change.

The book is organized into five sections—Managing the Business, Managing People, Planning, Financing the Business, and Governance. Each chapter contains specific advice on a topic along with examples of actual business experiences. Chapters are fairly brief and to the point so that they can be read in one sitting. An average chapter length is about 10 pages.

Running a business, division, or department should be exciting and fun. The problems and frustrations we all experience inevitably pass. It is the effective manager who can rise above the day-to-day problems, stand tall, and look out at what's happening in business, the economy, and society.

I sincerely hope this book adds to your enjoyment and success in the business world. As you gear up for the new century, use those ideas that make sense for you and will enhance your effectiveness as a manager and leader.

Good luck——have fun——make it happen!

Section I:
Managing the Business

Chapter 1

Recently, my faith in the future of American business was buoyed by a bunch of guys who sometimes smell like home-heating oil. Allow me to explain....

I have a client in Connecticut who requires my presence twice a year. The most recent trip was a success from his point of view and from mine, but several minor events and observations accumulated to make marked impressions upon me. In no particular order, they were:

• The unfillable plastic cup. As the attendant on my flight to Hartford eased the beverage cart down the aisle, a passenger requested orange juice. The attendant opened a new stack of 6-ounce, clear-plastic glasses, dropped in a couple of ice cubes, and began to pour. Almost as quickly as the juice left its container, it ran into the glass, out an invisible crack and down the attendant's arm.

"Look," she said to her fellow attendant. "Another batch of those glasses that leak." She poured the juice and ice into three more plastic glasses before she found one that didn't seep. Without additional fanfare, she and the cart moved off, down the aisle.

I was so awestruck by this little vignette that I let my coffee (in an apparently trusty coated-paper cup) grow cold. If the attendant knew these glasses had a history of leaking, why didn't she tell someone? More than that, why didn't she tell a number of people with the airline until she caught the attention of whoever buys the sievelike containers? A more pressing question may be, how can a manufacturer worthy of the name produce "another batch of those glasses that leak?"

• A habitat is not a home. My seatmate and I had a conversation that touched on many things and lasted much of the flight. We got on the subject of nonprofit organizations, and he told me about his unfortunate experience with Habitat for Humanity.

"I read in the paper that a Habitat group was forming in my hometown. I've always enjoyed carpentry, so I threw on some work clothes, grabbed my tool belt, and showed up for a meeting. The first meeting was devoted to how the organization would be structured, who would head which committees, and so on.

"I understood that administration had to be addressed. But at the second and third and fourth meetings, all we did was shuffle papers. I finally asked the chair if she would call me when the time came to do the work. That was in July. It's October now and I haven't heard from anyone. This is the time of year all of the for-profit builders wrap up their outside work. When do you think I'll hear something—when the wind chill is 40 below?"

- The president who thinks he's day labor. My client is a wonderful, well-educated man who began a successful manufacturing operation some 20 years ago in a one-car garage. He radiates that special something all entrepreneurs seem to share. His only problem is, he would rather be on the shop floor, breaking in a new employee or running a lathe, than attending to functions related to continued growth and prosperity.

I always leave him with dozens of small tasks that will keep him thinking about the company as a whole and in long-range terms. I can only ask so much of him, though, before he delegates it among his 60 employees and heads back out to run a forklift truck or inventory the tool crib. This person sees so many things so clearly that I wonder if we aren't all somewhat myopic when it comes to our own business. Stepping back for an overview evidently is much easier to do in theory, even if the firm's well-being should be threatened.

- Close, and not-so-close shaves. Because I always forget something, I had forgotten my safety razor and blades. Luckily, I discovered my error early the first evening and bought a packet of disposables.

Shaving with a disposable razor was a real eye-opener. The light plastic handle with the thin, silver blade embedded in one end gave me a vastly superior shave than did my non-disposable, made by the same company. I continued using the disposables for the next several weeks, discovering that blade-life was at least as good as with my regular razor.

How can a company sell a premium-priced product that doesn't work as well as its disposable brethren? If anything is ripe for testing at home, it has to be a razor and blades. Do all the folks in the home office wear beards, or is there another reason? I keep promising myself I'll write them a note about it.

• Names on a wall. I also called on a prospect in west suburban Boston. Arriving 90 minutes early, I killed time visiting Concord, the Revolutionary War site where the Minutemen fired "the shot heard round the world." Ironically, it wasn't the American Revolution that made an impression.

On a memorial to Concord's war dead, there is a single name under the words "Dominican Republic." Let's call him Adam Jones, Jr. I had forgotten that we lost anyone in the Dominican Republic in 1965. My eyes ran up the memorial, then stopped amid the dozen or so names of people killed during World War II. There was the name of Adam Jones. In a village the size of Concord, the two must have been son and father.

I chatted with my prospect and headed back to the Hartford airport, but I couldn't get the Joneses out of my mind. How can we believe we are making progress in areas such as planning and governance when we can't prevent the loss of a father and his son in separate far-flung wars?

• As long as we're eyeing the government, how long will it take us all to grab the reins of the deficit? Who will take a chance with a political career in order to solve a problem that, like overpopulation, grows geometrically, threatening to choke off the collective futures of our children and grandchildren?

Since this is being written during the first term of a new president from the 1960s generation, let me advance a cynical but necessary thought. During the campaign, the candidate said anything to get elected. Once in office, he planned to do what was needed rather than business as usual. Unfortunately, he lacks vision and the ability to lead. Government could demonstrate how to run a business, if it only would.

The Heating-Oil Guys

I thought about all the things I'd seen and heard as I neared the airport in my rented car. The radio was tuned to a local station, and an ad for a group of area businesspeople came on. The spot was done for several Hartford-area retailers of home heating oil.

The ad informed the listener that, while gas was a popular, efficient, and inexpensive way to heat a home, the cold and impersonal little line from the main would never replace the personal touch and responsiveness of the local home-heating-oil dealer. As winter winds swirled in the background, the ad noted that oil-truck drivers are neighbors and friends.

The ad made me as happy as I had been in days. Somewhere in Connecticut there is a group of people who know that their business is superior in only one way to the competition, and they are playing that trump card to advantage! Every time I feel I've witnessed or contributed to a business breakthrough, I hope I recall the well-bundled home-heating-oil truck drivers in Connecticut. They know something about advancing their product.

That oil company will succeed if it grabs hold of the new tools available while maintaining core values of friendly service and really caring about its customers.

Think of how the explosion of information has impacted the pricing strategy for the company. The price of oil these days is volatile, often moving from $.50 to $1.00 per barrel in a single day. Cold weather in the South, the threat of war in the Near East, an argument among oil ministers all impact the price our Connecticut delivery company pays.

It faces many new decisions. Should it hedge its inventory? How fast does it pass a price change through to its customers? How can it compete against efficient, faceless natural gas, in surplus today and perhaps in short supply in just a few months?

Business today is more complex and difficult to manage. Besides information availability, there's globalization, new competitors, the environmentalists, government regulations, constantly changing technologies, and new materials. At the same time, customers have higher expectations and will fight any price increases. It seems that each week some new challenge presents itself.

This book examines these changes and suggests strategies for emerging companies in today's more difficult environment. I am excited about how companies using these initiatives have changed. It's not just incremental gains that have occurred, but dramatic breakthroughs. Not only are product quality, deliveries, and productivity greatly improved, but the whole attitude infusing an organization changes. People look at their responsibilities differently, feel important, and see their contributions recognized. It's a win-win situation.

One word of caution. Change takes time. Initial suspicions at all levels must be overcome. It takes a while for the right people to be identified and trained. Processes and procedures must be altered. Customers and suppliers should be brought into the loop. Making it happen demands that top leadership has a fervent belief in what it is doing, some patience, and an insatiable demand for continuous progress. Leadership from the top is critical.

I truly believe that "more of the same isn't good enough anymore." However, in many ways, the new initiatives are not all that different from the way we did business in simpler times. People empowerment... work teams... just-in-time... these are today's words and phrases.

Yet how different are these concepts from the time when four or five people sat together in one room and ran the business? They would take orders, assemble the product, pack it, and send out an invoice. Just what a cell does today. And the team would stay until all of today's orders were out... just-in-time.

The principles for business success really have not changed all that much. Methods change, principles don't. It comes down to people serving people, whether that be in the corner tavern where the owner serves a group of steady customers, or a high-tech plant where the manager must attract, motivate, and empower a group of skilled technicians.

I can't wait for my next visit to Hartford. Will the home-heating-oil people still be playing their personal-service card against the stacked deck of pipeline gas? Or will they throw down a new trump such as more competitive pricing or some sort of you'll-never-run-out customer guarantee? Theirs is a risky business but, frankly, all businesses are risky. Meanwhile, we can learn from others, namely, the clients, friends, acquaintances, and authorities in the 30 chapters that follow.

These men and women have overcome challenges or learned from their failure to overcome a challenge. They've grown as they apply new techniques to businesses where "it's always been done this way." Not all of them are young or highly educated. Several might take offense if they were labeled progressive. Yet these CEOs and other managers share a common vision that cuts through the traditional layers and impediments to connect with the future. And since the future is where we're all headed, we might as well find the best way to go.

Personally, I can't wait!

Key Points:

○ Successful organizations will make use of available new tools while staying faithful to their core values of friendly service and concern for their customers.

○ Managing business today is more complex and difficult than ever before and the pace of change is accelerating. Customer expectations are high.

○ To be successful in the face of today's rapid changes, leadership from the top is critical.

○ Methods may be different but the principles for business success today still come down to "people serving people."

○ We can learn much about business success from others— from clients, friends and authorities in our field.

Chapter 2

Leadership, Setting the Tone, and Keeping Score with Money

Money is a good servant but a bad master.
 —French proverb

Watching the National Collegiate Athletic Association's annual men's basketball tournament, I was struck by the different ways in which leadership manifests itself among the great coaches. One looks funereal, sitting and shaking his head quietly as his team stretches its lead to 30 points. Another dashes up and down the sidelines from the tipoff, breaking into a sweat sooner than his players. Still another goes through an entire box of chalk as he envisions and then draws up plays to execute.

One of my favorite anecdotes about leadership concerns the Marquette University basketball team that won the NCAA tourney in 1977. Al McGuire was the head coach and Hank Raymond was an assistant. During timeouts with the score close late in a vital game, McGuire would take on a faraway look as he narrated incredible verbal panoramas for his players, comparing them to outnumbered Serbs facing the Ottoman Empire, or to Finns repulsing the Soviet Army. Meanwhile, Raymond would have seen an opportunity created by an opponent's weakness. He would draw a play on the chalkboard, tap a forward on the shoulder, point to the board, and say, "Run this route on the base line and look for a quick bounce-pass from the center."

Who can argue with this—or any other—method if the goal is envisioned and achieved? Like coaching, there is no single, sure-fire, superior method of leadership in corporate America. But all great leaders enjoy superior results because they can step back and foresee a strategic vision. Let's talk about them....

Al McGuire and Hank Raymond were making constructive change happen by approaching the same strategic vision from two different angles. McGuire offered almost messianic leadership; Raymond made sure the key people knew the plan to implement. Marquette's 1977 team had less raw talent than several other squads in that tournament. But the quality of leadership provided Marquette with a goal and a sense of purpose that was second to none. Just ask 1977 runnerup, Dean

Smith, whose strategic vision did not focus for the University of North Carolina until five years later against Georgetown.

We all know good managers. They are organized and run their plants well. Salespeople meet their call-frequencies and results are within a few percentage points of projections. Everything is in order. People march to the drumbeat of the plan as they generate sales, control margins, and manage expenses. Things go well for years, even decades, until one day the market changes. Suddenly, the organization does not have the resiliency or the resources to react.

Recognizing Opportunity

Compare such operations to ones where a new chief executive officer, within two or three years, revamps a business, its product, and image. We aren't talking about individuals who, through charisma and forceful leadership techniques, make a difference. We are referring instead to men and women who have the ability to recognize untapped resources and the imagination and creativity to redirect such resources to markets of opportunity.

Nowadays, we have a tendency to equate opportunities with high technology. However, opportunities extend far beyond computers and electronics. What about a metalworking company in the business of cutting, stamping, soldering, and assembling? At one such company, a leader with strategic vision anticipated the physical fitness trend and moved the company into production of rowing machines, stationary bicycles, and home gymnasiums. Results were spectacular.

The same thing has happened at Reebok International, the Avon, Massachusetts, tennis shoe manufacturer. Its sales have grown from $50 million to more than $1 billion in just a few years. Special-use athletic footwear, ancillary products, and effective promotion did it. There are a lot of people out there who believe they can perform step aerobics only in specialized Reebok shoes, hopping rhythmically on and off a Reebok-marketed step. That is anticipating a trend and then making yourself an indispensable part of it.

The food industry is hopping on the bandwagon today, but what about those who pioneered low-calorie, low-fat, low-sodium foods? It was tough sledding at first, but recent gains have been dramatic. The CEOs of such companies had strategic vision and the ability to mobilize their organizations behind an idea.

There are similar stories here in southeastern Wisconsin. Several years ago, a company housed in a loft on the southwest side of Milwaukee had annual sales of less than $100,000. The founder's vision was to use electronics to produce programmable message displays. First sold to commercial and retail markets, electronic boards today are incorporated into systems where they report machine breakdowns on automated production lines.

Another company supplied components to the agricultural market. Executives there saw 60 percent of their market disappear as original-equipment sales plummeted. The CEO looked beyond the traditional market and repositioned the company to serve faster-growing, more diversified markets.

What does it take to be a leader these days? If leadership has strategic vision, consider these attributes:

• **Customer-oriented.** Visionary leaders are out in the field seeing the customers and finding out what they think of the company's product or service.

• **Aloof.** Visionary leadership means standing a bit above the fray and refusing to get buried in the minutiae of daily activity. It isn't snobbery, that's social aloofness. Rather, it's knowing what doesn't pertain and ignoring it in order to get the job done.

• **Involved.** The visionary leader devotes enough time to outside activities that provide exposure to emerging trends. The person I'm talking about is miles wide and at least an inch or two deep on any subject you'd care to name. How else to prevent being blindsided by social or cultural change or acts of God? Look at what happened with the El Niño current in the Pacific Ocean and its effect on North America's winter fruit and vegetable prices.

• **People-sensitive.** The true leader spends a lot of time talking to people, learning about their skills, interests, and ideas for the company. The leader is bright enough to seek and recognize vision in others.

• **Action-oriented.** A leader with strategic vision gets things done. The methodology used is less important than having the organization respond with interest, commitment, and enthusiasm. The determined, low-key individual can be as effective as the charismatic flag-waver.

Flying Low

There was a time when, even as a CEO, I wondered if any single leader really could influence a company of any size. Then, a casual conversation a few years ago with an old friend altered my thinking. We were waiting for the same flight when the subject of good and bad airlines came up. We named our own favorites, which happened to be different, before turning to the subject of the worst.

Simultaneously, we blurted out, "Eastern!"

"Why do you think Eastern is so much worse than any of the others?" I asked. "Is it that everyone hates the same wiggly piece of chicken served on every meal flight? Or is it the flight attendant, tired and frustrated after a day of inadequate support, who snaps at a passenger who is in turn irate after still another delay?"

"It's the CEO," said my friend. "I have to think that, in a service business, even a large one with the capital commitment needed to fly planes, the CEO sets the tone for the entire company. And if he or she fails to set the tone, why is that person being paid an enormous sum of money?"

"So in a manufacturing business, there is less tone to set?"

"That's not what I said. What I'm saying is that Frank Borman may have been a great astronaut but now that he heads Eastern, the bad food, disinterested help, and dirty planes tell me his mind these days is on other things. Perhaps he's out to show the union he's the boss. I don't know. But I do know that Eastern's years are numbered."

In Eastern's defense, other airlines have bitten the dust following deregulation. But the fact that a frequent business traveler surveyed a huge company and saw bad leadership indicates the importance of the way a corporation is led. I wonder how often Mr. Borman, or his successor, walked past his employees and into his office caught up in his own thoughts. Just showing up and failing to acknowledge one's valued people can infect the entire organization with gloom, if not downright apprehension.

Reading so much into one person's attitude or conduct hardly is justified, but it happens every day. How many people feel a quiver when they see a long meeting take place behind closed doors? The boss may have no problem at all, or be occupied with a purely personal matter. Still, one of the qualities of an effective leader is the ability to exude confidence and enthusiasm. When things are going wrong, the need for positive leadership is even more critical.

Recently, Warren Bennis, a professor at the University of Southern California School of Business Administration, surveyed 60 chief executives and 30 leaders in government, cultural institutions, and foundations. He was searching for the common leadership characteristics possessed by the top executives in these organizations and was able to identify five overriding qualities. It's interesting to try to compare oneself — objectively — against the "ideal" leader.

Five Crucial Qualities

The first key characteristic Bennis uncovered is **"compelling vision."** Successful leaders, he found, know where they want their organizations to go. There is a clarity to their thought processes, and all their actions support that vision. None find it easy to identify or articulate a definition for the future of an organization. However, when it is achieved, the focus will be clear, and the energies and capabilities of the entity can be targeted on attaining the vision.

The second characteristic he identified is a **"flair for communication."** Most everyone would include communication skills as a critical attribute in an effective leader. These skills extend, however, beyond formal speeches or written presentations. What any leader wants to impart also can be conveyed convincingly and enthusiastically in personal conversation and through the use of imagery that captures the imagination of the listener. How many times does one see an individual commanding and holding the attention of a group in the midst of a large and noisy gathering? It's a difficult skill to attain, and it can't be counterfeited. But the ability to make a message clear, understandable, and interesting is one of the strongest motivational assets of the successful leader.

"Constancy" is the third important characteristic identified in the study. Persistence, coherence, and continuity all are evidenced in the actions of successful leaders, and these qualities are prized highly by fellow workers. They see these traits in a single, desperately needed trait — reliability. In fact, people generally prefer to work in an atmosphere where they are sure "where the boss is coming from," even when they disagree with that position. Most find uncertainty counterproductive and unsettling.

The fourth attribute of the successful leader is **"positive self-regard."** This isn't to be confused with egotism. With positive self-regard, leaders know what they can do well, and they build on their strengths. With positive self-regard goes the ability to know what tasks or projects to delegate, recognizing they can be carried out more effectively by someone else. Know thyself and thy strengths are good self-imposed commandments.

Finally, Professor Bennis identified what he calls the **"Wallenda Factor."** The Wallendas are the famous family of acrobats who performed worldwide for the Ringling Bros., Barnum & Bailey Circus. More recently, they have performed daring tightrope stunts in baseball stadiums and other unusual locations. For years, Carl Wallenda never considered the possibility of falling, but, several months before a fatal plunge from a high wire, he had begun to think about it. Wallenda, his family believes, actually kept himself from falling all those years by refusing to think about it.

The analogy applies to successful leaders. They do not recognize the possibility of failure. They do, however, constantly evaluate the positive and negative forces that are always at work. They examine problems and react to them with solutions that "manage" difficult situations. They don't procrastinate or hope adversity will disappear of its own accord. They want to hear bad news promptly and know how to handle it constructively. Like Carl Wallenda, leaders do not consider failure.

Objective self-evaluation in terms of these characteristics is a taxing exercise, but if leadership traits can be developed and employed with sincerity, they can be very productive. The sense of confidence and directed power real leaders possess and communicate will instill confidence in a subordinate group. With trustworthy, credible leadership, almost anything is possible. The great people of history, all of whom possessed these attributes, demonstrated that one person can move entire nations to greatness. Think about that the next time you wonder if an executive influences the tone of a corporation. Good leaders, through committed and inspired people, make success happen.

Rewarding Success

Cynics point out that democracy is the worst possible political system, but no one has come up with a better system so far. The same can be said of rewarding CEO success in a monetary way. The ultimate reward for running a company well is a well-run company. But the directors must show their support of the boss, and money is one way to do it. Past a certain point, money and perks become counterproductive and subject to harsh criticism. Potential regulation of executive compensation through limits on tax deductions came about because of excessive pay for some high-visibility CEOs.

I've met several CEOs who discovered what children have always known: the chase is at least as satisfying as the capture. There are a number of successful executives out there who would rather be put in charge of a foundering company ripe for rescue than receive another stock option or an added bonus.

Where a lot of companies, large or small, fail is that they do not connect CEO performance to CEO compensation. The American public en masse saw the U.S. executives who accompanied President Bush on a trade mission to Japan in 1991 as spoiled and sputtering compared with their lower-paid, stunningly successful Japanese counterparts. *Business Week,* in its March 30, 1992, cover story, suggested the following remedies:

• Limit the boss's salary base to $1 million a year. Every cent over that should be paid only when the CEO meets tough performance targets.

• Give boards discretion to reward improvement in such key areas as quality, customer satisfaction, and management development.

• Charge stock options, which do have a value, against earnings.

• Price large option grants at a premium, so shareholders benefit before executives.

• Encourage stock ownership among executives.

Until we come up with a better system, such as an executive National Honor Society, money will have to do. The CEO of Coca-Cola, Roberto Goizueta, recently was handed approximately $80 million in company stock. By buying up independently owned Coca-Cola bottling plants, forming a separate corporation with them, and then selling them as franchises, he has realized an astonishing amount of money for the corporation quite apart from anything related to retail sales of the soft drink. In fact, under his leadership, Coca-Cola stock has increased in value 14-fold in the last 10 years. Who's to say the decisions he made based on his goals and vision weren't worth what he was paid?

Key Points:

○ While there are many kinds of effective leaders, the most successful ones have a strategic vision of the future.

○ Successful companies recognize a trend and then make themselves an indispensable part of that trend.

○ Visionary leaders are close to their customers. They stand above the fray of daily activities, are open to new trends, sensitive to people, and get things done.

○ The most successful leaders today share five key qualities: compelling vision; a flair for communication; reliability; positive self-regard; and a failure to consider the possibility of failure.

○ Company performance should be tied directly to CEO compensation.

Chapter 3

What is corporate culture and what makes it more than just another faddish business topic?

Corporate culture has been defined as "the way we do things around here," as "what keeps the herd moving west," and, more precisely, as "what makes meaning for people."

Every company, large or small, yours or mine or the competition's, has its own culture. The subject was discussed in depth here in Milwaukee a while ago by senior officers of some of America's largest corporations. They spent a full day studying the ways corporate culture can enhance or impede their ability to change behavioral attitudes and results. Serious consideration of corporate culture is a long-overdue recognition of what is really going on in every company.

The keynote speaker at this meeting was Terrence Deal, who has written several books and numerous articles on the subject. His latest is *Modern Approaches to Understanding and Managing Organizations.* He has served as a consultant with many major corporations including American Telephone & Telegraph, Anheuser-Busch, IBM, and Kimberly-Clark. Deal is one of the new breed of young, articulate academicians who are helping managers of major corporations to better understand their organizations and then to use that insight to bring about positive change.

Culture consists of shared values and beliefs that define the essential character of an institution and shape its behavior. Normally, where strong cultures exist, they are supported by a rich tradition and well-entrenched principles, many traceable to the founders.

These values are established and perpetuated by corporate "heroes." They are not necessarily professional managers but are the creators of new ideas who will take risks and are obsessively tenacious in their beliefs. Historically, they are the Don Quixotes, the trailblazers, the legends, the characters.

I can think of several. Charles Percy, the former Illinois senator, came out of graduate school in the '50s with his MBA and was hired by Bell & Howell. He quickly and correctly sized up the corporate organization and told his superiors they could best save money by eliminating jobs like the one for which he had been hired. This and a few other actions and observations propelled Percy into Bell & Howell's chief executive suite almost overnight.

Another example involves the famous Lockheed "skunkworks." This oversize shed at one time or another housed every harebrained scheme and wild-eyed engineer in Lockheed history. The quality and quantity of space-age technology that came out of the skunkworks dates from World War II and is staggering. Many skunkworks alumni have gone on to become manufacturers of everything from titanium-framed mountain bicycles to movie-studio special-effects equipment. To this day, Southern California's racing-car builders, custom-boat makers and amateur-aircraft designers rifle the dumpster used by Lockheed's most innovative department for bits of exotic metals and blueprints of strange designs.

Perhaps the ultimate example of a business legend is the late Sam Walton. Sam and his family created an incredible retail empire built on openness, honesty, thrift, and a willingness to forgo personal comfort in the early days in order to open one more outlet. The Walton children gave Dad their newspaper-route money and he gave them stock. That stock today is worth thousands of times its original value. Contemporary Wal-Mart employees really feel as if they are part of an extended family and that someone is looking out for their fiscal and personal well-being. That's quite an accomplishment.

One of Deal's favorite examples involves 3M. Years ago, the company refused to accept clear tape as a viable new-product concept. The project was killed, but the inventor persisted despite warnings to abandon the idea and get back to his assigned work. When he wouldn't, he was fired. But, typical of this breed, he refused to leave. Finally, someone at 3M listened and recognized the value of that tenacity, if not the idea. The inventor was permitted to work in isolation and develop his product. Thus Scotch-brand tape was born and a new hero joined the 3M legend.

The same story was repeated more recently with Post-its, the small yellow paper squares backed with adhesive that we see and use everywhere. The 3M market research "experts" insisted there was no market for such a product. This inventor also persisted, sending samples to secretaries of the chief executive officers of the Fortune 500. Those secretaries quickly let 3M know that this was, indeed, a valid product.

Building on Developed Values

Company heroes assume different roles. Successful organizations find ways to build on the values they develop and reward people who respond to them. The pink cars of Mary Kay Cosmetics are a good example. Highly visible signs of achievement, these automobiles broadcast the message that anyone dedicated and willing can earn one.

Corporate cultures also contain rituals or routines that bind people together and set standards and limits of acceptable conduct and behavior. When these rituals are changed, it disrupts the organization because they are viewed as positive influences in the workplace. Corporate rituals take the form of ceremonies or special events—parties surrounding retirements or promotions, methods of recognizing superior performance such as the president's cup for outstanding sales, the plaque for quality control. These rituals, Deal points out, are often forgotten management tools.

No one I know of has more or better rituals than Harry Quadracci, the CEO of Quad Graphics. This immensely successful southeastern Wisconsin printer of many national magazines has parties for himself and for his employees where guests may be entertained by an elephant or a helicopter or an elephant being lifted by a helicopter, for all I know. The Quad Graphics messages are several: It's a great place to work, the benefits are terrific, the owner is benevolent, hard work is rewarded in many innovative ways, there's a time to work and a time to play, etc.

Corporate culture doesn't always need a three-ring circus or an oompah band. Often, a pleasant personnel decision can make waves. For example, many companies give their people Friday afternoons off in the summer. They are able to maintain production levels by tacking on an hour to each of the four preceding workdays. No one seems to mind putting in a nine-hour day in exchange for an early start to the weekend. McDonald's, Inc., and others also make Fridays casual-clothing days. Besides giving some relief to wardrobe budgets, casual Fridays help to humanize officers in the eyes of the troops.

In time, a kind of mythology emerges about what a company really is, with wonderful stories to support it. They are spread and perpetuated by a cultural network, present in every company. The members of this network—whom Deal defines as the priests, storytellers, gossips, whisperers, spies, dummies, and cabals— are the carriers of a company's culture. They perpetuate the memory of "our founder, good old Al," despite the fact that he may have had the disposition of a grizzly bear and died 20 years ago.

If you doubt the existence of such a web in your company, test the system. Drop a bit of "confidential" information into the right ear and see how long before it is "confidentially" reported back to you. With a strong cultural network, it will travel faster than by jungle drums or smoke signals. Just don't confuse corporate culture with office politics. Many a worthwhile employee has walked away from an office because he or she rightly feared that the next promotion would go to the person who most often complimented the boss's tie. Office politics is the soft white underbelly of business, whereas corporate culture can be the very soul.

The cultural network and the embedded tradition of the corporation can be barriers to positive change. Deal notes that people become attached to a culture and that change creates ambiguity—something most individuals don't want to face. The best example I know of is a company that has just merged with or been acquired by another. Employees walk around on eggshells as they try to detect the first signs of change in—what? The level of activity? The number of notations on their paycheck stub? The new guy no one knows in the corner office? To achieve change while recognizing the importance of culture, Deal suggests looking at the new in terms of underlying values, heroes, ceremonies, and rituals, and defining and communicating change within that framework. In other words, spend an evening or two at the library studying the recent history of your new partners.

The Transition Ritual

For deep-seated change to be effective, an organization must go through what Deal calls a "transition ritual." There is a mourning for the old ("We weren't so bad, were we?"), followed by the wake, the funeral, and, eventually, the resurrection ("We really *have* turned things around, haven't we?"). Every fundamental change must go through this ceremony before an organization can put unwanted tradition to rest and move ahead.

When change is done right, managers pay attention to and build on the good elements in the structure of the organization—its skills, its politics, and also its culture. Suppose you want to motivate your sales staff. What does it say if you double, even triple, the number of annual awards? Simply that instead of 10 winners, there are 30 who deserve that recognition. What kind of message do you send when eligibility for the bonus program based on profits encompasses two or three additional staff levels?

Maybe greatness will be thrust upon people. A senior manager at Chrysler Corporation, following the Iacocca-led (and government-assisted) return from the brink of bankruptcy in the early 1980s, said there was one strong undercurrent at company headquarters. "A lot of people walking around here, ordinary-looking people, are heroes," he said, almost misty-eyed. "They know who they are."

In my consulting assignments, it isn't difficult to identify the culture of a corporation and spot barriers to change. It is important to view culture not as a negative but as a building block. While the old ways in time change, there are always underlying values that can provide a springboard and lifeline as the organization moves forward.

Several years ago, I worked with a high-tech company that had a number of young, outspoken, and talented engineers on its staff. When the economy slowed, a tension developed between the creative engineers and those anxious to install more "efficient" work rules and performance standards. The conflict was resolved through a natural process of change. Some of the traditional influences left of their own accord. A number of uninvolved shareholders were bought out, and those who came up from the engineering side recognized their responsibility to deliver an acceptable level of profitability.

A strong board of directors helped this process and encouraged management to give young engineers increased profit responsibility. A product-manager concept emerged, and with it, greater accountability and responsiveness to the marketplace. It also helped maintain an atmosphere where technical innovation flourished and younger people had a chance to run with their ideas. There has been a natural harmonizing of legitimate organizational needs. Results in terms of spotting market trends, technical innovation, resource development, and financial success have been completely positive.

Levels Of Culture

It should be pointed out here that corporate culture can have more than one level. John Kotter, a Harvard University Business School professor, notes that there are visible and invisible levels of company culture. Visible levels might include whether there is a formal or informal dress code, or whether all employees wear badges at all times on the property. Invisible levels could include phenomena such as the values shared by members of a team, even as team membership changes. In some companies, for example, people care very deeply about money. In others, technical innovation or customer satisfaction may be more highly prized.

Look at your own organization and try to define, preferably on paper, what its underlying values are and how they have been ritualized and perpetuated by your people. It shouldn't take many words to capture its essence. This exercise will answer three questions: Is the culture still valid? What are its positive values? How can they be used to support the changes you need for continued success?

Until you define your culture, you will have a hard time coming up with those answers. Let's look at some widely differing examples. If you insist that prospective employees and prospective suppliers submit to drug testing, you are sending a strong message. If you want the message to stick, make sure you're prudent about alcohol, too. If you have a company picnic and make a big deal out of inviting families, think about liberalizing maternity leave, which also has a positive effect on families, especially the ones just getting started. Are you a good corporate citizen? Then give your key people time off to serve on nonprofit boards.

It's even more important to be consistent where line decisions enter the picture. Do you believe in quality? If so, does every employee have the power to stop an apparently faulty product in its tracks? Do you ship on time? If so, can any supervisor authorize overtime to get a product to the customer as promised? Are you customer-driven? If so, you and your marketers and engineers know that a product will sell before the first production model rolls off the assembly line.

Where Are You Headed?

If you're running a new business, all this talk of corporate culture may be confusing. Why, you may ask, should we ponder corporate culture when everyone gives 100 percent every day and we have a great company? My rejoinder is, a great company isn't an end in itself; where are you going with your great company? To find that answer, and to nudge you down the road toward your own corporate culture, think about what your mission is. Once you've decided, express it in a few words.

The Quill Corporation, a family-owned office-supply firm in suburban Chicago, has as its mission the creation of "an atmosphere in which people can develop to their fullest potential." Quill has a "two-way bill of rights" that spells out what is expected of employees and what employees should expect of the owners. Its mission statement sets the tone for the whole company. The delineated rights bill not only gives everyone standards but also is itself a crucial piece of Quill's corporate culture. Your motives may not be quite so noble as Quill's, but I'm guessing an introspective look will turn up similar goals.

Here's more food for thought. Richard P. Cooley, chairman and CEO of Seafirst Corporation, recently gave a meaningful speech before a major human-resource management conference in California. He said that the corporate culture of his shipping firm is based on customer service. "You have to be better today than you had to be yesterday." Serving customers at Seafirst includes getting to know local businesses and consumers first hand; getting involved in the community; selling as an inseparable part of corporate culture, not something that is here today and gone tomorrow. Other requirements include

retaining the customer; being the low-cost producer; and hiring, training, and keeping good employees.

Those are ambitious demands. If you incorporate them
into your own business, your status as a legend, as an inseparable part of the corporate culture, will be guaranteed.

Key Points:

○ Every company has its own corporate culture—shared
values and beliefs that define its character and shape its
behavior.

○ Company heroes who develop new ideas and values
should be rewarded.

○ The cultural network of a company can be a boon or a
barrier to positive change.

○ For deep-seated change to be effective, organizations
must undergo a transition ritual where the old traditions
become the springboard to new values.

○ In analyzing your corporate culture, be aware of both its
visible and invisible levels.

○ Establishing a mission statement is a first step in creating
a corporate culture to set the tone for your company.

Chapter 4

Robert Townsend's *Up the Organization* was written in 1970. Should you pick it up today, you might find some of his contentions fairly familiar and obvious. That's unfortunate, because Townsend's book—and its sequel, *Further Up the Organization*—did to corporate structure what a Cecil Fielder line drive does to outfield fences. Townsend rifled innumerable dents into the excessively rigid framework that is corporate structure. Yet corporate structure still stands. How come?

If patriotism is the refuge of the scoundrel, rigid organizational structure is the hiding place of the old-fashioned, inflexible, or excessively satisfied administrator. How many people do you know who, when their point of view is at risk, their thinking is skewed, or they fear a decision, automatically call a meeting? Or take refuge behind company policy? Today, management cannot afford to give an administrator a private fiefdom, let alone a chance to toy with a personal pyramid of bureaucracy.

Robert Townsend saw this earlier than the rest of us. He had, after all, served such major corporations as 20th Century-Fox and American Express before revitalizing and then selling Avis Rent-A-Car. I'm guessing that his book was produced almost spontaneously, the result of years of impatience created by wasted time and effort adhering to rigid organizational dictates. We've all been victims of rigidity; I'd like here to address several organizational problems and their solutions. I'll try to be a little less, well, brassy, than Townsend, who is nevertheless one of the most forthright business thinkers this country has produced.

The reason Townsend's thoughts may sound dated is that they have been popularized: everyone agrees with him. We can look at America's leading companies and see mirror images of what Townsend dismantled at Avis. General Motors, IBM, Sears—these corporate stalwarts seemed rudderless in the late 1980s and early 1990s. There's a surprising amount of agreement on the cause.

The many functions at such large corporations—accounting, engineering, finance, human resources, marketing, manufacturing, and more—have become isolated from each other and from the individual purposes of the corporations. A hierarchy develops within each major function that inhibits, rather than facilitates, what that corporation does. Besides separating all of the auditors from all of the engineers from all of the marketers, this so-called "functional-silo syndrome" loses sight of the customer and the products or services the company delivers.

Reaching Critical Mass

Some may point out that we can still get by with a vast and unwieldy governmental bureaucracy. But the truth is, an institution—any institution—obsessed with and controlled by its own structure will never survive. As this is being written, the federal government is reaching critical organizational mass. We are all looking for federal leadership that will make hard, perhaps unpopular, short-range and long-term decisions for eventual and ultimate benefit to our children and grandchildren. Corporations all over the country go through this. Some find the leadership necessary to dismantle the outmoded organization, and some fail to survive organizational implosion.

Leadership is needed to dismantle the great organizational frameworks that served us so well for the 30 years that followed World War II. Those three decades will be most accurately remembered, I think, not as a time when America was preeminent, but as a period when the country had little or no manufacturing competition. Without competition, our industries looked for things to do. They began to toy with and inflate organizational structure, a pastime that has cost us dearly, especially now that Japan and all of Europe compete with us for global markets.

Bob Townsend has a sharp eye for the bloat created during those years. He points to the cadre of corporate public relations people, for example, and bluntly advises their elimination. The craft of public relations, he contends, is really just being open and honest and pleasing the customer. "We called in the top 10 or so people in the company and the telephone operators and told them they were the PR department," he says of his Avis days. "The telephone operators were given the home phones of the 10 people and asked to find one of them if any of the working press called with a question."

Improving the organization is not just about job elimination. In fact, it has more to do with people, and the way in which they are treated, than does even the most secure PR job. Townsend advises his readers to turn first to his chapter on people. He tells them there that it's more important that people be put to productive use than that the "right" people are hired. Productivity and depth of management will come if the organizational structure is more nearly horizontal than vertical.

What do we mean by a horizontal organization? For centuries, institutions such as government, church, and school operated pyramidically, to use an awkward word. The only structure that made sense was a single, absolute leader. A few people passed on the leader's edicts to more people, who in turn barked the orders to more, and so on down the line. The broad base of the pyramid consisted of the people closest to the actual, physical work. Anyone can look at such a structure and see that the leader in the scheme is furthest from the action. Conversely, those with personal knowledge of the organization's daily operations are the most numerous but also are utterly powerless.

Today, we have an unprecedented opportunity to control our collective, corporate destinies, and part of the way to do this is to organize horizontally. The focus for any company looking to develop a product or service is teamwork—adding employees, customers, and key suppliers to the decision-making process. Modern teams are *in*clusive, not *ex*clusive. They include so many strata that the traditional organization chart becomes meaningless.

Let's take development of the new, high-performance Dodge Viper from Chrysler as an example. Do you think the $50,000 sports car would have seen the light of day without Chrysler finding out first if there was a market for this kind of vehicle? Once the market was apparent, Lee Iacocca put together a diverse team of 85 employees with real decision-making authority. With strong and continuous support from management and with the inclusion of new technologies and flexible suppliers, the car came off the production line in three years instead of the normal five- to six-year development cycle.

This is vital from the standpoint that the consumer wants and needs change. The shorter the period between input from consumer focus groups and actual production, the more successful the product is likely to be. Let's think of a service example.... Your research indicated several years ago that cellular-telephone networks would be viable. This concept, which would compete with everyone from AT&T to GTE, took six years to get up and running. Meanwhile, many other service providers had entered the market and captured customers as the cost of the phones declined from $1,000 to $100. Had you put your cellular network in place quickly, you might not have been the one who had to call it quits.

Why Go Horizontal?

Getting to the market quickly isn't the only advantage of a horizontal organization. Let's tick off other benefits of horizontal thinking:

• **Your people will be empowered.** Everyone from the receptionist to the laborer loading semitrailers full of product will be making meaningful decisions as part of a team. Their judgment is at least as good as yours because they have been trained and they know their own jobs better than anyone else in the company. Parameters is a $2 word, but it applies here, since every employee will know the parameters of his or her position—and who to consult or where to turn when a decision requires knowledge outside the usual boundaries.

• **Your product will improve.** If your employees know what they are to do, understand how to do it, and are a part of the process—and if supplied parts meet rigid standards—your product will be world-class competitive. You've assured success by eliminating the winding avenues failure takes. Yes, there will be compromises. For example, a manufacturer of welding rods may find that the alloy that works best for the product is no longer available. He or she will have to search for a supplier offering the best alloy still on the market. If there is demand for the rods, customers will continue to buy the best there is.

• **Your costs will go down.** Why? Because everyone will know that simpler is better, and simpler always is less expensive. Why create a production line if 20 percent of the finished products have to be reworked? Won't you be better off with fewer steps, slower production, and zero defects? You will save money, too, by being told by your confident, empowered people that some operations are done better by subcontractors. Ford Motor Company has become more and more an assembler and less and less a manufacturer. Its quality and sales have risen along with the number of outsourced goods it uses.

• **Your mental health and the mental health of your employees will improve.** A horizontal organization is an open organization. Everyone knows that everyone else is about the business of maximizing productivity. Doors stay open. Research and development, which may at times require the utmost secrecy, can be done in a separate building. But since your company has greatly reduced the span between discovery and production, you've further reduced the possibility of a security leak.

• **Concurrent engineering will take place.** While R&D is perfecting the new widget, engineering is perfecting the fixtures that will help make it. Packaging and shipping are working to ensure that it will reach the end user in the best possible condition. Why will all this happen simultaneously? Because there are no barriers between or among people with all these talents at work on the project. The end result is a design for manufacturability that will gratify everyone with its straightforward purpose.

Other benefits will accrue, but among the intangibles are the prestige and mutual respect that a horizontal organization will generate. In a traditional pyramid, no one in marketing has any idea what an industrial engineer or a millwright does. Your staff and line personnel will come away from a project with an understanding of your company that the very best MBA program could not teach. "You should see this guy from the mill," I can almost hear a market-research analyst say to his or her spouse. "The guy has no research experience whatsoever, but he looked at the product and knew right away no one would buy it until we made the locking mechanism a one-hand operation."

From Pyramid To Great Plains

If you are by now convinced that fully integrated, horizontal management is the way to go, how does your company adopt it? That question is being faced by Sears, General Motors, and other troubled companies at this very moment. You—and they—need to obliterate any kind of labor-management line forever, since anyone in your organization may come up with the manufacturing innovation or assembly mechanism that will give you a competitive edge.

Robert Townsend believes one way to go about this is to put everybody, including the janitor, on salary. He further believes that everyone should have the same benefits package and that perks such as reserved executive parking, company planes, and executive dining rooms should be eliminated. Humane beneath his leathery exterior, he wants workers' locker rooms scrupulously clean, air-conditioned and in the executive building, right alongside the (modest) offices of all the executives.

The former Avis wizard has a number of related suggestions. He advocates offering the employees stock, but he's dead set against giving them shares in the company without payment. If they are handed shares, even as a bonus, they will subconsciously think that the stock—and perhaps the company—isn't worth much. Besides, if employees know they are in for a bonus, they are thinking in terms of what they will do with the cash received. *Don't* disappoint them. *Do* offer shares of stock without any sort of handling or brokerage fees, and let them know when big blocks of the stock move and the effect it may have on their holdings.

Several companies in Wisconsin would agree with Townsend's views. Northwestern Mutual Life Insurance, here in Milwaukee, has always prepared a free, hot lunch for all of its employees. Oshkosh Truck Corporation executives are hard to spot in the plant because they wear sweaters or open shirts. More importantly, they post safety rules prominently and point out to a visitor that assemblers can't be expected to wear their shatterproof lenses if an executive strolls through the plant without eye protection. This will sound terribly egalitarian to middle-aged middle managers. They may require special attention.

How to prepare a veteran middle manager for the horizontal organization? Actually, it's easier than you may think, because you are opening lines of communication rather than closing them. If you take Townsend's advice and force the managers to rid themselves of their assistants and sub-assistants, do it gently and incrementally. Do it in such a way that the managers won't feel as if their feet have been cut out from under them, and in such a way that the assistants won't suddenly feel they have no value. The most humane method is enhanced incentive to retire early, or a well-thought-out retraining program. But do it.

Receptivity

Line management, on the other hand, will be jubilant. They're perfectly capable of picking up most of the chores done for them by the staff, whom they've always suspected of mysticism. In exchange, they will gleefully help you pitch the rigid policy manual, which went out the window anyway whenever a real crisis occurred on the line. But don't take my word for it—here are a couple of thoughts from my clients.

"Reorganizing this place saves money on a daily basis," one reports. "We never order more than we need, and new-product lead times have dropped dramatically. I'm a softball player, and I would compare it to a high-pressure, league tournament game versus a pickup game with friends. You play just as hard with your buddies, maybe even harder, but the atmosphere is more relaxed."

Andy Lapczynski, former executive vice president and general manager of Manitex, Inc., is quoted in my chapter on scheduling. Manitex is the McAllen, Texas, subsidiary of the Manitowoc Company, a manufacturer of cranes for construction and marine applications. Lapczynski has several thoughts that pertain to organizational structure. The goal of any organization should be "optimal utilization of capital resources. That involves plant and equipment as well as labor.... It has to be a constantly changing system, one that shows you are in a dynamic environment. When a (positive) change occurs, the entire mechanism must react."

Key Points:

○ Successful companies must be flexible. Administrators cannot hide behind a rigid organizational structure or hierarchy.

○ A company controlled by its own structure will not survive.

○ An organizational structure more horizontal than vertical leads to greater productivity and management depth.

○ Empowered people; improved products; lower costs; greater openness; concurrent engineering—all are benefits of a horizontal organization.

○ Horizontal management obliterates labor-management lines and enhances communication.

○ The goal of any organization should be optimal utilization of capital resources.

Chapter 5

Is your product or service in all the top markets? Are you sure? If cities such as New York, Los Angeles, and Chicago are all that come to mind, it may pay to expand your horizons. America's three most populous metropolitan areas are only the 5th-, 12th-and 25th-largest markets, respectively, on earth.

Chicago, for example, with its stable and relatively mature population of 6.5 million residents, will never be as large as Tokyo (26.9 million) or São Paolo (18.1 million) or even Essen, Germany (7.4 million). By comparison, Bangkok now has 5.8 million residents but will have 7.8 million by the year 2000. In addition to having a much younger population that helps create a higher birthrate, Thailand is the destination of some 5,000 people *each day*, who migrate there and do not leave!

No company, no matter what its current size, can expect to succeed in the decade ahead if it fails to think globally in relation to everything it does. In this period of rapid change, instantaneous worldwide communications, burgeoning off-shore markets, and technological change, no company can afford to limit its thinking to what's going on in its local community, state, or nation.

Look at what happened in just the last few years. New markets have opened in Eastern Europe. The European Common Market is becoming a reality. Trade barriers between the United States, Canada, and Mexico are crumbling. Economies in a number of South American countries are surging ahead. Perhaps the biggest growth area in terms of economic development is the Pacific Rim, with countries such as Thailand, Malaysia, and mainland China beginning to take the spotlight away from Japan, Korea, and Taiwan.

Even if you have no immediate intentions of entering export markets, it is important to be aware of worldwide developments in relation to your product line, raw materials, and competitors. The United States is not an island. Successful organizations will be evaluating their futures in terms of worldwide opportunities.

In 1992, I attended a conference in Brussels on corporate globalization, with emphasis on the new European Community (EC). A number of interesting conclusions emerged from the wide range of speakers, who included government experts and representatives of American corporations and banking interests, as well as EC diplomats. Among their contentions:

• The lifting of trade barriers within EC countries is occurring but will make very little difference to companies that have been active in Europe for some time.

• To succeed you must "think globally and act locally."

• Successful companies use nationals to run their operations, with great emphasis on understanding the culture of the country.

• Tremendous patience is required to develop relationships with European corporations. Their leadership will want to know you well before proceeding.

• In-depth involvement of the chief executive officer of the American company is critical to make a deal work. One CEO friend made 17 trips to Europe over 18 months before completing a major joint venture.

• Any initiative should be managed by a team of advisors headed by the CEO and should include a well-connected national from the involved country.

In no particular order, let's discuss some of these points. Your first question may be, "Where do I begin?" Let's assume you want to explore export markets. A CEO should turn to the marketing department to find out which parts of the world will be most receptive to the company's products or services. An excellent source of country statistics and market analysis is the Department of Commerce. Its job is to help you, the American businessperson. Take advantage of its expertise.

Another option is to undertake market research that is targeted to gather information about your product line, competition, trends, and access. Don't pick a country merely because a friend or a competitor enjoys success there. The reasons for that success may hinge on something over which you have no access or control.

What Will Sell?

Meanwhile, you should assess your line of products or range of services. Should you enter a market with a single item, then add items one or more at a time? Or should you introduce your entire line simultaneously? American companies with marked success overseas include H.J. Heinz, Procter & Gamble, and Tiffany. Yet none of these companies markets all of its products abroad. A globetrotter for a company in southeastern Wisconsin reports that his firm made a costly false start in the '60s that has taken it years to overcome.

"Our overseas sales manager at the time was a very aggressive guy," the friend recalls. "He attempted to introduce every product in our line into every major world market at the same time. Consequently, we hardly scratched the surface anywhere. And we paid no attention to the subtleties that make business in one country slightly different from business in another."

Several years later, the firm re-entered a single, carefully analyzed market with one kind of product, expanding slowly but surely. After that success, other products were added. Then, another carefully chosen country was approached, and a single product established. Today, the company has a presence in almost three dozen countries. The firm operates in a world-class way, as opposed to trying to operate in every country on earth. There is a real difference.

"If a company is serious about foreign markets, then I would strongly urge the chief executive officer to get involved." Those are the words of Roger Muencheberg, former director of export sales for the West Bend Company's Premiere Cookware Division and a man who for 17 of his 26 years with West Bend spent a great deal of time opening and improving markets for the Wisconsin manufacturer.

Muencheberg, now a special-account executive and director of governmental affairs with his company, has a unique perspective on doing business abroad. That's because the cookware division's products are sold direct—through dinner parties given in homes from Japan to South America and into Europe. "There are minor variations due to cultural or religious demands, but the cookware needs to be demonstrated and the story needs to be told so that features and benefits are understood."

Consequently, Muencheberg opened up a market not by finding a prosperous trading company but by identifying people in that country who had direct-sales knowledge and experience. Perhaps they were selling cosmetics, which are very popular direct-sales items. In any event, Muencheberg and his company screened and trained people but did not micro-manage. Results met expectations.

The West Bend Company found that Southeast Asia is especially receptive to in-home sales, that sales in the Middle East are, for religious and cultural reasons, made almost exclusively to non-Muslim foreign nationals working there under contract, and that "our next big market may be Eastern Europe. We're finding a lot of 'mattress money' there. People hoarded and hid money there in the past because they felt they would eventually have a better form of government."

Does Eastern Europe offer potential? There were as many questions as answers in Brussels. The size of the market, for example, is very impressive, but how large it will become depends on whether the Eastern Europeans and the Russians join the European Community. At the moment, Europe (excluding Russia) has more than 500 million people. If your goals are global, Europe must be a significant part of your marketing plans.

Geography isn't the only uncertainty. No one is sure at the moment just how far the European Community will go beyond the initial stage of a free market. Political union as yet undefined is under discussion, as well as an economic and military union now scheduled to occur no later than January, 1999. It's difficult to imagine a rock-ribbed Conservative member of the English Parliament linking arms with a Scandinavian Socialist, but in terms of trade, we in the United States certainly have benefited from a lack of barriers among our states, which are as different from each other as are the countries that make up today's Europe.

Yet another issue is membership expansion. The EC could eventually include the entire Eurasian land mass, though most speakers at our forum believe the market will not spread beyond Eastern Europe. How the European Community could act as a supernational organization to deal with such issues as drugs, anti-terrorism, subsidies for industry, immigration, and even abortion is an open question.

Setting the rules

This brings up yet another facet to consider for the CEO interested in selling abroad. If you believe that world trade rules were established by the United States and then taken over by the Japanese, you had better prepare for Europe. The EC, together and functioning as intended, will become the largest single trader on earth. That means Europeans will be increasingly in charge of the rules and guidelines for foreign trade. America and other nations will have to adapt to assure their continued ability to compete. The less rigid you and your corporation are, the better prepared you will be for change in the way things get done internationally.

Much of the information imparted in Brussels was hopeful. We are, after all, on the cusp of world-trade opportunities unparalleled in human history. Yet the forecast is not entirely sunny. One top U.S. military official speculated on the future of the United States in Europe. He suggested that a revolution similar to Yugoslavia's could take place in the former Soviet Union as economies deteriorate and various ethnic groups try to take control. Such internal warfare could involve nuclear weapons and nuclear terrorism, a specter counterbalanced by the continued strength and presence of NATO in a unified Europe.

A number of friends visited the huge and turbulent land in recent months. One was present for the failed coup in 1991. They agree that the situation is deteriorating rapidly. Few believe the former Soviets can make the transition to a free-market economy; marked progress will take decades.

Some believe that the former Soviet Union could evolve as China has, with progress on the local level rather than from the top down. A number of the independent states may have the resources to survive. However, the only groups in the area with any management understanding are the Communist Party functionaries, who are now out of power, and the military. The position of the former Soviet army is of great concern. It was described as an explosive force prepared to turn back current liberalization.

To appreciate the change in the former USSR, I did some reading upon my return from Brussels. In 1980, a Rand Corporation expert writes, our big concern was that the Soviet Union would invade Iran from Afghanistan and gain control of Persian Gulf shipping lanes. Today, there is speculation that a Gulf country might grab Soviet territory should the Central Asian republics, with their heavy Muslim populations, spin out of the Soviet orbit. That's quite a change.

A Perilous Market

The situation today was viewed as untenable for any American corporation interested in making investments in the former Soviet Union. A government-to-government, foreign-aid program similar to the Marshall Plan has started to keep the former USSR from falling into turmoil. Figures of $50 to $70 billion have been mentioned, amounts that few Americans are likely to swallow in view of the federal deficit and the needs of most U.S. cities. But without some continuing aid, the chances of a military takeover in the former USSR are high. The ultimate cost to the United States of increased defense spending could be considerably greater than any foreign-aid program.

With such a clouded outlook, is it still wise to explore overseas markets? Indeed, it is. A salesperson for the Milwaukee-area division of a major manufacturer points out that, when one part of the world is troubled, another can be undergoing incredible expansion. He also notes that some products, in addition to weapons, are needed regardless of political stability.

"I sell [a capital product] to hospitals. There are hospitals in all parts of the world that want and can afford such devices," he says. "Now, I grant you, we have a big advantage because so many top physicians come here to study. When I visit a hospital in Athens or Tel Aviv or Buenos Aires, there is someone who has learned to use this kind of equipment while studying medicine in the U.S. My point is, they will buy a quality product they really want and need whether times are good or there are riots in the streets. And speaking of riots, I've been in places like Peru, where guerrillas cut the power every night and hold Lima hostage. Yet, the Peruvians continue to buy medical equipment."

That brings up another point: how are U.S. products perceived? The medical-equipment salesperson says U.S. and German devices are recognized as the best in his field, with American goods enjoying a slight price edge. Roger Muencheberg found worldwide competition from several brands of quality European houseware manufacturers. Curiously, in some parts of the world, he says, the last thing you want to do is hold any kind of sale. "If you knock money off the price, some people assume something is wrong with the merchandise. If you have a quality product, they believe you should hang onto it and it will eventually be purchased. They're not concerned with your excess inventory."

Muencheberg can stand the competition from Europe and the inexpensive, low-quality cookware that is produced locally in many countries. His major complaint is about U.S. manufacturers who sell low-cost, low-quality, export-only goods that damage the reputation of American products as a whole. Perhaps such shoddy goods would not be created if U.S. companies took a long-term look at international markets. "You have to be willing to sacrifice short-term profits to create a quality image—good design, good products, good service. We began selling internationally in 1965, and it didn't really start to pay off until the early '80s. Now, foreign sales represent one-third of the Premiere Cookware Division total."

Non-tariff Barriers

Muencheberg's only other caution about international sales is the specter of non-tariff barriers. Wars and unrest represent one kind of barrier, but there are others. In order to enter the Korean market with a durable good such as cookware, for example, 3 percent of goods shipped into the country must be submitted to destructive testing. The Japanese are known for the number and kind of barriers they erect, yet both Korea and Japan are large and growing markets for some American goods. "I can have an affidavit in my hand as to the composition of the product and they will still cut apart 3 percent of every shipment," he says.

CEOs may have to look no farther than the annual meeting for other non-tariff barriers. Empowered shareholders with strong political, religious, social, or environmental agendas may object to offering goods and services in certain locales. With today's numerous brush-fire wars and the clear-cutting of tropical rain forests, chief executives will have to learn to deal with these owners of corporate America, who are, by and large, well intentioned if not always on the same page of the agenda as the corporation.

Let's close on another note from our friend Roger Muencheberg. He fears that some executives may be looking beyond our shores before they have done their homework. "Your manufacturing process here had better be absolutely nailed down before you try to sell abroad." The days of "it's not selling here, let's make it an export item," are gone forever as Americans, Europeans, and all other people become increasingly interdependent. Banking, marketing, planning, managing—none of it matters if the product isn't produced with the utmost possible quality and efficiency.

Key Points:

○ No company can succeed in the decade ahead if it fails to think globally. Successful organizations will evaluate their futures in terms of worldwide opportunities.

○ Use market research to test receptiveness to new product ideas in export markets.

○ More and more, Europeans will set the rules for foreign trade. American business must adapt.

○ Don't let turbulent political climates dissuade you from marketing overseas. A country will always need some products, regardless of its political stability.

○ Understand non-tariff barriers before marketing overseas.

○ Take the long-term view—only export top quality products.

Chapter 6

Recently, I spent some time with a client whose manufacturing facility is on the outskirts of Minneapolis. I was introduced there to one of the hourly employees, a young man I'll call Mark. I made hurried notes while Mark talked to me about his responsibilities. I think you will find his words of great import.

"I work for [name], a 20-year-old company. It specializes in metal stamping and metal fabrication. I began here three years ago, right out of high school, running a press. The work was boring but the pay was all right, and I had no idea at the time what I wanted to do with my life.

"Then, a year and a half ago, the company purchased its first robot welder. There were about a dozen welding operators here at the time. Amazingly, none of them wanted anything to do with the robot. I saw the factory rep create a couple of programs for jobs to run on it, and I became curious. I told [the welding supervisor] that if no one wanted to learn how to program the robot, I would give it a try.

"Not that I was an expert. I'd taken one semester of welding in high school, and I've never had any kind of computer course. But programming is logical and I guess I have a logical mind. Anyway, within six weeks I was creating the programming. My first program called for seven or eight welds on a piece that looked like the headboard of a metal bed. Once production began on the piece, the robot was completing 38 of the pieces an hour, compared to our fastest welding operator, who was turning out eight."

Let's interrupt Mark momentarily for a few words from his welding supervisor: "Maybe because Mark had no experience, he saw the real potential rather than a threat with the robot. He watched it operate and was the first person here to realize that the fixture or jig is at least as important for productivity as the robot's ability to move around with the welding gun."

Service Means Speed

"If [company] wanted the most out of its investment, we had to be able to move more quickly from one job to another," Mark said. "But how were we going to do that, since the fixture for one job may be completely different from the next? We came up with what you see here—two large, flat metal tables with a lot of little holes in them and with the robot and its power source between the two. Each hole is numbered and will accept the same kind of adjustable clamp. Now, when we run a new job, we figure out which holes require the clamps. The clamps are placed in position, and the program is written. Then, if we ever run that piece again, we'll just call up the program and it will tell us where to put the clamps. It takes about five minutes to switch from one program to another."

In the first year of robotics production, Mark filled the robot's memory to capacity with 250 different welding programs, one for each job run for a variety of customers. What was he to do with the 251st program? "I wondered about that for awhile, but the answer was right here, in the office. They have a PC that will let me store programs for the robot on a disk. So the capacity of the robot really is infinite."

As you may visualize, Mark clamps parts onto one table as the robot welds on the opposite table. He moves to the just-welded piece as the robot swings into position where he has just secured the parts. He removes the completed weld, stacks it with identical, completed pieces and begins to clamp parts onto that side of the table. The robot's speed is adjustable, so Mark has enough time to do his job before moving to the completed piece on the opposite table and replacing it with parts to be welded.

That's not the end of the story. The company now has three robots, all programmed by Mark. The very first robot turns on five axes, whereas the two later models are six-axis robots. The newer acquisitions can run more complex jobs because they can execute welds that the five-axis robot cannot. With the assistance of the personal computer, Mark has made sure that the initial robot's memory has the 250 easiest jobs stored in it. The newer robots hold the more complex tasks. There is now a separate, supplementary storage disk for each of the three robots.

While Mark programs all three, it is, of course, impossible for him to remove welded products or clamp down parts to be welded on three pairs of tables. Consequently, he has two laborers who now answer to him. He's looking forward to a one-week school for programming new robot models that will soon come on stream. "I've learned everything about these machines but the terminology," Mark said, adding that he's eager to attend the programming school, put on by the manufacturer of the welding power supplies.

Mark's superiors are happy, too. "We're billing these jobs as if they were done manually," said the company president. "We've gotten a lot more business because the robots are so responsive. They've created our reputation, which is that we fabricate quickly and very well. Until our competitors have their own robots and drop their prices, we won't have to."

Robots were seen as the scourge of American labor when they first came on the scene. The experience at the Minnesota plant has been exactly the opposite, as Mark noted. "It's nothing for us to run three totally different jobs on the same robot in one eight-hour shift. I'm told what needs to be run when, and I call up the program from the robot's memory or from the PC disk. After that the clamps are moved to accommodate the new job. It can all be done in five minutes. Even if I have to modify a program, we can be running new parts within 30 minutes."

The company's welding operators are as busy as ever; there are some fabrication jobs for which no program can be written. The three robots have caused Mark's hourly wage to virtually double, and they have necessitated the hiring of his two assistants. Each robot is fed welding wire from separate 500-pound spools. These barrels of wire last up to three months, which means that downtime from threading a new spool into the robot is almost nonexistent.

Flexibility Equals Customer Service

I wanted Mark to tell his story, which is a study in customer service, as a counterpoint to new techniques the Japanese are using. A recent issue of *Fortune* told of the heightened importance of flexibility in Japanese manufacturing. Here's how it was explained:

"The theory behind flexibility is simple. If you and I are competing, and I can read the market quicker, manufacture many different products on the same line, switch from one to another instantly and at low cost, make as much profit on short runs as on long ones, and bring out new offerings faster than you—or do most of these things—then I win. I can parry your every thrust, attack niches in your market that you're too bulky to squeeze into, improve faster, and maintain or even fatten profits while forcing you to follow my lead on prices."

Not many in the United States are addressing the advantages of flexibility, according to the magazine. Americans are more intent at the moment on rapid handling of orders, strong supplier relationships, rapid and reliable delivery, broad channels of distribution, durable products, and a flexible work force. Flexibility allows the Japanese to offer enhanced product features, products with a high research-and-development content, lower prices, rapid changes in production volumes, rapid changes of product mix, the introduction of many new products, and a state-of-the-art manufacturing process.

If you feel we have a long way to go, you have to remember how far we've come in the area of customer service. Marketing 1960s-style meant that corporations had millions of dollars to spend to precisely profile potential customers. These marketers were very, very good at their tasks. They polled and probed and test-marketed and otherwise queried, using exacting methods. One result was that a manufacturer of small appliances, for example, could tell how well a product would sell in different geographical areas, in different seasons, in urban or suburban or rural areas, in black or white or Latino households, to young and to old, among the more or less educated, ad infinitum.

As admirable as this exactitude was, we see now that it was only a partial answer to acceptance of any product or service. That's because the marketers found people willing to buy the product instead of first finding out what people wanted in the product. They paid little or no attention to the point of sale, where the customer came in personal contact with a retailer. Marketing was great at identifying potential customers, but we realize now that much of the effort was wasted because service to the customer was in a primitive state.

Service-Sensitive Businesses

Customer service is both wide and deep. For years I have been fascinated with the challenges certain businesses faced in appeasing customers. Daily newspapers and oil companies come immediately to mind.... A few years ago, newspapers were buying each other like crazy because they all made money. That's no longer true, and not all of the blame can be pinned on television or on the disinclination to read. Think about it—a chain of newspapers may own forests and mills and railroad cars that deliver newsprint to the dock. It may own multimillion-dollar presses that thunder with power in turning out 100 or more pages of news and advertising every day. It has local and national sales representatives skilled at culling every ad dollar available. This investment all hinges on a 12-year-old, who may toss your copy of *The Evening News* on the roof!

A friend sells automobile advertising for *The Sun Times* in Chicago. She's good at her job, is well-compensated and can offer automobile dealers the city's best-read car section. "After I've been making calls all day, it's discouraging to see a carrier's bicycle, loaded with papers, parked at the playground. The kid should have passed those papers an hour ago. I get this urge to throttle him."

Declining circulations are being slowed in several ways. Many newspapers are studying the St. Louis area, where adults deliver *The Post-Dispatch* partially or entirely by car. These part-time jobs pay $150 a week, enough money to ensure that the papers are passed promptly and delivered in waterproof envelopes when it rains. Yes, newspapers have other problems, but better service to the customer is a step in the right direction.

Then there are the oil companies. I'm guessing Mobil and Exxon and everyone else who retails gasoline breathed a collective sigh of relief when self-service became the way of doing things at the gasoline island. Prior to self-service, the customer was greeted by an untrained, frequently unkempt person who resented being asked to check the oil or the tires. Nowadays, that employee is hermetically sealed behind a window, or we can pay at the pump. Assuming the attendant doesn't short-change you or the machine keep your credit card, little else can go wrong.

Ironically, this has paid off for the diminishing number of stations still willing to cheerfully pump gasoline for their customers. Older customers—and those of us who don't want our hands to smell like 87-octane unleaded—find and then frequent stations where the people are friendly. I'm guessing that an overwhelming percentage of the full-service stations are run by the owners.

Contemporary manufacturers are spending time and money to retain the customers they have and to offer a "whatever it takes" approach in securing new business. I tend toward manufacturing examples of customer service because many of my clients happen to be manufacturers. Companies that deal in services are even more vulnerable to the whims of customers. Richard C. Bowers, senior vice president of Milwaukee's North Shore Bank, has instituted a customer-service program that was extremely well-thought-out and produces measurable results.

Not Order-Driven

"About four years ago," Bowers reports, "it was apparent that we could not depend on being an order-driven institution. We conceived a two- to three-year plan to become a selling culture rather than an order-taking culture. We began holding quarterly and annual sales banquets, and we took a program, Bankers Who Sell, and drafted our own plan to fit our needs.... The growth of the money market, sales of six-month and 30-month certificates, IRAs—such business had become deregulated, and we floundered for several years before becoming more customer-relationship-oriented."

Bowers is responsible for the branch system, for consumer lending, and for human resources, so he was the obvious choice to convert bank employees from catchers to pitchers. He established sales standards, put in a sales-tracking system, and hired sales-training consultants. He also put together a very deliberate plan. "We could have done it faster, but we wanted to do it slowly," he says. "The time can work for you.

"For us, the best customer is one who has multiple accounts. We used the 80-20 rule, believing that 80 percent of the business comes from 20 percent of the clientele. If a customer had a total of $25,000 with us, all service charges for checking and savings accounts and for safe-deposit boxes were waived. We even picked up the charge for MasterCard.

As it turned out, about 70 percent of the business was coming from 17 percent of the customers."

A shaking-out took place as customers with only one kind of business with the bank declined and persons with multiple accounts increased. Meanwhile, Bowers bought a training package that brought customer service representatives (formerly called tellers) up to speed. Today, any customer who fails to be called by name or who has to wait more than five minutes for a representative is handed $5. There are about 100 customer service reps; with normal turnover, the reps can be taught contemporary customer service by one full-time trainer. I can tell you that North Shore Bank has a customer-oriented ambiance, backed by service guarantees that make banking much less of a chore.

By now you may be wondering how robot operations connect with prompt delivery of a newspaper or with knowing the names of all customers. The only obvious definition of customer service is this: it is whatever the customer wants it to be. Those wants may become more complex as your customer service improves. *Fortune* notes that the Japanese aren't standing still while we grope toward better service. Among the items on their agenda are custom orders, even when the orders may run to hundreds of thousands of items. They are also able to make multiple products on one assembly line, using such devices as laptop computers to take the assembler through the proper steps.

Even more exciting, the Japanese see their salespeople entering a potential customer's place of business without any kind of order sheet or system. "We are in the cosmetics business," the salesperson announces. "What do *you* want?" Knowing the customer is one thing. Being able to immediately react to each one as an individual is something else entirely.

What an exciting time to be in business!

Key Points:

○ A flexible approach will result in an ability to change volume and mix rapidly as well as enhanced product features, fast development of new products and state-of-the-art manufacturing.

○ The success of any product or service always comes down to customer service.

○ Successful companies spend time and money on retaining the customers they have and offer a "whatever it takes" approach to securing new business.

○ Good customer service provides exactly what each customer wants.

Chapter 7

I like almost everything about niche marketing but the name. To my mind, "niche" connotes something small and perhaps insignificant—a cranny or crevice or fissure of some kind. Active niche marketers will tell you that such openings can result in years of heightened opportunity, sales and profits. Let's talk here about marketing from the perspective of several people who have helped market their companies to real success.

Incidentally, if customer service is whatever the customer believes it to be, marketing and sales are whatever chores the companies themselves choose to perform under those twin banners. Similarly, a niche can be either a large or small market for any given company.

Marketing and sales are physically close at the Williamson-Dickie Manufacturing Company, a privately held maker of men's apparel based in Fort Worth. A friend there, Jim McLaughlin, is vice president of sales. He points out that he and the marketing vice president share the same office. How, then, do responsibilities break down?

"The marketing vice president's position is more promotionally oriented," McLaughlin indicates. "At times he almost takes on a public relations function. He's charged with getting our name into trade and consumer publications, running the cooperative advertising program—if Wal-Mart places an ad featuring Dickie pants, it will have been a co-op ad that has the blessings—and partial underwriting—of marketing."

Speaking of Wal-Mart, what does McLaughlin think of the fact that the huge retailer insists on dealing directly with the manufacturer? "We've always had that arrangement. We sell direct to everybody except those who have no credit. In Los Angeles, for example, there are several large wholesalers who buy our products and then sell them to small, Korean-owned and other ethnic stores."

A Middle Eastern Niche

Sales of his products, he continues, are very sensitive to the economy. The moment consumers believe they have less discretionary income, they decide to make their pair of Dickie pants last another year. "Business has not been strong in the U.S. in the last couple of years. We work to overcome that by finding niches overseas that are very strong and steady. An example is the Middle East, where there are a large number of guest or foreign workers employed by the state. The standard uniform for these people is Dickie's short-sleeve coveralls, purchased by the government and furnished to guest workers."

On the road almost constantly, McLaughlin remembers that he responded to a Dickie's classified ad in a Syracuse newspaper when he was a senior in college. "I moved to new York City and became a showroom salesperson. Actually, as the junior salesperson, I became the coffee boy. I was then given a territory, the Cleveland area, and was fortunate enough to triple sales volume. It sounds cliched, but all I did was make calls 12 hours a day, six days a week. After that, I was brought here in a junior management position in sales."

But back to niche marketing....Williamson-Dickie manufactures work pants and blue jeans (including such private labels as L.L. Bean—private labeling being a niche in itself) here and abroad. McLaughlin spends much of his time exploring foreign markets by opening new accounts and expanding the product line in existing markets overseas. Besides such Middle East locales as Bahrain and Saudi Arabia, strong markets include Belgium, the Netherlands and the United Kingdom. Sales in the U.K. now total about 20 percent of U.S. sales. There is a very good reason for such strength.

"We are the largest employer in Belize, which used to be British Honduras. Belize still enjoys favorable trade tariffs with England and Canada. We manufacture goods in Belize and ship them direct to England and Canada, thereby avoiding tariffs we would pay shipping from Belize to the U.S. and then overseas," he says. Clearly, numerous niches add up to prosperity for the Texas firm.

Flexibility is the key to doing business overseas, since offshore markets may be as volatile as domestic markets are steady. With that in mind, McLaughlin is looking at the former Soviet Union somewhat gingerly. "At the moment, we're more interested in the relatively stable economies of Central Europe such as Czechoslovakia. K-Mart has developed a strong presence in Czechoslovakia and that is a logical outlet for our products. The problem with Russia is that there is incredible demand for U.S. goods, but you can't get paid for them. Levi-Strauss and Pepsi-Cola have barter agreements. They are paid with cases of Stolichnaya Vodka, which they then market in Europe and the West."

Reality — knowing when not to enter a market — is as important as flexibility. Due to the incredible amount of inexpensive and poorly produced clothing items that come out of China and Southeast Asia, Williamson-Dickie does not market at the moment in the Far East. "But I would be willing to bet you can find knockoffs (imitations with authentic-looking labels) of our products in Thailand and elsewhere." Until Far East governments show concern and control over fake merchandise, it will not pay McLaughlin to further examine that market—though populations are young and large, a jeans marketer's dream come true.

The niche enjoyed by McLaughlin in the Middle East hinges on a history of strong demand for U.S.-made goods. "These people are all but overwhelmed by poorly made, Third World goods," he says. "But money is not an issue. They want our garments, even though they may be three or four times as expensive as the competition."

The buyers of Dickie coveralls in the Middle East lack neither sophistication nor capital. They have seen that McLaughlin's products wear very well, wash easily, hold their color, provide comfort and fit properly. Third World knockoffs cost only a fraction of the Dickie product, but they lack quality. By the way, Williamson-Dickie sells direct overseas, just as the company sells to Wal-Mart or K-Mart or other large, domestic accounts.

Beware The False Niche

McLaughlin clearly decides which markets have potential and which do not. The same can be said of a major U.S. manufacturer of children's furniture. A spokesperson for that company has a fascinating anecdote to relate about a false niche for which her company almost fell.

Jan Smith (not her real name) says her employer has for decades successfully reached expectant and new mothers, the people who usually make the buying decisions for the nursery or the young child's room. "A few years back, we began to hear about more and more women putting off the birth of their first child until the age of 35 or older. We'd never attempted to reach women of that 'advanced age,' and we were worried about overlooking an important segment of the market.

"As it turned out, there's a lot more *news* about women having their first child after 35 than women actually doing so. We paid an outside market research firm a bundle to find out that we were reaching as high a percentage of expectant and new mothers as ever. What was happening was that perhaps 2 or 3 percent of all married women were putting off having their first child until they were older. Because they were frequently professionals and managers, they got noticed. We haven't changed our marketing approach one bit.

"Researchers told us that the small number who were postponing childbirth sought out the same things that younger mothers did. One of the people here (a small Midwest town) pointed out afterward that we could have saved ourselves some money by looking around. No one here knows anybody who is waiting until the age of 35 to have a first child. In fact, most local women are done having children by the age of 30."

Smith notes that the same kind of false niche can show up in other areas. "Think about a woman who chooses to marry after the age of 35. There aren't any magazines out there called *Older Bride* or *Finally Married.* If these women want to have traditional weddings, they access themselves to the same things as the 18-year-old or 25-year-old brides-to-be."

An All-Niche Market

Richard Osborne, vice president of marketing and gas supply for Wisconsin Gas Company, faces a changing set of challenges. As a public utility, the energy business once was heavily regulated. Now, due to deregulation, he deals with four markets that once were three. The gas company has always had residential, commercial, and industrial customers. But deregulation has allowed Wisconsin Gas and other gas companies to sell outside their territories. In other words, they can successfully market energy wherever it can be profitably delivered.

"There are 460,000 Wisconsin Gas customers," Osborne says. "Some 420,000 are residential. Most of our residential marketing is through trade allies—dealers, contractors, and builders. We set up programs to market through them, offering our allies incentives. We also offer customer incentives, such as rebates, primarily via direct mail. Industrial customers view us as consultants who can evaluate their needs and deliver cost-effective energy."

But the opportunity to sell to anyone, anywhere, is a niche not without peril. Osborne predicts that this opportunity will spell the end for some smaller companies. "We are no longer prohibited by the structure of the industry, or by the pipelines, as to where we market. Now we can sell excess capacity anywhere. The trouble with this market is, all gas companies have overcapacity at the same times. There are other problems—we have real concerns about maintaining the quality of service, and such selling doesn't make for very attractive margins. Gas these days is very much a commodities market or a financial service; we line up supply to meet demand.

"There is now trading and hedging and spot markets. It's moving very quickly and it's hard for the small municipal energy company to exist. It takes more investment in a faster-moving, more complex environment. Like financial services, we have to have a good back room, administering contracts on a daily basis. It used to be on an annual basis. We're all having a tough time adjusting."

Marketing Velocity

Dick Osborne brings up a cogent point: marketing is moving faster than ever. Decisions that we could probe for weeks are now being made in minutes. Responses to the velocity of the market vary, but here are several I've encountered among my clients:

• The traditional adversarial relationship between a manufacturer and that manufacturer's suppliers is breaking down. Suppliers are being winnowed. Those that survive receive a larger percentage of the business. They are present from the design stage on, helping reduce costs and eliminating incoming inspections, with capital expenditures to accommodate the manufacturer. Their role is to cut the manufacturer's indirect costs wherever possible. The reward is designation as a certified vendor, which means among other things that the manufacturer can audit the supplier at any time. Risks are higher, but so are rewards.

• Once certified, a supplier may find that the manufacturer has linked the supplier directly to one or more customers. The customer can "pick" parts and subassemblies from the supplier's inventories, thanks to electronic data interchange, orchestrated by the manufacturer's computer system. This type of system, particularly on consumables such as welding rods or excavator bucket teeth or computer memory boards, eliminates busy work that may have been necessary but unprofitable for the manufacturer. And it speeds crucial parts to the customer.

• These days, it's not just the sales force that interfaces with customers. Several prominent manufacturers are connecting their officers to their best customers. A vice president, for example, will monitor activities of the team or teams that are responsible for the needs of two or three major customers. This is a great concept. It frequently energizes the manufacturer's officers, and it puts a responsible voice and a face with the product.

• Contemporary marketers worry until the product or service is in the customer's hands. You probably recall your Federal Express representative scanning your delivered envelope. The device being used transmits time-of-delivery information that can be called up immediately in any Federal Express office to confirm that the job has been completed. DSC Logistics, a major hauling and storage business headquartered in Des Plaines, Illinois, stays in contact with its truck fleet nationwide via the ARDIS System, a joint venture between Motorola and IBM.

• DSC Logistics can tell a customer exactly where the customer's goods are and how soon delivery should take place. It can even divert the driver from the anticipated route in an emergency. Dennis Waliczek, vice president of information systems, says customers often call to find out where trucks bearing their goods are, only to discover that the DSC Logistics trucks are awaiting unloading at the customers' own docks! The system requires only a small antenna, it works inside buildings, and it creates non-customer-related data such as the driver's log sheet. It costs an estimated $3,000 per unit, and Waliczek estimates that payback is in two years or less.

• Companies everywhere are re-examining their advertising and promotional efforts. Procter & Gamble, for example, is backing away from the use of coupons. Many food and related manufacturers view couponing as a bucking horse they have to stay on. Leave it to P&G to emphasize lower standard pricing rather than coupons. Coupons, after all, can be abused. Some grocers buy the couponed product at a lower price, then stash the inventory until the promotion ends. Or, they violate the law by turning in coupons to the manufacturer for which no products were sold.

• In contrast, here's a place where coupons work well. Richard P. Ross, vice president of marketing for North Shore Bank in suburban Milwaukee, was among the first persons anywhere to use coupons to increase sales of financial services. He contends that the line between marketing a product and marketing a service is a thin one. And though "Geritol may have been first," banks were among the first and best at realizing the potential of customers over the age of 50. "Some institutions thought they should give free checking to young people, but they found there was no profit in it. We view the checking account as a tool to get savings-and-loan business, though this is a bit more difficult than getting their savings account and safety-deposit business."

If by now you are daunted by the complexities of marketing and selling, take the advice of our friend Mr. Ross. A college teacher of marketing for a decade and a brand or product manager for companies such as Pillsbury and Jergens, the banker reminds us that there remain just five elements in the marketing area: research, advertising, promotion, public relations and sales. "Just find out what customers want and get it to them. The toughest thing continues to be making the actual sale. Once you're in front of potential customers, you must convince them of the need for your product or service."

Challenging The CEO

Beyond that, Ross continues, "the marketing person has the responsibility to present new ideas—to challenge the CEO. The CEO, in turn, must encourage fresh thinking in the marketing person. I was hired here at the bank because of my background in marketing products. Specifically, the boss told me he liked me because I didn't know what could *not* be done."

Key Points:

○ Flexibility is key to doing business overseas, since off-shore markets may be as volatile as domestic markets are steady.

○ Reality—knowing when not to enter a market—is as important as flexibility. Beware the false niche.

○ Today's market velocity means decisions are often made in minutes.

○ Manufacturers are winnowing their suppliers. The survivors can become certified vendors, part of your customer's team.

○ Top officers, not just the sales force, should meet regularly with their best customers.

○ Distribution is a key concern of manufacturers.

○ Companies are re-examining advertising and promotional efforts.

○ The actual sale is the toughest part of marketing. You still must convince the customers they need your product or service.

Chapter 8

Total Quality Management:
Two Sides of the Same Coin

"Quality is an organization-wide effort conceptually based on the continuous improvement process. This activity ulti-mately focuses on the customer-supplier chain, both internal and external, creating a culture in which everything is seen in either the customer sense or the supplier sense in order to con-tinually improve the process."

—Quality manager

"If you want this plant for yourself, forget about quality. But if you want it for your son, then you'd better initiate a total qual-ity management program."

—Quality manager

"In the race for quality, there is no finish line."

—David T. Kearns

"Quality is free — only it ain't."

—Philip Crosby

This is the story of two managers. They work for separate compa-nies in the same Midwestern state. Neither has quite reached his 40th birthday, and each is charged by the respective corporation with the same daunting task: getting a total quality management system up and running. One works for a company financially extended in the face of a recession that has sharply reduced mar-ket demand. The other is employed by a smaller, more stable firm. Which manager is encouraged by results, and which suffers from occasional dejection? The answers may surprise you.

Let's call the first manager Bill. About a year ago, he came to the sizable, publicly held manufacturer of durable goods that now finds itself scrambling. He had worked for nearly 15 years with manufacturers of varying sizes. Bill has earned several degrees, yet he points out that the only institution currently offering a quality management sheepskin is unaccredited. "That's just as well," he says with a smile almost visible over the telephone, "because nothing but experience will prepare you for some of the things you'll learn on the job."

Bill's resume includes two familiar names in different manufacturing fields. Neither had any sort of quality man-agement program when he arrived. The larger of the two is the more fascinating. "I was never impressed with the design or performance of their products. But their approach to quality has always been fairly effective—they constantly test the hell out of every product that comes out the factory door." Bill persuaded his current employer to initiate a testing program, and the program has detected defects that were quickly solved. He was able to convince senior management that the cost of testing could be recouped by reduced time and effort spent honoring warranty claims.

"If you test, look at your priorities, find the most troubling attributes of your product, then test again, you can put a solid product in the field that will increase your market share and build customer confidence," he says. "We build a very durable product here, so seven years is a long time to live with poor performance. When the customer replaces what he has, he won't come back to one of our dealers. It takes a long time to build a customer base in a mature market with durable products. That's something we just can't afford to lose."

The customer focus is less straightforward with Jim, our other quality manager. He has been with a privately held manufacturer for about a year and a half, after earning praise from a larger corporation for getting a total quality management system off the ground. That was a rewarding experience.

'If Japan Can, Why Can't We?'

"The president of the company where I was formerly employed and I both happened to watch the same television program. It was an NBC-TV white paper entitled 'If Japan Can, Why Can't We?' We came away convinced that total quality management was the best way to ensure the company's future. We implemented a program soon afterward that proved to be a success."

Jim came to his present position, manager of quality assurance, with a pledge from the chief executive officer that he could introduce total quality management. It hasn't been easy. "Some managers thought we could install a program overnight, sort of like off-loading and plugging in a new photocopy machine," he recalls. "They believed that, because there was someone on board with 'quality' in his title, it would all just magically happen."

Jim faults himself for not sufficiently explaining to fellow managers what would happen right away. "When you first start to measure and keep track of your quality, it will be a real sore spot. You are accounting for the things that really do go on, all the rework, all the matters that are swept under the rug or that have always been left hanging. The negative numbers will shoot up dramatically, and you will be blamed because no one ever documented how bad the quality really was. You then have to convince management that there will be no solutions until you have shown the magnitude of the problem."

Some managers within the company resisted the process another way. Those who dealt with suppliers didn't want Jim working with these outside sources, even if it meant better parts, delivered in a more timely and cost-effective manner. "It's a re-education process. You're asking a lot of an experienced manager. Sometimes, what you want is for him to admit that he may not know what he's doing. You're telling him that his supplier must be certified; otherwise, the supplier will make the same mistakes we're making here.

"Another thing, the whole process is a little too democratic for some managers. You need for them to loosen their grasp on the reins so that fellow managers, and especially the rank and file, who are closest to the manufacturing process, can help with the solution.

"Today's workers are more educated and intelligent," he continues. "They want to be part of the process. The worst thing you can do is to fail to adequately explain total quality management to them, because they've seen new programs every two or three months for years, and each time they've been told, 'This is really different, this is going to succeed.' So you have to get their attention. To do that, they must be given control over what they're asked to do. Otherwise, they'll think of it as just another slogan, as more hot air."

Bill would agree. "There are certain employees who are harder to bring on board than others. It has worked here because we've taken the time to get to know them as individuals, and we respect them. Once everyone here knew what each person had to do, peer pressure forced the stubborn ones to either get on board or face being lost forever at sea."

Jim cites the contention of the late quality guru W. Edwards Deming that 85 percent of all quality problems are caused by management. He had only one disagreement with an hourly employee, and that was over a task the employee did not want to do because he thought it violated the union contract. The employee set about the task immediately after Jim hauled out the agreement and the two read over it. "Actually, the union here isn't bad. They don't care who pushes the broom as long as the work area is clean at the end of the shift. That's pretty progressive."

That same employee was the first one to stand in the way of a finished product he knew to be wrong. According to Jim, "I never met a customer who would complain if you said, 'We're shipping this tomorrow instead of today because we've had a quality problem we want to fix.' That one-day delay will soon be forgotten if the product gives the end-user an extended period of trouble-free service."

Management and workers alike must understand that "this is not a fad," Jim repeats. Bill made sure everyone at his company knew what he wanted to accomplish when he began. Posted wherever line or staff personnel work are his goals, in the following order:

- Improved customer satisfaction.
- Improved internal employee morale.
- Improved productivity.
- Increased market share.
- Accelerated continuous improvement.

"I would much rather pursue these aims than chase a Deming prize or a Baldrige award," Bill says. "They become too much like contests or bowling trophies. Management can get pretty relentless, and it can adversely affect morale. Florida Power & Light, for example, won a major quality award, but the pressures put on people resulted in a lot of turnover, and it did not improve their bottom line.

"There are a number of prizes and experts out there, but you have to pick and choose what's right for your own environment," he says. "That has happened here, despite the fact that we're constrained financially. We still believe that, if you offer a product of greater value, even in a mature or declining market, you will gain market share and improve profitability."

Absentee Ownership

Jim thinks his major obstacle may be an absentee owner. "When the owner of a privately held company isn't running the show, there is tremendous pressure on management for continuous, short-range profits. That may eliminate the spending necessary for a total quality management (TQM) program to work."

I met Bill and Jim, who do not know each other, while providing strategic planning consultation for their respective companies. I was struck by their intelligence and intensity. Intensity can be a pejorative term, but both of these managers had the ability to step away from their tasks and offer a relaxed, objective overview. They then were able to immediately return to their jobs with a single-mindedness I envy. If your total quality manager is as capable as these two, and if quality is such an obvious goal, what can go wrong?

Chief executive officers can be deeply committed to TQM, but if they fail to convey its importance to everyone in the organization, it won't work. Do staff personnel at your company feel they have little or nothing to do with quality? If so, this vacuum needs to be addressed immediately. Everyone in an organization must address quality, from the CEO on down. If every employee reacts to every other employee as a valued customer, you've come a long way toward nailing down the elusive process that results in quality products and quality services.

Is your company set in its ways? Does it strike you as being too inflexible to change? Is your market so mature that you fear moving off dead center? There are no easy answers, as executives at Polaroid have discovered. They found that their mature, instant-photo market could be influenced by changes in quality, but the administrators are divided to this day over whether concentrating on incremental change would prevent breakthrough technology. After much soul searching, that question has yet to be resolved. But the company feels the tough questions must be addressed and that some sort of quality program is needed.

What sort of quality strategy will work best for you? There are several, ranging from comparing your products to world-class competition, to total employee involvement, to wonderful new methods of cost management. But the key, whatever you choose from the quality menu, is commitment. Our friend Bill has worked at places where quality circles were formed and nothing was accomplished. The participants did not know why they were in attendance, and the managers did not know what to do with the circles once they were formed. Perhaps that is why he signed on with his present employer, even though it has profit-and-loss problems. He was offered a blank slate and detected a company-wide desire for quality.

Jim will continue to serve his company, in large part because he has perceived more willingness among hourly employees to improve than he had anticipated. "The U.S. Department of Labor in 1985 did a study to find out if American workers were productive. Using Americans as the benchmark, they compared us to British, French, German, and Japanese workers. The results were gratifying—American workers are more productive than their foreign counterparts. Even in a product-oriented industry, labor accounts for only 6 to 8 percent of the cost of production. So if you have productive, willing people, properly trained and empowered, you will have the classic win-win situation. Your product will be produced better for less money, and worker morale will climb as employees feel more and more a part of the process."

Ten TQM Benchmarks

How important is company-wide involvement? It is the first rule among 10 laid down by Armand V. Feigenbaum, president and chief executive officer of a Massachusetts engineering firm and a renowned expert on competitiveness and quality. Feigenbaum says a company-wide TQM program will create quality leaders and quality followers and that the followers will want to join the leaders.

Here, in order, are the remaining rules:

• **Quality is what the customer says it is.** Not even the most competent engineer or market researcher can ever *assume* what the customer wants, needs, and perceives as quality. He or she must go to the customer and *ask*.

• **Quality and cost are a sum, not a difference.** Companies that make quality a priority enjoy a 5-to-10 cents-on-the-dollar competitive advantage.

- **Quality involves both team and individual zealotry.** To paraphrase the old antiwar slogan, "Quality begins with me." The very best employees will think like team members in team situations and like distance runners when they're alone.

- **Quality is a way of managing.** It's the realization that quality will make everything in the organization right.

- **Quality and innovation are mutually dependent.** Quality is the equal partner of product development. They should reach their goals simultaneously.

- **Quality is an ethic.** It's deep recognition that what you are doing is right.

- **Quality requires continuous improvement.** In a very real sense, Bill and Jim will always have their goal in sight but never reach it. Quality is always moving away from you, and that movement must always be upward.

- **Quality is the most cost-effective, least capital-intensive route to productivity.** It will eliminate the need for departments that exist due to bad work.

- **Quality is implemented with a total system connected with customers and suppliers.** Quality leadership is systematic, "by the numbers." It doesn't just happen.

I chose Bill and Jim for this chapter because I wanted to underline the fact that nothing just falls into place on the way to TQM. Unreasonable expectations and impatience have downed more than one quality management program as soon as it started to fly. Despite the number of get-quality-quick books and tapes and shows, TQM has worked for some, is working for others, and could work for you. How confident does a successful program make you feel?

Bill may have articulated it best. "Regardless of ideology, if the United States government were to apply TQM and make it work, that government would be responsive and efficient, and the national debt would wither away." Pursuit of governmental quality also would greatly reduce the probability of wars and the severity of social problems, he firmly believes. If an experienced quality manager feels that deeply about TQM, it must be more than a fad.

Key Points:

○ Test and identify a product's negative attributes—then test again. You can put a solid product in the field that will increase market share and build customer confidence.

○ All managers must understand and commit to TQM before it can succeed.

○ Management causes 85% of all quality problems.

○ Even in a mature market, a product of greater value will gain share and improve profitability.

○ TQM won't work unless the CEO can convey its importance to everyone in the company.

○ Company-wide involvement is the most important TQM benchmark. Quality followers will want to join quality leaders.

○ Nothing just falls into place on the way to TQM. Unreasonable expectations and impatience have downed more than one quality management program.

Chapter 9

The plant manager called the welding operator into his office. "You've been here—what's it been? Five years? What do you think of this operation?"

"It's all right," said the welder, toying with the company badge clipped to his shirt pocket.

"Is it?" The plant manager's eyes traveled to the ceiling and back. "I don't think it's such a great place. You come here every morning clean and full of energy, and you leave dirty and drained. If that's all that happens, this can't be an 'all-right' place."

"I have to earn a living—feed my family, make house and car payments, those sorts of things," the welding operator replied, showing a flicker of interest.

"Sure you do, but you shouldn't have to go home too tired to work on your son's dirt bike or too grubby to sit in the living room without a shower and a change of clothes. Why do you think you end up like that every day?"

By this time, the welder was too puzzled to reply.

"It's not the work—the welding—that wears you down and covers you with grime. It's all the things you have to go through to successfully execute a weld. You know—chasing parts, lifting heavy objects, blasting a piece of metal with the air gun to remove scale, trying to read instructions marked faintly in chalk on a piece of metal, that sort of thing. If your biggest exertion each day was the nod that drops your welding mask into place, how would you feel at the end of the shift?"

"Better," said the welder. "And cleaner."

"Let me tell you," said the plant manager, "welders in Japan go home clean and with energy to spare. It's past time that we provided you a clean, comfortable, and efficient cell in which to do what you've been trained to do, whether it's a massive metal-arc pass on a big piece of pipe or one of those surgical tungsten-arc welds on a solenoid. What do you think of that?"

"I'm not sure," the welder said. "But why do all this for me?"

"Because it's not just the best possible solution for you and your well-being; it's the ultimate solution to this plant being world-class competitive. And now that it's here, I guess I'm as bewildered as you are that it didn't happen sooner."

The above dialogue is fictitious, yet I'm sure analogous conversations are taking place all across North America these days. I thought about such a conversation after touring a world-class manufacturer of car and truck seats in southern Wisconsin. The welders, at work on seat frames, perform in cells inside a plant that is at least as clean as the average school cafeteria—and much quieter and more orderly! The new era in manufacturing is upon us, and it's equally exciting from the worker's and the manager's points of view.

Next To Godliness?

I spoke above of cleanliness and order. Those are good places to begin if you intend to compete with anyone, anywhere, with your products. A clean and orderly workplace means that the forklift bringing parts to a machine and taking finished parts away enters and exits efficiently. There is no scrap to dodge, no tool cart to avoid. If you're going to do this right, you might reach the point where you spend a great deal of time on such facets as optimal lighting and the best possible location for the drinking fountain. What you're doing, besides improving efficiency, is conveying that orderliness is the natural human condition. You'll know you're on the right track when this good housekeeping expands to other areas.

Cleanliness is an inseparable part of workplace organization, yet being tidy is no end in itself—surfaces don't need to be clean for the sake of appearance. Instead, they more readily show oil leaks or cracks, and even more important, they will be less likely to contribute to any sort of accident. Once the plant is clean, you can easily move machinery and equipment around to improve workflow. That will reduce the repetitive movement our welder friend found so exhausting and it means you may be able to cut back on personnel by arranging several machines for one person with multiple skills to monitor.

Having machines and equipment aligned so they work best also will reduce setup time. As companies become increasingly responsive to the marketplace, setup time or changeover will become more and more crucial. The injection-molded plastics firm that can produce a toy one day and an auto aftermarket component the next will find it has the jump on the competition. Setup time can be reduced by separating the work that can be done when the machine is stopped versus when it is running. All prep work possible can and should be done away from the machine. Reducing the time needed for adjustments and test runs also is necessary to minimize production lost from changeover.

Another area where efficiency matters is the conveyor area. A decade ago, I paid a visit to a manufacturing operation in southeastern Pennsylvania. This place had a monorail inventory system where parts dangled on hooks and moved along as four miles of aerial inventory. The company believed that, because inventory wasn't underfoot, it was efficient. Nothing could have been further from the truth, as assemblers relied on this excess to cover up for the fact that there was a high rate of rework. Happily, just-in-time inventory has replaced this seemingly endless array of dangling parts, and the New York Stock Exchange-listed company is in the black. In other words, conveyors can improve productivity, but they can just as easily decline into storage points for excess inventory and, therefore, unnecessary investment.

The small manufacturer, perpetually fearful of being overwhelmed by a global company, can compete worldwide by going after the small-lot production business. If the firm is tenacious, it's difficult for a large company to compete toe-to-toe when only a few hundred or a few thousand parts are needed. Increased speed of changeover will help companies large and small make more profit from mature endeavors, too. If you're convinced that you'll be producing the same widgets in the same sizes, shapes, and quantities forever, you need to look at the process. If you don't, your complacency could cost you customers when the competition ups quality, lowers manufacturing costs, and speeds deliveries with new processes.

Smaller, short-run firms face increased pressures from the constant changes caused by product variety and volume. One answer is to mix the production of various products. Productivity will be maintained as one of several products is dropped from the line and another is added. If you're running four different products, for example, and you experience some kind of glitch, that can adversely affect only one-quarter of your inventory, production, shipping, etc. And with a multiple-product line, you will be able to realize economies as you fine-tune the system.

Serving The Producer

Looking at the same tidy production area from on high, there's a lot to be learned from patterns of movement. Are your production people, the heart and soul of your process, in one place? Or do they move about, searching for wrenches or welding rods or electrical outlets? Production support should revolve around the producer. But even the most efficient worker and machine will bog down if preproduction and postproduction aren't equally efficient. A magnificent new machine will pile up inventory in its wake unless you are as concerned about moving those freshly assembled pieces efficiently to shipping as you were about keeping the machine in parts.

From our perch up above, we can also see whether inventory is handled excessively and whether the intelligent features added to the machines (warning lights, gauges, etc.) improve or impede productivity. While we're up here, glance at your inventory. If it takes up more than a very small percentage of the building, you need to improve. Now is a good time, too, to think about an ultimate flow to production. What would it look like?

The plant where car and truck seats were made did have a cadre of welders in cells, but this wasn't the end of their careers. Operators spent one day every other week servicing the line, which allowed them to learn the process from before it hit the welding department to the point where upholstery was added to the freshly welded and painted frames. Such job rotation is another mark of a world-class competitor. Equally important, the modern tools and methods allowed operators to use different physical and mental processes without any strain and to see how the finished products of their peers stacked up. I have to think the results were a heightened sense of being part of a team and a high level of concern for quality.

All of these good things were being accomplished without an inch-thick employee handbook or rules posted everywhere you looked. Instead, the welders and cutters and sewers and painters and shippers in the seat plant had been trained to look at everything in a standardized way. The *way* in which every employee approached his or her assignment was the same. Management was constantly at work on taking the wasteful, potentially dangerous, tiring and mind-dulling activity out of even the most mundane task. In return, the employees were alert to constant improvement rather than to rules written by someone half a continent away in corporate headquarters.

Let's back off a bit more and look at the plant as a single unit. If what we've discussed so far has taken place in each department, the level of awareness of the plant's function will be uniformly high among all employees. Once you reach this point of awareness, it's easy to convince your people that they must treat other departments as if those departments were valued customers. The plant will become more self-controlled as it becomes more decentralized, with fewer emergencies being bucked upstairs to the manager's office. This gives the manager the time to continue improvement and to contribute to the corporation's requests for managerial input in the planning process.

As operators become more familiar with and attuned to their machines, defective parts should decrease in number, and downtime should dwindle. This is because the production worker is attentive to changes in the process and can catch altered conditions at the moment they occur. Consequently there is less scrap, since the operator may have detected an abnormality while the machine was still producing acceptable products. To attune your people, make them responsible for routine lubrication and maintenance. You will be surprised at how eager many of them are to learn the intricacies of the equipment. You may find, too, that the small monetary reward you add for their maintenance chores is only a fraction of the amount being saved by decreased downtime.

Another area being influenced by new thinking in manufacturing is the relationship with suppliers. A small number of strategically important suppliers who are seen as extensions of the line will result in constant communication, sharing of technology, decreased defects, and similar philosophies. If you are a supplier, your increased attentiveness will result in more security as superior performance, knowledge of the client, and mutual prosperity make you difficult to dislodge.

Kanban

Kanban is a proven way in which departments can communicate. This can be done with kanban or instruction cards that are attached to a group of parts. The information on such a card tells where the parts are headed, where they are from, when they are needed, the part number, the quantity, and more. Any employee in a world-class manufacturing setting should be trained to examine a kanban card and take appropriate action. After the parts are assembled into finished products, the cards are collected, and inventory and production are adjusted accordingly. In this way the plant keeps inventory at the absolute minimum (requiring minimal investment), and no more parts or products are assembled than are required (no excess inventory, no orphan subassemblies). This has been done for years with bar codes and other data-processing methods, but the relatively simple kanban system seems to work as well as any.

You may by now realize that many of the techniques under discussion were first attempted and practiced to virtual perfection in Japan. There's a tendency here to congratulate the Japanese for their manufacturing methods, but to fault them for looking at people only in terms of numbers and productivity. Not only is that bigoted, it's untrue. Kiyoshi Suzaki, in his recent book, *The New Manufacturing Challenge,* warns that successful managers must abandon traditional work styles and enter "into an unknown and open environment where titles, responsibilities, and office space mean little." He recommends daily mingling with operators, group-improvement activities, awards, bulletin boards devoted to news of worker improvements, and, above all, a sincere concern for each person's problems.

He further advocates implementing all of these suggestions and others by undertaking an individual project. Following a single success, the manager can then segue to more ambitious undertakings, though he or she must bear in mind that improvement is continuous and therefore is never finished. The just-in-time inventory techniques, total quality control approaches, and productive maintenance techniques aren't ends in themselves, but means to the impossible goals of producing perfect products under perfect conditions.

I'll close by recommending another book, one that reaches many of the same conclusions as the Suzaki work, but does so in a much more entertaining way. *The Goal,* by Eliyahu M. Goldratt and Jeff Cox, is the fictionalized story of a plant manager who has received an ultimatum from his boss: either make the plant productive and profitable within three months, or it will be closed. The hero, Al Rogo, is responsible for a factory with all of the tools but none of the techniques so necessary to fill orders correctly and in a timely, quality-conscious manner. To complicate matters, the more time he spends at the plant, the more he alienates his wife and becomes distant from his children.

Against All Odds

But since this is fiction, there is hope. Al Rogo is coached episodically by Jonah, a brilliant Israeli management consultant who leads the plant manager toward efficiency and productivity by asking him provoking questions—then flying to one coast or the other without offering easy answers. Working with factory supervisors, Al uses Jonah's unconventional wisdom to eliminate production-line bottlenecks and soon turns around the sluggish and inefficient plant and its processes.

Like all good fiction, there's a tension that's maintained until the very last page. Besides battling corporate inflexibility, Al isn't sure of what his goal as the plant manager should be. When he realizes that his only goal is continuous improvement, and that continuous improvement moves away as you step toward it, he becomes a Jonah-like guru, dispensing advice to an old friend as the two fly back from Japan after a successful selling trip.

Whether you like the straight approach that Suzaki uses or the creative approach favored by Goldratt and Cox, it behooves you to learn all you can about modern manufacturing methods. In an increasingly global economy, it's your best long-range plan—your goal, if you will.

Key Points:

○ To be world-class competitive, start with a clean and orderly workplace.

○ All personnel should constantly search for ways to reduce setup time.

○ Pre- and postproduction must be as efficient as the actual production process.

○ All workers in a plant should approach their assignments in a standardized way and be alert for possible improvements.

○ All employees in a world class manufacturing setting should be trained to examine a *kanban* card and take appropriate action.

○ Just-in-time inventory techniques, total quality control and productive maintenance aren't ends in themselves, but means to the goal of producing perfect products under perfect conditions.

○ Your best long-range plan in an increasingly global economy is to learn all you can about modern manufacturing methods.

Chapter 10

It's the 11th working day of the month. The chief executive officer is, as usual, on edge. This is the day the computer spits out last month's financial results.

The CEO's nervousness escalates until 4 p.m., when he can stand it no longer. He charges into an adjoining office. Here he finds the chief financial officer shaking his head in disbelief over the first computer run. The CEO snatches up the printout and groans, "It can't be, it just can't be. No way!" The shock, furrowed brows, and disbelief point to the fact that the company's information system needs work—intensive work.

Compare that with the office where the CEO calmly reads monthly financial reports without surprise. After all, throughout the month information has been available daily that indicates with a high degree of certainty what the month-end results will be. The 30-day report of forecasted versus actual results rarely shows a variance of more than 5 percent. Amazingly, this company doesn't have a sophisticated computer. Nor are internal control systems automated. Why the difference?

You probably know CEOs who fall into both classes—companies where it's a surprise every month, usually unpleasant, and others where results are consistently and amazingly close to forecast. The difference lies in a good, effective management information system. When you're a two-person shop, management information can be passed easily. All you have to do is yell across the shop floor that the XYZ order came in. But, as your business grows and becomes more complex, with more people, products, and processes, tracking developments is absolutely essential to your success.

Several years ago, I had some preliminary talks about consulting with the owner of a company that purchases, modifies, and then rents expensive pieces of capital equipment to business and industry nationwide. The founder and CEO introduced me to everyone and noticed my shock on seeing large and ponderous ledgers on the desk of the chief financial officer. Behind the CEO's closed door, he told me that the CFO was highly accurate, but that he dispensed no information on a regular or organized basis, and he had a phobia about automating the company's records.

"If that's so, how do you get timely information?" I asked. "And if you don't get timely information, how are you able to make timely decisions or accurate forecasts?"

A light went on inside the CEO's head (I suspect the bulb had been burning all along). "You know, that's one of our big problems. We've always had trouble with forecasts. Do you think regularly scheduled financial input would help?"

I would like to report that the chief executive officer convinced his CFO to better organize or automate. I don't know either to be the case. The company continues to do business, and I never did learn if the founder was able to solve his information problem. I do know this—without timely and accurate information, this is a company that will be unusually vulnerable to even mediocre competition. If that mediocre competition has an informational advantage, our friends will wither on their previously very lucrative vine.

There are two main elements in any information and control system. First, you must identify the key result areas—call them KRAs—that really make a difference in your operation. Track them every day, or every shift, if necessary. Second, provide immediate information feedback to those who can act on it, not to those who can criticize or second-guess results. By the way, the key result areas are all line-driven.

Your system must go on red alert whenever troubling anomalies pop up. These anomalies differ somewhat in order of importance from one company to another, but usually include such areas as backlog levels, scrap or shrinkage, daily production, machine downtime, setup time, customer complaints, sales by product class, number of late deliveries, indirect labor, and speed of orders through the system. You know your company will be affected when your top salesperson is lured away by your most aggressive competitor. But do you know the impact and the consequences when one of your machines goes down because of poor maintenance on a die?

Resistance to the idea of a management information system often occurs, but there are really no valid reasons that preclude its installation. You can be prepared to experience such comments as:

- Our industry is different.

- Our manufacturing processes are such that we can't make accurate forecasts.

- Our raw-material costs fluctuate, so it's impossible for us to put together a system that provides appropriate controls and immediate feedback.

No Excuses

Don't accept any of these cop-outs from yourself or your managers. The truth is that companies of all sizes in all major industrial categories rely on management information systems to provide for control and responsiveness when it is important: at the time a critical variance occurs. An on-line system as part of a decentralized information system is the trend nowadays.

How does it work? Let's look in the paint department of a manufacturer of machine parts. A painter enters into the system that he or she is using a drum of flat-black paint intended for one of your products. The system will check to see that there is sufficient paint inventory and that there are enough of the parts produced to be painted. It calculates whether the paint being used is the right amount, and it decides how much paint should be expended or left over, based on the number of parts coated. A thorough system will prevent errors and reduce rework. Ideally, if you inadvertently create defective parts, it will also tell you how best to recoup your loss. In short, anything that affects profit or loss will be analyzed and passed on.

Histories of troubled businesses testify to the fact that two or three weeks after a historical document (the monthly profit-and-loss statement) reports a variance, the time for correction is long past. The cost of delay has proved to be significant and is compounded by a frantic scramble to define causes and identify responsibility, with important day-to-day tasks being relegated to second-class priority.

Those companies that have effective controls in place have thoughtfully examined critical points in their business. There are not that many key areas. Based on the backlog, data on projected volume and margin against plan are put in place at the beginning of each month. Adjustments are made daily to cover production, shipments, cancellations, and new orders received for shipment during the month.

For example, perhaps you operate with standard manufacturing costs and have an information system that responds to volume and mix variances. If you are on top of your manufacturing operations, you probably have an hours reporting system. Standards of performance for each job are related to volume or some other activity indicator each day. Your supervisor can receive daily reports showing performance against those standards and reasons why variances occurred and what corrective action was taken. Even better, you are organized in cells and know your costs by day for each cell.

Every well-run manufacturing operation records scrap daily. It's a clear indicator of a whole range of concerns—from raw material defects to labor or machinery malfunctions—that merit immediate corrective action. Scrap with rework virtually doubles the negative impact on production schedules, making this a critical element of attention and control.

Typically, your utility costs are predictable and also under control. If they are an important part of your manufacturing expense, they are monitored daily so that you know immediately when usage changes. Go right down the list of other major expense classifications, whether they be repairs, supply purchases, or rail or truck demurrage. Whatever the expense, variances are your early warnings—the clues that will give the people responsible opportunities for timely reaction. Speaking of timely reaction, any time- or money-saving suggestion can be evaluated quickly with an on-line system. If the painter says more parts can be covered with the same amount of paint, you will learn very quickly if the idea has merit.

You need not, on the other hand, pay much attention during any one month to most so-called overhead expenses. Ongoing costs in such functional areas as research and development, marketing and sales, engineering, and administration will not vary materially if your annual planning for each department has been thorough and thoughtful. You will have provided the resources that are necessary for each group to carry out its responsibilities and meet key objectives for the year. Your monthly personnel chart shows individual department staffing by jobs against the plan.

Imparting The Message

The second key element for an effective management information and control system is communication—how the information is disseminated and used.

Certainly you should not keep bad news a secret from the CEO. But rather than requiring that your managers rush right to the top with a disappointing report, isn't it better to let those individuals directly responsible receive the results of the day's work before the next person up the line reviews the reports? It's more effective to give these persons and each level of management about half a day of lead time to respond to variances. In other words, give them time to find the answers, talk to the production workers, make suggestions, and get things straightened out. Then, when asked why a variance occurred, they have the answer ready and can indicate the corrective measures taken. You, as the next-level supervisor, get the information you really need. The same philosophy should extend all the way to the top, with the information consolidated and presented in a manner that meets the needs of the individual receiving it.

This is important. A digest of information, as opposed to a stack of unedited facts and figures, will result in increased efficiency and fewer delays in the decision-making process. Every U.S. President in the 20th century has employed a cadre of experts to note all that has happened in the last 24 hours, boil it down, and tell him of its relative significance in a report the following morning. Running the country is no different from running a corporation here—to make timely decisions, the right information and the right *amount* of information are both necessary.

Those who work day in and day out with management information systems talk about the difference between data and information. Data is everything entered in the system, whereas information is a meaningful interpretation of that data. The difference between data and information is usually a matter of organization. Your best people should oversee the setting up of the system. No vendor will be aware of your corporation's priorities—the order of importance of the information gathered from all that data.

All this may sound simple and logical in the abstract. However, examining in minute detail the pertinent components of your business takes time and patience. Organization-wide understanding of the importance of these key factors also is critical to efficient control. It is equally true of a packer on the floor or a financial vice president responsible for short-term investments. Each person involved must be part of the communication chain.

Training your employees to operate your management information system is a critical part of the setup and requires continuous commitment, so says a friend, Frank Koch of Genco Distribution System in Pittsburgh. "Besides classroom time that results in understanding of an ample user's manual, some type of help screen should be a part of the software."

Koch advises you to ensure that the management information expert you deal with has a strong support arm. He also believes a sound way to screen these experts is to note whether they have experience with corporations similar to yours in size and intent. A retailer with a single outlet can read a couple of computer magazines, go to a store, and purchase a piece of software that will more than meet the company's needs, Koch indicates. "But if you're a manufacturer of any size, you will need people who can take what you have told them and create a good relational system, then analyze it for you, and explain how it will run your business better.

"Software is fairly easy to change, based on your type of environment," he says. "So what's important is finding someone who will be your consulting firm, who will work hand-in-hand with you."

Insist that the consultant not only set up your program but also put into place methods of preventing the information from becoming unwieldy. If your firm is fortunate enough to grow, to acquire divisions, and open new markets, you will need an information system that is programmed to receive new data, weigh its importance, and provide the information needed for continued success.

I can't begin to tell you how accomplished some information management systems are. *Fortune* recently told of several companies that excel in "haystack searching." One firm, Verity, Inc., of Mountain View, California, produces a retrieval system that can rank documents in order of importance. The program is called Topic and it is not only capable, says an expert, "of giving you everything on a subject, but of putting the good stuff on top."

No Surprises

When controls are in place, when the information is carefully monitored, when responses to variances are prompt, it's easy to see why there are no surprises at month's end. Then the monthly financial statement becomes more of a report for government authorities than a source for operating decisions—and is certainly less of a source of anxiety. The key, of course, is that however your information system is designed or implemented, it must respond to the needs of your company.

Good management works each day to deliver its plan. Those without the tools are in a constant flurry of activity and discover only after the fact what really happened in a given time period. Then explanations become overstated and overbearing and degenerate into excuses. Reports flourish and the appropriateness of response becomes an exercise in fault-finding. The business becomes enmeshed in disputes and meetings that, at best, do nothing to move the company forward and are often more likely to be destructive.

It's in your power to take the afternoon off to play golf on the 11th working day of any month. If you subscribe to the cult that manages by "inner voices," or belong to the group that relies on once-a-month reports, it's not likely to happen. But a good management information system can be your ticket to a relaxed and pleasurable 18 holes.

Key Points:

○ An effective management information system is crucial for timely decision-making and accurate forecasting.

○ You must identify and track the key result areas that really make a difference in your operation and give immediate feedback to those who can *act* on it.

○ Imparting the message is key—how the information is disseminated and used.

○ The right information and the right *amount* of information are both necessary.

○ Training employees to operate management information systems is critical and requires continuous commitment.

○ Information systems must respond to the needs of your company. There should be no surprises at month's end.

Chapter 11

"Change starts when someone sees the next step."
—William Drayton

"Discoveries are often made by not following instructions, by going off the main road, by trying the untried."
—Frank Tyger

Economic woes were only partly to blame for the recession of the early 1990s. Lackluster sales of new products have a deeper cause: companies are focusing too heavily on the finished product and not on who is buying the product. Too often, industry leaders wait until after a product has been placed on store shelves to find out why it isn't selling, or why it simply doesn't work.

The new focus for any company looking to develop a new product is teamwork—adding your employees, the consumer, and key suppliers to your team roster. Better approaches to new product development result in increased market share. Let's first look at the consumer as he or she relates to new product development. The consumer-based approach is a three-step process:

- Identify and research your target audience.
- Gain consumer identification of wants and needs.
- Develop consumer input on product refinement.

The development of any new product will be a failure unless you adhere to these three steps and listen to your customers with an open mind. Try to understand what you are hearing in focus groups. Behind every product there are specific consumer attitudes that direct behavior. And if a customer approaches you with a problem, solve it in a simple way and do it fast! The pace of product development in this country is slowed by breakdowns in planning and production.

When developing new product concepts, gear them toward a significant need not already addressed on the market. Start with a clear picture of what your company is trying to accomplish, and prioritize your objectives. Involve your customers, employees, and suppliers in these discussions. Here, two-way communication among all participants ensures that everyone is hearing the same thing. This isn't always as easy as it sounds, as a recent conversation at the local camera store will show.

Too Good A Product?

The retailer asked if I wanted to try Kodak's relatively new Ektar film, touted to deliver the most vivid color prints in the history of 35-millimeter photography. I said I was pleased with the results I'd obtained with Kodak's Kodacolor Gold Plus print film. "That's the trouble," he said. "So is everybody else."

Kodak no doubt put together consumer-focus groups after their research and development people produced Ektar. They probably asked group members if they wanted even better pictures than they'd obtained in the past. No consumer in his or her right mind would say no, but perhaps Kodak did not realize how pleased the public was with Kodacolor. When Ektar came out, consumers saw the higher price, glanced happily through photos they'd shot, and opted once again for Kodacolor. Amateurs shoot more than 95 percent of the color print film in this country, and to amateur eyes, the quality difference was not worth the money. To spark sales, Kodak has widened distribution and has begun offering 55-cents-a-roll discount coupons on Ektar film.

Kodak has been one of America's strongest companies, a real blue-chipper. In an era when U.S. products are sometimes hard to find on foreign shelves, the familiar yellow Kodak sign is virtually as common as Coca-Cola or Pepsi. So we're only guessing why Ektar has not been a smash hit. Did the company feel there was a significant need not already addressed on the market? What were Kodak's objectives? Were they clear and understood by everyone, in their order of importance? Does Ektar process even more easily or more quickly than Kodak Gold, which can be turned into prints in hours by processors all over the country? Or has Kodak reached that bittersweet point where the product is so good that consumers cannot detect—and will not pay for—further improvement?

We have to assume that the company involved its consumers, employees, and suppliers in the product development process. Communication among all participants ensures that everyone is hearing the same thing. At Ford Motor Company, internal-communications skills and teamwork are so important that they are part of the overall performance-review process. That may be part of the reason Ford is realizing a string of product successes and increased market share.

Speaking of automobiles, the high-performance Dodge Viper took me aback when it was introduced. What was the intent of Chrysler's Lee Iacocca in producing a radically styled, high-powered, gas-guzzling sports car? Again, I have no access to Chrysler corporate motives. But I have to think that Iacocca backed development of the Viper for one or more of the following reasons:

- Research indicated that there was a market for such a car. Perhaps there are drivers who dislike the General Motors Corvette but do not want to buy a foreign sports car.

- The interest generated by the Viper will increase traffic at the company's dealerships. People who have never purchased a Chrysler product will be drawn by the Viper, and could come away impressed with everything from a Jeep to a sedan.

- Iacocca needed to test the development of his new, $1 billion product development center. You never know if your massive investment will work until it goes through the cycle for which it was intended.

- After learning that the Viper would be no more than a break-even proposition, Iacocca authorized production because he felt the company needed a flagship car that was unique. From that flagship could be developed car models that will make money and influence the corporation in other ways for years to come.

- Could his suppliers have had any influence? Could the Viper have been the sum total of all the new, subcontracted thinking that serves Chrysler?

Several automotive magazines named the Viper "Car of the Year." So did *Fortune* magazine, but for a different reason. "Accolades go to Chrysler for meeting its goal of producing a car from start to finish in less than 36 months—just like the Japanese.... The No. 3 auto maker restricted the development effort... yet the $50,000 Viper is winning raves for—believe it or not—design. More than 4,000 people wrote Chrysler saying they wanted the Viper even before the company began accepting orders."

A tantalizing follow-up question may be this: will the product development center's increased responsiveness turn product failure into product success for the car maker? Can management make the difference where a new product is concerned? Chrysler may have introduced the Viper for one of the many reasons that new products are needed: product obsolescence and life cycles, market need, growth, and survival. Those who watch the domestic automobile industry are aware of other benefits. Every time a new model is introduced, assembly-line attendance improves. Workers want to be a part of the new product! If the product is prestigious, so much the better. Goodyear points out that its racing-tire department has less absenteeism and is more productive per person than its passenger-tire or truck-tire counterpart.

New Products And Failure

Despite this upbeat note, most new products fail. I believe that the failure rate will be lower in the future as new products are smaller in number but reach the market much quicker and are more in sync with the long-range plans of the corporation. Knee-jerk reaction is a synonym for poor management; but someone will have to make a go or no-go decision on hastily assembled information. That person must keep in mind that a new product has to fit the corporate scheme of things for it to prosper. For example, Subaru has a dramatic new sports car. Yet sales for this technologically interesting piece of equipment are disappointing. It must be due to the highly dependable but not very exciting image that seems to be a part of Subaru's long-range corporate strategy.

Or do some companies fail to give their new-product programs high visibility, putting them in the mainstream of corporate activities? While developing your new product, you are also developing a structure within your organization to bring ideas that will work into the marketplace. Gear your specialists to become "specialized generalists." Will the bells and whistles really add value in the eyes of your customers?

If the answer is no, confront the technological expertise of your designer with what the customer wants and will pay for. Arrange a time to have your designer meet face-to-face with the customers and present ideas for refinement using qualitative research. Don't design something that isn't consistent with consumer needs or the manufacturing capabilities of the organization. Kodak may be able to produce the richest and most sumptuous color print film on earth. But does it know without doubt that there is a substantial market for the product?

Don't let my conjecture about Ektar film prevent you from implementing Continuous Improvement Programs. By definition, improvement on a product never ends as employees search for ways to "do it better." I have to think that Kodak's reliable Kodacolor Gold Plus film has been subjected to, and benefited from, continuous improvement. And if there's no way to make Ektar better, it can always be made faster and with less capital outlay.

One of my clients, Adaptive Micro Systems (AMS), successfully executed new product development using a team approach. Several years ago, AMS, a manufacturer and marketer of Light Emitting Diode (LED) message displays, identified wholesale buying clubs as a potential market. Sales of the LED signs in the clubs were growing. The company believed it could develop a product for this market that would represent a significant improvement in quality, offer unique features that the competitors' products did not and at a comparable or lower price.

Assembling The Team

AMS began with market research, promotion, product management, manufacturing, and engineering people working together. Market research indicated that the product was price-sensitive. It also identified the buyer's critical needs and the major customers who dominate this market. Their requirements for delivery, packaging, and support were all known well in advance. At the same time, the product development process was under way with manufacturing and engineering working together on the design and manufacturability, calling on common components used in the past whenever possible.

In four months, a production prototype was ready and the product successfully introduced to the buying clubs.

Customer acceptance has been excellent. The customers are buying. It appears that the product meets or exceeds the company's sales goals. This was a team effort that covered all bases, did it right, and did it fast. AMS built a product using a multifunctional team's talents to respond to customer needs.

While focusing on customer needs, look to projected costs and serviceability from a maintenance and repair standpoint as it relates to product reliability. Here, too, goals should be clearly articulated. Product testing should confirm that these goals have been achieved and the product meets or exceeds the performance of competitive products.

Throughout the process, the team challenges its approach and searches for ways to reduce development time and cost even further. You cannot overdo planning. The temptation is to pick up the CAD system or pencil and begin drawing. This is premature until you clearly identify and validate all product criteria.

The same principles apply to a service organization. Another client, North Shore Bank in Milwaukee, has implemented these proven principles. Recently, it has been promoting a program offering unconditional guarantees.

As previously mentioned, customers receive $5 if the customer service representative doesn't call them by name and another $5 if they have to wait more than five minutes for service. The latest guarantee offers $5 if any errors are detected in an account.

The first two may not appear all that risky. They certainly require trained customer service representatives, flexible personnel, and accurate schedules. You can be certain the branch manager will jump behind the counter whenever it appears that a customer may have to wait more than five minutes. But isn't that what service is all about?

The third unconditional guarantee, however, is a little more challenging. Here a team went to work to identify where errors most often occur and put into place a simple, permanent solution. More important, the organization rallied to meet the new challenge. It's also important to note how North Shore has positioned itself with its customers. It gives them personal recognition, prompt service, and assured accuracy in recording and reporting each transaction.

The product development process appears simple, logical, and easy to implement. It's not. Old habits, relationships, and turf boundaries change slowly. What is needed is a firm, enthusiastic, and unyielding commitment to the customer, product, and program. The goal must always be to design a product that is cost-effective, fulfills the unmet needs of the target audience, and is appealing to new and existing customers.

Why not give it a try? It works, and it will give your organization another leg up to becoming world-class in every way.

Key Points:

○ Companies run into problems when they focus too heavily on the finished product and not on who is buying the product.

○ Teamwork is key to the product development process. Teams should include employees, consumers and suppliers.

○ New products will fail unless you listen to your customer with an open mind.

○ Most new products fail. Don't design a product that isn't consistent with consumer needs or your manufacturing capabilities.

○ Product improvement is a continuing process. During product development, the team constantly challenges its approach and searches for new ways to reduce development time and costs.

Chapter 12

"We find comfort among those who agree with us—growth among those who don't."
—Frank A. Clark

Wanted: Consultant to straighten out the administrative (or, alternatively, marketing, wage and benefits, business planning, financial, communications, organization effectiveness) problems of XYZ Co. Must be brilliant, trustworthy, fearless, flexible, and indestructible. Qualified saints will be considered, but martyrs need not apply.

That is exaggerated, perhaps, but not atypical of the gulf that sometimes separates perceptions and realities in management consultant relationships. There are, however, some guidelines that one can follow in selecting and working with people who can help you out of these problem situations. When observed, these rules may help to achieve about 60 percent of the above description.

I might add here that, while consulting is my profession, I'm also on the buy side and use consultants in my business when their special skills are needed. Both my clients and consultants have heard what follows.

As a preliminary caution, make the distinction between those problems that you can deal with internally and those that require special expertise or a disinterested, objective perspective. You may often find that use of consultants can be less costly and equally as effective as adding staff.

Consider some of the questions companies may face:

• Can you restructure your company to meet the challenge of rapid growth, or is it more effective to retain a firm to conduct an organization development study?

• Do you want to undertake a search for an acquisition on your own, or would a specialist speed up the process of identifying candidates, doing preliminary screening, and assisting in the negotiations?

• Would an outside facilitator be of value in guiding you through a formal planning process, or can you undertake the effort without assistance?

• Will it be better to hire a full-time human resources person, or would your needs be best served by drawing on the part-time services of a team of legal, communications, training, and search specialists to handle your human resources requirements?

• Does your marketing staff have the capability to undertake the research for a new product?

Once you have decided to hire a consultant, it is most important to know the firm and the people you retain. Inquire into experience in your industry, background, and areas of specialization. If the problem is actuarial-based benefit planning, rule out firms without experienced, qualified specialists on staff. Request a current client list and ask to interview past and present clients. Make inquiries of clients who have worked with the specific consultants who will be assigned to your project. No ethical consultant will take on a project without the expertise to do the job well.

Can They Communicate?

In your preliminary meetings, evaluate carefully the communications skills of the entire group. You will depend on them to communicate their findings to your people and motivate them to implement the agreed-upon program. How well they do will be critical to the success of the assignment.

The second guideline is equally important. Be sure the chemistry is right. That is an absolute for success. It must exist between the client's chief executive officer and the top officers and associates of the consulting firm. Ask to meet all the members of the team who will be working with you and your staff. As the assignment progresses, never hesitate to request a change if tension develops or you have questions about the qualifications of someone working on your project. Clients are not in the "educating" business.

Speaking of education, a client recently told us about his experience with an ex-academic who is a leading consultant in a manufacturing field.

"We're growing but are not large, and we knew that this consultant had a national reputation," says the manufacturing VP. So we offered him a small retainer, which he accepted. It was only $1,000 a month, but I began to worry about taking enough or too much of our consultant's time. Eventually, I told him my thoughts, and he said he worried, too, about giving us our money's worth.

"We reached an agreement within a few minutes that he would not work for a competitor while he was advising us, and we settled on an hourly charge. The consultant knows he will be paid for all hours he works, and we understand the financial impact of any assignment. We always receive an estimate before the work begins. Everyone is happy. In fact, I don't know why I ever considered a retainer."

Retainers do indeed seem to be losing their cachet. When there were only one or two consultants in a fairly broad field, a company might retain a consultant to keep him or her away from the competition. But with the growing popularity of hiring consultants, the retainer has lost much of its appeal. Speaking as a consultant, I want neither of us to worry about compensation once it's agreed upon. There should be no surprises for the client when the bill arrives.

An important exception to the no-retainer concept was pointed out by Linda Glembocki, a former corporate attorney for Autotrol, the Milwaukee manufacturer and seller of valves and controls, primarily water-related. A retainer is used when you hire an attorney on an isolated, out-of-state matter, such as a product-liability lawsuit, not covered by insurance. This attorney may want a retainer because he or she doesn't know your company or method of payment. We have no local retainers."

Attorneys, by the very nature of their work, are in the consulting business. "A corporation's general counsel doesn't have the time or the licenses to practice in every state, even though a corporation may have operations in several states," Glembocki says. "If our insurance company doesn't provide counsel, I find one through peers who are members of a professional association, through our own outside counsel, or by consulting a state list."

Euphoria May Be Brief

Consulting engagements often begin—as they should—in a rosy glow of warmth and enthusiasm. But that euphoric state lasts only as long as it is supported by a businesslike relationship. Even if your project has a narrow focus and a predetermined termination, be sure the consultant provides a plan and detailed programs. Ask about the frequency of progress reports and evaluation meetings.

Be sure about fee structure, including hourly rates of the persons assigned to your project, the method for handling expenses, and billing format. An experienced firm will provide a realistic cost estimate on its own initiative.

Consultants deal in two commodities—experience and time. When the expenditure for an assignment is a significant expense for the client, that fact should be understood in advance. Progress billings should be provided as the assignment moves along, especially if unexpected circumstances indicate that changes may exceed the original estimate.

Clients, on the other hand, can contribute to cost efficiency by making sure the consultant's time is well spent. Don't require consultants to perform tasks—calculations, projects, or basic fact-finding—if data is available or your staff can produce it more economically. Use the firm to bring a new creativity and perspective to a problem. Conceptual thinking should be high on your priority list. Scratch bean-counting. Expect your consultant to discern nuances, to see things you may be missing through day-to-day familiarity.

Like all mortals, consultants function poorly in a vacuum. To be most effective, all members of the consulting team must feel they are true members of your team.

Don't withhold information, especially that which might come as an unpleasant surprise. This is especially important at the highest level of communication—between the chief executive officer and a senior partner, for example.

Spreading The Word

Be sure the consultant's mission is understood within your organization, and your staff recognizes that this venture has your full support. Document the information that is to be provided from internal sources, its scope and importance to the total project. It is not unusual for people who are insecure to sandbag an assignment, or at least impede its progress. Reassuring your staff will keep that from happening. They should also know they are part of the problem-solving team in order to assure enthusiastic participation in the implementation phase.

Finally, keep expectations at realistic levels. That is a point, perhaps, to resolve before interviewing the first firm. Miracle workers are hard to find. Let's talk to some consultants and those who hire consultants to hear what they have to say about expectations as viewed from both sides of the business.

A friend of ours is a former accountant who now serves as business manager and part-time instructor at a major university in upstate New York. He told us recently of his worst-ever consulting assignment, which occurred a number of years ago.

"[Name of major accounting firm] hired a huge number of us fresh MBA graduates in 1970 to serve as business consultants," he recalls. "Pairs of us would be farmed out to companies that needed to streamline financial functions. On my first two assignments, things went well. The companies were pleased with recommendations, we saved them a lot more than we charged, and the work was so interesting I didn't mind living for weeks at a time out of a suitcase in a motel in Ohio or in rural Massachusetts.

"But the third assignment was a place run by the founder, a control freak. We analyzed the functions, talked to the people, and concluded that the place was about 98 percent efficient. We handed the owner a report to that effect, and he hit the roof. He refused to accept our conclusions—and I mean he was livid!

"We went back to our offices in New York City and discussed matters with senior people," he remembers. "They said there were only two things to do, stand by the report, or hand the guy a piece of fiction he would swallow. None of us wanted to be deceitful, so the company ended up losing money on the assignment because the owner refused to accept our report."

A Consultant Defined

A technical consultant, Bill Coan of Neenah, Wisconsin, reminds us that: "A consultant is someone who borrows your watch to tell you the time. In other words, consultants can't tell most companies anything they don't want to hear. From the consultant's perspective, it is most important that you find out what the options are. You have to look for the solutions consistent with the mentality and implementation capability of the people who are there. You have to stay within those limits.

"My biggest impediment is that people within an organization frequently have their own agendas. Some feel that what's good for engineering can't be good for purchasing, and what's good for purchasing may have a negative influence on R&D. A consultant has to balance the competing demands of various management functions in order to do the job."

Coan has been consulting for more than 10 years, after success in engineering, production, and business-to-business advertising. In all that time, he can think of only two clients who made his job difficult:

- "Employees at one large manufacturer were extremely territorial. Every department blamed every other department for shortcomings. They would cooperate with me only if we were dealing in an area where they had no interest. Before trying to improve their productivity, I told management they would have to flatten the pyramid by de-compartmentalizing their plant."

- "The other company was even larger. They produce retail products in massive quantities, and the plant ran very well, based on systems that were in place. The systems were extremely well-thought-out, but a program would be running full blast one day and shut off the next. It seemed capricious to me and to hourly employees, but I suppose this will happen more rather than less as companies become more and more responsive to their markets. Nevertheless, I went home each evening not knowing if the line for which I was writing troubleshooting procedures would be in place when I returned the next day."

Coan adds that in the last decade he has seen quantum leaps in handling consultants efficiently. "At first, I would show up at a plant and sometimes sit for a couple hours before the people who had hired me could meet with me," he says. "Now, I'm about 90 percent productive, and it's because no one—including me—wants to see me loiter. I can't begin to tell you how much more intelligent and efficient my clients have become when it comes to getting the most out of what I have to offer."

The Client Side

Let's look at the consulting equation once again, this time from the perspective of the client. The director of marketing services for a very large and prominent maker of retail food products says he learned early to inform every employee that consultants would be on the premises, as well as the exact functions in which the consultants would be involved. "That eliminates fears of any sort of head-count reduction. I can't overemphasize the importance of putting your employees at ease with these people, because your own employees are the raw material from which solutions will be generated and implemented."

In addition to market research and consumer promotions, our acquaintance oversees design and graphics for packaged foods. He deals with several different sets of outsiders. "I don't see The Cambridge Group or other big-league consultants, but I frequently deal with The Nielsen Company and similar marketing experts. They survey the public and give us data from which we can better aim our efforts. We also deal with printers, graphic designers, etc., but those people are suppliers rather than consultants. From my point of view, a consultant is someone who will come in, survey your operation, and make suggestions designed to maximize productivity."

Can a firm function without outside help? Of course. On the other hand, if no outsiders except the vending-machine route driver ever get a look at what goes on behind your walls, how are you sure your operation is state-of-the-art? Consultants not only can bring you to up to speed, they also can delineate programs that make you the standard by which your business or industry is judged.

K e y   P o i n t s :

○ Before bringing on a consultant, you must distinguish between problems you can deal with internally and those needing special expertise or an objective perspective.

○ Carefully check a consultant's experience, skills and references.

○ Make sure the consultant can communicate and motivate. The right chemistry is an absolute for success.

○ Agree on fees and expectations before the assignment begins. There should be no surprises.

○ Your organization must understand the consultant's mission. Make your full support of the project clear to all.

○ Be well-prepared so the consultant's time with your people is productive.

○ Good consultants not only can bring you up to speed, they can help install programs that make your company the industry standard.

Chapter 13

Scheduling

When the history of the 20th century is written, it surely will be done using that marvel of our time, the computer program. I hope the writer will remember to give sufficient credit to the power and versatility of the personal computer, which today is able to instantly accomplish what a mainframe could not tackle a decade or two ago. Virtually anything the mind can imagine has been reduced to an intelligently conceived program on a small disk. Since our subject is scheduling, let's look at an appropriate personal-computer program to see how far we've progressed.

Among several low-cost programs that adapt to scheduling is Act! 2.1. The $229 product is recommended for "any business user who needs to track daily activities and manage relationships with others." I think the people who produce this savvy software may be too modest. Act! includes database, word processing, telemarketing and time-management functions. It has features such as tickler files, instant location of any record or group of records, and formats for to-do lists. It is offered in two-user and five-user versions and can serve as the basis for building a network of any size. All for less than the price of the most inexpensive facsimile machine.

I spoke with a Deep South manufacturer of electronic components about the feasibility of running an entire plant schedule on a personal computer. "You have to know what results you want, of course, but in terms of power and speed, a personal computer and the right program is all you need. I considered myself the last holdout before we purchased this little system, and I learned enough to be dangerous the first week. By now, about one year later, everyone is comfortable with it.

"Drawbacks? I don't know of any. The computers we purchased have enough memory that they can tackle anything," says the manager. "About the only thing I am unable to master is reading extended pieces, such as spreadsheets, on screen. I have to have it printed out so that I can hold it, mark it up, think about projections, and so on. But that's my own shortcoming and my only complaint, so you probably can tell that it works well," he says.

Computerized scheduling has saved the company $110,000 since the start of the firm's fiscal year seven months ago. "The program can tell me on any given day since it went on line what the payoff is. We went into the black with this system, which is a five-PC network, nine weeks after installation. That's pretty amazing when you consider that it took us two to three weeks to load all of the pertinent information."

Just as amazing, according to an expert we know, are the non-computer improvements in scheduling. Lynn Remillard is manager of marketing services for Weasler Engineering, Inc., in West Bend, Wisconsin. In her seven-plus years there, the time between when an order was taken and when production began has been cut in half.

"When I began, we had a backlog of orders totaling $1-2 million. Today, that figure is $100,000 to $200,000, so we've made great strides," Remillard says. The increased efficiency, she adds, was customer-driven. As more of Weasler's customers went to just-in-time inventory procedures, order sizes decreased from approximately 120 pieces to fewer than 70. Lead times were correspondingly reduced from eight weeks to six and to as little as one or two weeks in emergencies.

While Weasler is fully computerized, much of the success of production hinges on one clerical person. "He decides when to release the order, then he issues the material to the shop," she says. "He tries to release the order based on the difficulty of the product—on how many machines it will have to cross in order to be produced at maximum efficiency ...Despite the computer, there is more manual follow-up, at least one weekly meeting and constant communication with suppliers."

It's impossible to overemphasize supplier importance in scheduling. "If you can't ship, communicate!" the old sign says. Suppliers must be impressed with the fact that you've adopted new methodology. They have to discern your new ordering patterns and new standards, shipping the right parts at the right time and being rewarded when their quality and responsiveness meet or exceed the needs of your plant. If you want suppliers to provide the best possible service, it behooves you to open up your system and invite them to attune their operation to it.

That's what Gary Ford, vice president and director of total quality management (TQM) for Accu-Rate, Inc., a manufacturer of dry-materials feeders in Whitewater, Wisconsin, did in the fall of 1992. He played host to a conference for all of his suppliers to ensure that they understood scheduling and his company's adherence to ISO standards of production. Ford also has cut in half the amount of time between when an order is received from a customer and when the item is manufactured.

"We eliminated all of the paperwork possible. We also took a team problem-solving approach to order entry. We looked at each step, decided whether that step added value to the product, made a flow chart, redocumented everything, and ran a trial. We reduced the time between receipt of the order and production by 50 percent," he says, adding that the key to productive scheduling may lie with the beholder. "Today, you have to take an operations perspective rather than a departmental perspective if you want to maximize scheduling."

The Benefits Of Scheduling

Once Act! or your own equally efficient scheduling program is in place, what are its benefits? Andy Lapczynski, former executive vice president and general manager of Manitex, Inc., a maker of marine and construction cranes in McAllen, Texas, says precise scheduling will provide optimal use of capital resources, including working capital and plant and equipment, as well as labor. "The goal is maximum revenue with minimum inventory."

Lapczynski advises beginning by comparing the level of work being scheduled against shippable backlogs. "This is a good indication whether you're building what you need and how readily it converts to revenue. That gives you a clear idea as to whether you're piling up excess inventory."

"Schedules are impacted by any inherent problems, and you have to compensate for them. In fact, you have to *solve* those problems if you ever expect maximum revenue from minimum inventory. The system has to be extremely flexible. Management needs to get involved by pinpointing the systemic problems and then eliminating those bottlenecks or machine breakdowns or excessive accumulations of scrap.

"Look at the entire system. It should be changing constantly, which shows you're in a dynamic environment. Whenever improvements occur, scheduling should change."

Gary Ford sees scheduling and quality as inseparable. "Taking for granted that you already have management rapport, there first should be an assessment of the current system's strengths and weaknesses. This can be done with a total-quality-management tool kit, the contents of which can vary from one company to another.

"Our kit has 230 tools. Some that we are using include policy deployment or planning, task teams, progressive management techniques, safety, ergonomics (working in cells), just-in-time (JIT) manufacturing, etc. I worked for the Japanese for a number of years, and I studied total quality management in Japan, so I have an advantage most people do not."

The Lone-Guru Error

In putting together a schedule that will maximize revenue with minimal investment or inventory, most companies make an elementary error, Ford believes. It is a common error made by any firm trying to solve the quality/productivity equation. "They subscribe to only one guru's philosophy. They may be committing to a philosophy that doesn't really fit that company's needs. Forcing a philosophy into an organization that may not fit will prevent optimal scheduling forever. You have to know what's out there, but you also must know your own company."

Regardless of which tool a company uses, "it is important that they pilot the tool. Pick an assembly area where it will be most successful. Once workers see the benefits of the new system, they will become more involved, making decisions in the work area. That's why it's called psychology of management."

State-of-the-art scheduling will indeed foster a cultural change, he says, no matter whose idea it was and whether it is called TQM or JIT or *kanban* or materials requirement planning. Implementation, says Ford, should follow four steps. "First comes the **vision.** Second is **commitment,** active commitment on a daily basis. Third is the **discipline** to a formal operating system, then improving it and documenting that improvement. Fourth is **leadership,** educating, counseling, rewarding, and delegating responsibility that results in team building. Those are the four TQM fundamentals."

Everyone even peripherally involved in scheduling has his or her own contention about what's needed for success. For Keith Clark, manager of manufacturing services for the John Deere Company's lawn and garden tractor division in Horicon, Wisconsin, it is this: "The assembly line must execute."

Deere products command top prices because of their excellent and long-standing reputation for quality. "In our environment," Clark says, "we have both materials requirement planning and JIT production or triggered production. We start at the assembly line and work our way back, maximizing efficiency in the press area, the manufacturing area, etc. Wherever a part produced under MRP is used in a department that triggers its inputs, we have inventory. The least desirable scenario is a supermarket or warehouse of parts. The most desirable, of course, is zero inventory. Again, to approach zero inventory, your assembly line has to execute."

Clark says the trigger theory of production works well if you are dealing with large capacity in a primary facility and if setup times are short and few in number. "The master plan sends a physical trigger that results in the material being produced.... Here, we have presses with perhaps 100 parts going across them at a time. There is no way to trigger and get a priority that makes any sense. So the system is prioritized, and that's MRP. This is all textbook stuff, yet the key is making your assembly lines work."

I don't know about you, but I find the thoughts of people such as Ford and Lapczynski and Clark reassuring. Their contentions tell me that they understand what must be done to move relentlessly toward zero inventory and maximum income via scheduling. They are modest to a fault, having in one generation set aside a century of thinking that America automatically knew best how to run a plant and manufacture a product.

Thoughts From The Past

As a point of reference, I picked up a 1967 book in the local library, *Production and Inventory Control, Principles and Techniques*, by G.W. Plossl and O.W. Wight. This volume shows how far we've come. Under "the objectives of production and inventory control," the authors furnish the following information:

"Three of the major objectives in most manufacturing firms intent on earning profit are:

- Maximum customer service.
- Minimum inventory investment.
- Efficient (low-cost) plant operation.

"The major problem in meeting these objectives is that they are *basically in conflict*. Maximum customer service can be provided if inventories are raised to very high levels and the plant is kept flexible by altering production levels and varying production schedules to meet the customers' changing demands. The second and third objectives thus suffer to meet the first. Efficient plant operation can be maintained if production levels are seldom changed, no overtime is incurred, and if machines are run for long periods once they are set up on a particular product— this results in large inventories and poor customer service while meeting the objective of maximum plant efficiency."

How times change! It's obvious from the above that we once looked at the changing demands of the marketplace as a liability rather than as a path to increased sales and income. The authors go on to relate that "inventories can be kept low if customers are made to wait and if the plant is forced to react rapidly to changes in customer requirements and interruptions in production." In a nutshell, that line of reasoning was why we turned to the Japanese to sharpen our production methods.

Is there anything to be learned from this 27-year-old book? There is. If you ever wonder how America slid into a less-than-productive state, the information is here. Plossl and Wight point out that: "Production control and inventory control developed separately. In its very beginnings, production control was only one of the many functions performed by the line foreman. He ordered material, set the size of the work force and the level of production by hiring and releasing people, expedited work through his department, and controlled customer service through the inventories that resulted from his efforts....

"Inventory control, on the other hand, developed—at least in theory—along more scientific lines. The basic concept of the economic lot size was first published in 1915, and the statistical approach to determining order points was presented by R.H. Wilson in 1934. However, these fairly sophisticated techniques of inventory management had very little application. Perhaps this was because the 1930s and 1940s were not years that encouraged scientific management. For most companies during the depression of the 1930s, the most important objective was survival... long-term profit and growth became subordinate."

This compartmentalization of functions, vertical management, and short-term thinking made us all less productive. Plossl and Wight believe that the biggest problem in applying advanced management techniques was the fact that they were tried before the firms had solved basic problems in controlling manufacturing. Had managers mastered scheduling earlier, it is not inconceivable that much else would have fallen into place.

What does 1990s-style scheduling do to quality control? John Deere's Keith Clark believes modern methods improve quality because "it becomes impossible to cover up manufacturing mistakes with inventory—it just won't work. But any attempt to reduce inventory will improve the quality of the product."

Scheduling And Quality Control

Carl R. Green, Sr., an engineer with McDonnell-Douglas in Cape Canaveral, Florida, and an information source for the American Society of Quality Control, says that only under ideal conditions can you remove all inspection functions from your schedule. "Where there are human factors and machines not designed for rigid controls, you require inspection. There are some functions, too, that can only be performed by the human eye.

"Complete elimination of inspection is an unrealistic immediate goal, because we have evolved into what we are now. We have to maintain the assurance that the as-built product reflects the as-designed product. Where the culture failed us was that our own self-interest prevented us from seeing our customers. Quality control isn't something to be eliminated. Instead, it is the key to evolutionary product improvement."

Green knows whereof he speaks. He was part of the team that developed the Delta Two rocket, the most trouble-free such device ever launched. In the face of constantly changing technology, he advocates personal integrity. "All these buzzwords have to mean something to workers and managers. The quality philosophy has to be part of each individual's consciousness. The link between quality and scheduling is vital. It's also inseparable."

Key Points:

○ Computerized scheduling has been a tremendous boon to business.

○ You can't overemphasize the importance of suppliers in the scheduling process. Suppliers must adapt their operations to your system.

○ A total logistics, rather than a departmental approach, will maximize scheduling effectiveness.

○ Precise scheduling will provide optimal use of capital resources. The goal is maximum product output with minimal inventory.

○ The link between scheduling and quality is vital and inseparable.

○ State-of-the-art scheduling involves the four TQM fundamentals: vision, commitment, discipline and leadership.

○ Times have changed! New marketplace demands are not threats but opportunities for greater sales and profits.

○ Inspection is necessary so the as-built product reflects the as-designed product.

Section II:
Managing People

(

Chapter 14

There's only so much power in any organization.
Spreading it around could improve your plant's productivity.

The first sign of people empowerment in American industry was a subtle one. Ten or more years ago, among the many executives on any given airline flight, there were one or two hourly employees. These blue-collar people, who may have been employed by empowerment pioneers such as Digital Equipment or Procter & Gamble or TRW, were traveling on business. They were headed somewhere to evaluate a new wrinkle in a manufacturing process, or to decide on a major capital outlay for a new piece of machinery, or to interview a prospective engineer. Because these hourly employees worked with the process or the equipment or the people, they knew best what was needed—and their companies knew they knew.

Nowadays, the friendly skies are filled with small groups of a company's employees flying this way or that to make a decision that will affect the economic health of the firm for some time to come. Hourly employee, straw boss, maintenance chief, and supervisor—American industry is discovering the knowledge and potential of these people, and the results are encouraging. Who better understands what needs to be done than the people whose hands and eyes and minds will keep the process or equipment productive and profitable once it is off-loaded and worked into the line?

What empowers them is this: they are authorized to make many of the far-reaching decisions formerly left to executives, decisions based on their experience, decisions that allow these hourly employees and their peers to better and more efficiently produce the company's products. Where are the mid-level managers who formerly made such decisions? Many industrial engineers, for example, have become facilitators for the men and women on the production floor. Other office workers have been furloughed, or have retired, as the communications conduit runs more directly between the production floor and the CEO's office.

"Empowerment means gradually shifting responsibilities or power from the office to the shop floor," says Roger Ahrens, who is director of manufacturing for the Gehl Co., the country's leading producer of short-line farm equipment. Headquartered in West Bend, Wisconsin, the publicly held corporation has had to face the tough times that have afflicted agriculture and construction markets in the early 1990s. Ahrens says, "Trust is the number one ingredient for successful people empowerment.

"It is easier to understand power if viewed as a limited commodity such as water," he continues. "There's only so much of it. You can pour it from one container to another, but the volume does not change. Even though we often deny that producer empowerment impacts office staff, the truth is that it does. To empower producers, you in effect remove power from the office and transfer it to the shop floor. All things remaining equal, this usually means some office staff reduction. The remaining manufacturing-support people are reoriented to become facilitators for their customers, who are the producers."

There are numerous examples of such empowerment throughout the United States. Nowhere is it more dramatic than a few miles up the road from West Bend at the Johnsonville Sausage Company plant. There, a team of hourly employees helped CEO Ralph Stayer make the decision to proceed with a major plant expansion. The workers told Stayer, without benefit of input from any office, that they could produce more sausage faster than he would ever have thought possible. They noted that there might be some overtime required initially, but that expansion seemed feasible to them. In six years, these empowered workers have created a 50 percent hike in productivity.

Such stories abound, and not always in the production sector. Aetna Life & Casualty has steadily improved customer service while reducing the ratio of managers to hourly employees from 1 to 7 to 1 to 30. Cereal maker General Mills has a night shift at a California plant that is so productive it operates without any supervision whatsoever. And an empowered team of clerks pointed out a paperwork problem at Federal Express that was needlessly costing the company more than $2 million a year.

'Tremendous Knowledge Out There'

Empowerment of workers, happily, has reached the stage where it is no longer a buzzword. Carl Just, plant manager of the Gehl Company's Lebanon, Pennsylvania, production facility, says maybe American industrialists saw the potential in empowerment when they realized that the range of intelligence on the line was at least as wide as it was on staff. "There's just a tremendous body of knowledge out there," he says.

"I like to have the operators of the CNC equipment do their own programming," Just says, citing an example. "Here are guys who run the machines and wrote the programs that run the machines. This gives me the opportunity to compensate them better than if they were just the operators."

Just's plant makes two types of manure spreaders and a mixer-feeder. Later it will be producing a bunk-unloader. He had seen empowerment work earlier, when the company was making fewer products with fewer people in a smaller facility nearby.

"The 45 employees we had at the old plant were more empowered than the current group of 100 employees because it takes a while for workers to orient themselves," he reports. "Here, we have new employees producing new products. If you had unlimited resources, you could empower them first, but it's not always practical, so you have to limp along as best you can."

In other words, Just is responsible for meeting production goals and staying within his budget, two constraints that don't always mesh with empowering employees. "We've brought two new production lines up in the past two months, so we're just now beginning to re-emphasize empowerment. It's a question of resources—you have to meet production goals along the way. I believe wholeheartedly in empowering employees, but on the other hand I will err on the side of expediency, which can send a bad message. It takes relative sophistication on both sides for empowerment to work well."

The Gehl Company began to empower workers initially at its smaller production facilities in South Dakota, Pennsylvania, and Georgia. Its West Bend, Wisconsin, facility has now started employee involvement and currently has eight empowered manufacturing teams in place. All these teams are focused on quality improvement. "For the most part, they are anxious to take the initiative and willing to assume responsibility for process and production," Ahrens says.

"Many companies try to implement employee-empowerment programs in a relatively complex environment. This approach often leads to employee frustration and unsatisfactory results," Ahrens adds. "Streamlining and simplification of process flows and administrative procedures and practices are often required before producer empowerment really takes hold. A test I frequently use to informally measure the level of transparency and complexity is to ask employees what they are producing. If they must refer to a blueprint or shop order to read me the part description, it is more likely an indication the operational environment is too complex for effective employee involvement. In an effective, empowered work environment, every producer must be able to understand and visualize patterns of production and cause-and-effect relationships.

"There are many ways to create an empowered organization," Ahrens says. "Massive educational programs for all employees is the method some organizations use to begin the process. My experience indicates this is often not the most effective method. I prefer using a low-cost, train-as-you-go approach. I like to start a low-key implementation with a few small groups of empowered people guided by a trained facilitator, and then gradually enlarge the implementation by building on small successes."

Carl Just points out that there already is empowerment awareness among production workers nationwide, so when the announcement is made that it will be undertaken, there isn't a lot of resistance. In fact, empowerment may have enough of a track record that employees in your shop will realize it isn't just another slogan you hope they will take to heart. "But once you begin," he says, "you can't fail them in some way by being too slow or too bureaucratic. If there is a problem, you had better be able to explain why you couldn't deliver. It's humbling, but management has to admit its frailties, admit it's not all-powerful."

The second step for managers is to commit themselves to the frequency of contact empowerment requires. If necessary,

Just says, management must divert resources from production to allow empowerment to take place. "Management has had a responsibility to drive the work ethic. Once your people are empowered, they will create and drive their own work ethic. It's up to management to set the tone for the expectation level. Then, the teams will follow.

"I also talk to them about the dignity of work, the need for productivity, the need for efficiency. If they want to buy homes and cars and send their kids to college, they can only do it in the manufacturing environment, where they're adding value to a product. They understand all this, and they bring a lot of pride to the organization. That's empowerment."

A Siege Mentality

It's only fair to balance things by including comments from an executive of a firm where empowerment is on shakier ground. This middle-aged manager runs a plant in the Illinois/Iowa Quad Cities, "where labor relations have always been terrible," he says.

"When we began to talk about empowerment to union people, they were suspicious. They assumed we had tried everything else and failed, so now we were going to let the employees take over and run the shop into the ground, a direction they felt it was headed anyway. Union officials saw empowerment as a way for management to bypass their authority. Recent events such as the Caterpillar strike have really thrown a monkey wrench into empowerment, which is a great theory. But here, for the time being, it's just that—a theory."

By now, you may certainly wonder if empowerment is right for your organization. Despite the clear thoughts and careful definitions of the two Gehl Company executives, you probably remain skeptical. Here, then, are the questions you may be pondering and answers to those questions. Empowering employees won't throw a line to a drowning company. And all the empowerment on earth won't help if you don't maintain a clear picture of customer wants and needs. But empowerment should do enviable things to your quality and efficiency as it makes your shop a more exciting place to work.

Q. How do I keep empowered employees focused on the problem?

A. There is a tendency to wander off track as empowered people find they are able to solve a problem; they may move on to something that does not pertain. But that is where the maligned and neglected middle managers come in. The industrial engineers and their peers must say, "You solved that problem. Now, tell me what the second most pressing problem is with this process?" In other words, middle managers maintain the agenda, furnish information and statistics and hand out "Atta boys." An active group of empowered production people will give such middle managers all of the work they can handle.

Q. Is the middle manager my eyes and ears in this empowered team?

A. Your eyes and ears had better be your own. Ideally, you will be able to walk in and out of a meeting and be treated for what you are—one more intellect aimed at finding the ultimate solution. No more and no less.

Q. If empowered people improve the bottom line, how should they be compensated?

A. We live in a capitalist society, yet not everyone sees a direct correlation between their performance and more pay. Why not ask your people what they would like? If you're really candid, you can always tell them you have X thousand of dollars to reward them for their diligence, and, within the bounds of sanity, you'd like to give each of them what he or she wants. One may take the cash, another may ask for a trust for his child, another may want you to add to her retirement, still another may opt for a Christmas bonus. You may be surprised—an empowered employee might say, "I've always wanted to learn how to program a computer. Would you pay for an introductory course at the local tech school?" Hopefully, at least one member of this empowered team will use the money for a new motorcycle or car or truck so that you can point to it in the parking lot and tell everyone that it's rolling proof of empowerment!

Q. Speaking of money, do empowered people have the authority to make capital expenditures? If so, how much?

A. An empowered team is an integrated team. As a part of it, you and the engineer and the accountant may be able to say, "We can spend $5 million if we have to, but we all hope this much talent will be able to solve the problem for less. What do you think?" Obviously, empowered people understand that saving money on a project will improve their own fiscal well-being and will, of course, help everyone in the entire plant. CEOs tell me empowered employees aren't spend-thrifts. Like the rest of us, they spend money only to get the job done.

Q. Is there opportunity for advancement?

A. A horizontal organization means there is less opportunity to advance. On the other hand, there is much less dissatisfaction (we're assuming that the truly apathetic have drifted elsewhere by now). The empowered employee, like Carl Just's CNC operators, can learn to program. They can then learn troubleshooting of hardware and software, learn to write programs for other machinery, etc. In effect, you are telling each employee, "Here is what we make. How important a part you play is limited only by your motivation and ability."

Q. Is there a lot of squabbling among empowered people?

A. Empowered people *are* opinionated, but that's because they are more confident and have taken the time to study the problem on which they're working. There will be times when a team reaches an impasse over equipment purchases or production methods. One technique is to form a subcommittee of workers to study the problem and come back to the whole team with an answer. Actually, answers may be a bit easier to find, since there is less pressure to agree with the foreman or the boss. Properly trained and empowered people know how to reach a consensus without getting personal or damaging egos. A last-ditch effort may involve inviting a separate team in to assess both sides in a disagreement.

Q. What should be done when an empowered group makes a costly mistake?

A. Set that team about the task of finding out what went wrong. They can then go to other teams in the organization and say, "We've run across a costly mistake, and we think you ought to be aware of this pitfall." I don't think much of a hierarchy of teams, since managerial hierarchies are what caused many of our productivity headaches in the first place. You can always infuse a few talented people into a team that is not working up to snuff.

Q. Will that create distrust?

A. Not if flexibility is known to be a component you use. In the modern manufacturing environment, production requirements change all the time. Empowered people are confident employees. They should be as successful in one team as in another, because they know that, once the parameters are understood, logical decisions will result.

Q. What do I do first?

A. Educate your employees about what the company does, how it is done, who its customers are, who the competition may be and what the short-and long-range outlooks are. Don't be afraid to mention dollar figures, since some employees know them already, because that's a strong indication of your desire to be candid. Find a production problem and create an integrated group to address it. Get enthused about successes, and downplay momentary failures.

Encourage informal contact among departments. Explain how the best companies are customer-driven, then show how your company can better serve customers if employees will treat fellow employees as if they were customers, too. Point out the direct connection between how well the company does and the ultimate benefit to the empowered employees and their families.

Empowerment is as exciting a concept as the steam turbine was to Mr. Parsons or the assembly line to Mr. Ford. You and your company can share this light from the dawn of a new industrial era. As a Midwest CEO said recently, "When I began to empower people, I was eager to get it done so I could return to my job. Then I realized that empowerment *was* my job."

Key Points:

○ Empowerment is the gradual shift of responsibilities or power from the office to the shop floor. Trust is the number one ingredient for successful people empowerment.

○ Who better understands what needs to be done than the people whose hands and eyes and minds operate the equipment and maintain process flow?

○ In an empowered work environment, every producer understands patterns of production and cause-and-effect relationships.

○ Empowerment will enhance quality and efficiency as it makes your shop a more rewarding place to work.

Chapter 15

It's a funny thing about opinions—they can accrue into fact. For instance, I was listening recently to an automotive-industry expert on a National Public Radio business show as I drove along the freeway. By the end of the century, this industry analyst boldly predicted, the automobile business would have two universally recognized leaders, Ford and Toyota. They would, he said, be leaders for the same reason: they were the two large car makers that had best grasped the importance of quality and modern management techniques, and were headed somewhere with those ideas.

That same week, I read about a road test of a Ford truck. The nationally syndicated newspaper writer indicated that this particular model was an entire generation or cycle ahead of its nearest sales rival and corresponding model from General Motors, a Chevrolet. An ad in the same edition pointed out that 5 of America's 10 best-selling vehicles at the moment were Ford products.

I also spoke with a colleague who told me about a robot-welding device he had seen running in a northern Ohio auto-parts subassembly plant. This welding machine made side-guard door beams, the federally mandated steel bars built into car doors to protect driver and passengers in collisions from the side. The colleague was impressed by the speed, intensity, and precision not only of the welding equipment, but also of the entire plant. As you may suspect by now, the subassembler was under contract to Ford.

The clincher proved to be reading *A Better Idea*, the book by Donald E. Petersen, retired CEO of Ford Motor Company. I had expected a bloodless record of Petersen's rise to the top at a large corporation and a catalog of the number of people he had put in their place in doing so. Petersen *had* put people in their place, but not in the way one might assume. Working with the late Dr. W. Edwards Deming and others, he changed Ford from just another big American corporation overstuffed with managers who were as territorial as they were unpleasant, to a place filled top to bottom with teams of purposeful human beings. It's a readable book, one that should be examined by everyone in your corporation, from the CEO to the janitor.

Petersen spent his entire adult working life with Ford. To read of his early years, it's miraculous that he lasted. He tells of being pushed around by at least one executive who was so uncaring and abrasive that he drove Petersen to resign—in the middle of a recession as he and his wife were taking steps to adopt a child. Robert McNamara, who as Ford president had spotted qualities in Petersen he admired, talked him out of leaving, and convinced him instead to spend some time amid Ford trucks, where money was made and everyone was happy, but prestige and excitement were lacking. It was here that Petersen developed an appreciation for the hourly employee.

As Petersen ascended the organization, he became aware of several things. He saw that a Ford-sized business was by its very nature inefficient. Like the game where a secret is passed along in a line of giggling grade-schoolers, the end result didn't bear much resemblance to the original. So it was at Ford. Designers complained that engineers lacked the talent to translate blueprints into workable pieces. Engineers said designers were unable to create anything anyone could build. White-collar employees had nothing but disdain for their blue-collar counterparts. Hourly employees retaliated with attitudes and absenteeism.

Vehicles were put together on the line by people who used devices such as shims to ensure that all bumpers were roughly the same height. It became evident to the rising executive that workers drew on their own ingenuity to make the finished product work, but they had little control over how vehicles were designed, or materials chosen, or method of assembly. Why not harness that ingenuity, which seemed to the CEO to have a great deal of potential?

Teamwork In Stages

Though the idea wasn't original, Petersen can be credited with helping teach Ford employees from many different departments to take the team approach to problem solving. The retired executive says that creating teams that lead to greatly increased quality (and therefore larger market share and increased profits) can be done in six stages. It's tougher than he makes it out to be, particularly in an organization the size of Ford. Petersen deserves much credit. In abbreviated form, the six stages include:

Stage one. Get people together to talk about the purpose of the company. Is the firm doing what it should be doing? If not, why not? If so, is it being done as efficiently as possible? Petersen advises the creation of a mission statement that will put people ahead of product or profits, then realigning things to make the company fit the statement. He strongly endorses teaching everyone statistical methods, and he defines quality to include pleasing the customer and serving internal departments.

Stage two. Convince management that things are awful and need marked improvement. Petersen did this by assembling a focus group made up of California consumers (Petersen chose Californians because they are more attuned to automobiles than the rest of the country). Many of these people shocked Ford executives by stating they never considered purchasing a Ford when buying a car, and they weren't sure if they had ever even ridden in a Ford. Obviously, if they had, it was not memorable. He also advocates visiting competitors, and putting quality first by taking bold and decisive actions that prove the drive for a better product isn't just another tired slogan.

Stage three. Encourage every employee to think creatively and listen to what each employee has to say. The Ford boss began the company's team-building approach with an eight-step process that included opening up the books to show participants how what they did affected the entire corporation. Petersen spent time with his employees, finding cells or teams that were doing a good job, and spreading news of their accomplishments throughout the company.

Stage four. Wean managers away from their fixation on authority by developing participative-management seminars. Many loyal executives need some nurturing here as responsibility is pushed downward, allowing lower-level managers and production people to make major, possibly costly, decisions. Petersen rewarded the top team players, pressing all the buttons to show other employees how much teamwork mattered in the new order of things.

Stage five. Use all elements of the teamwork philosophy on a new program. This shows the start-to-finish influence and importance of teamwork and the importance of providing teams plenty of authority to complete their assigned tasks. Petersen doesn't come right out and say so, but such a vivid demonstration is for managers as well as hourly employees. The former CEO emphasizes the fact that besides involving suppliers in the project, successful teams are customer-driven. Once the project is under way, the power and effectiveness of the team effort can spread throughout the organization.

Stage six. Look for signs that your rate of quality improvement is slowing. That, says Petersen, indicates you've reached a certain level of maturity. It isn't the bell at the end of the fight, however, but is instead a call to action. Look for entirely new processes, check out what your competitor is doing, and search for ways in which to be pioneers. Again, Petersen doesn't say so, but the most successful companies beyond the year 2000 will be those that can cut the time between when a product or process is discovered and when it can be in the hands of the customer.

What A Manager Does

My favorite chapter in Mr. Petersen's book is "The Manager's Role." Regardless of your rank or experience in an organization, these pages are worth contemplating. They spell out what a manager faces in joining, helping operate, and then running a company. It probably would be a revelation to hourly employees that managers ever doubt the wisdom of their own decisions and those of their peers, that there come times in management careers when one wonders if the path chosen is the right one. And, most illuminating to many a traditional puncher of the time clock, guys like Don Petersen really are concerned with the mental, physical, social, and economic well-being of their people.

More than that, contemporary managers are turning to production personnel to help approach world-class quality standards and keep their companies there. How can you convince veterans of the assembly line that you're suddenly interested in their thoughts and their welfare? Listening well and not seeing issues in terms of absolutes is a start. Petersen says he was always quick to admit, "I don't know," when a production point was pondered. He then took the next step, asking assemblers, "How would you improve this operation? Is there a better way to address the problem? You're the person with the rivet gun—you tell us what you need to do this job in a better way." He stood patiently still and listened.

He was always equally generous with praise, delivered via a note, on the phone, or in person. Praising individuals in a team raised the median level of commitment. He also found that rewarding members as a team (with special jackets or caps, for example) strengthened the team and sent a positive message throughout the plant. Conversely, Petersen advises readers never to criticize anyone in front of anyone else. In a meeting where there was disagreement, he taught his people to say, "That's certainly one way to address the problem. I wonder if there are others . . .?"

It's also incumbent upon the manager, at least of a consumer-driven company, to know what customers want. The CEO at Ford spent time at a competition's driving school and in the company of everyone from racing drivers to homemakers to find out why consumers chose, or decided not to choose, a Ford product. Frequently, he was able to take a consumer complaint back to a Ford team, and the team would solve the problem, making the car in question more comfortable or more reliable or easier to drive.

CEOs And Shareholders

The CEO, he says, must know the company better than anyone else, not always to appease shareholders, but to chart the overall course. At Ford in the 1980s, there was shareholder pressure to keep up with General Motors, with its massive capital commitment to new machines and equipment. But Petersen and his fellow executives took a trip to Japan and saw that Toyota was making quality cars and encouraging profits with machines and equipment that were often less contemporary than its competitors. The American executives noted that Toyota, unlike Nissan, for example, emphasized getting the most out of its people and didn't arbitrarily acquire acres of equipment no one knew how to run. Ford shareholders dialed down their investment second-guessing as Ford market share increased.

To build teams you need team players. Ford executives began to recruit white-collar management talent from colleges and universities they respected. They looked beyond the degree to find out if a candidate participated in clubs or sports or related activities. Was he or she naturally inquisitive? Did the candidate strike the executive as a good fit? Petersen cautions against automatically ruling out candidates based on where they went to college or how they think, but he seems to prefer relay racers to long-distance runners.

I admire Petersen for Ford accomplishments, and I admire him even more because he is candid about Ford failures. Employee involvement at some Ford factories in Europe has been discouraging. The labor-management relationship in Britain is complicated by the fact that there are dozens of unions at any one plant. It's safe to say that no two unions share identical views of management, and management finds some more cooperative than others. In Germany, hourly employees and managers alike are represented by works councils. The head of a works council sits on the board of directors, so he or she has a pivotal understanding of what the company is trying to accomplish. After witnessing employee involvement on a visit to the United States, the German works council endorsed it and it is up and running. There's no reason why you can't "go global" with employee involvement.

Once production people are successfully involved, Petersen advises spreading the tentacles of teamwork to the service side of your enterprise. Ford has a financial arm that employs 26,000 people and has $120 billion in assets. Like the assembly line, this huge endeavor is a petri dish for better performance. When the team concept was explained to service personnel, they initially focused on their own minor annoyances rather than on impediments to improving efficiency. So Ford began finding individuals who excelled at their jobs—such as credit checks or collections or simple filing—and sent those people throughout the organization to teach their methods. Meanwhile, personnel from different departments were encouraged to gather and discuss ideas.

Widespread Application

Petersen points out that the principles of teamwork succeed at Ford, but can be applied to most other organizations. Final decisions must rest with civilian managers in corporations and with officers in the military, but employee involvement, teaming, and total quality management are being implemented today within the armed forces. Proof of the need for such a program comes from a recent U.S. Army statistic. It indicates that the Army wanted to give early discharges to 10,000 junior officers but quickly ended the program when 20,000 of the young officers applied. Clearly, the service needs the atmospheric improvement that real teamwork fosters.

Searching hard for something critical to say about *A Better Idea*, I believe few of Petersen's concepts are original. Yet I know of no other business book of late that has so succinctly explained how teams form and function, and how they can become an invaluable part of a corporation. Petersen has lived what he covers, so perhaps his experience is simply more real than the theories of others.

The former CEO ends his book with several prescriptions for restoring pride and productivity to the country. I'll let you read them yourself. Suffice it to say that the principles apply to virtually any kind of effort. Will we see more Donald E. Petersens and their management philosophy in American industry? I hope so.

Key Points:

○ Creating effective teams can lead to greatly increased quality, market share and profits.

○ Six stages in creating effective teams are:
  • Get people together to talk about goals;
  • Convince management of the need for improvement;
  • Encourage employees to listen to each other and think creatively;
  • Wean managers away from authority fixations;
  • Use all elements of the teamwork philosophy on a new program;
  • Look for signs that improvement has slowed and you've reached the next level.

○ Tomorrow's most successful companies will be those that can cut the time between discovery of a product or process and delivery to the customer.

○ Managers seeking to build teams should listen well and not see issues in terms of absolutes.

○ To build effective teams, you need team players.

Chapter 16

I have a friend nearing his 52nd birthday who doesn't think much of the good old days. If your math is solid, you can compute that he graduated from high school around 1960. You may recall the time—Dwight Eisenhower was in the White House, rock 'n' roll was young and fun and loud, cars looked sleek and ran well on 29 cent-a-gallon gasoline, boys wanted to swing like Mickey Mantle, and girls wanted to act like Sandra Dee. Those were the days, right?

For two consecutive summers, our friend was employed 40 hours a week in a local factory. Local to him was Richmond, Indiana, a city of about 40,000 people on the Indiana-Ohio line some 70 miles east of Indianapolis. He worked those long, hot summer days in an Avco plant that produced the inner workings of missiles for the military. Avco once was Crosley, makers of the first refrigerators with storage space in the door, and the first post-World War II car that could be called a subcompact. The company had been an important one in the Midwest for years; if you're a baseball fan, you know that the Cincinnati Reds' home park at the time was Crosley Field. But timing is everything and it seemed that Crosley/Avco's most ingenious projects often were ill-timed.

Back to our friend. He recalls a very constricting and compartmentalized environment throughout the factory. No one knew what anyone did in any other department. No one asked or answered questions. And no one ever saw a finished product: when boxcars rolled onto the siding to pick up whatever was being made, armed soldiers showed up to shoo everyone away from the loading dock.

"I was in the Army in Vietnam, and I played on a college intramural basketball team that never scored more than 20 points a game," he remembers. "Yet morale in either of those situations was stratospheric compared to morale anywhere in that Avco plant."

What was the problem? No one—hourly employees, clerical personnel, straw bosses, mid-level managers, senior managers—had any sense of accomplishment about the job being done.

Worse, no one even thought about what kind of work the plant should seek once that particular defense contract was completed. Because Richmond was a small city, our friend knew sons and daughters of the Avco staff. These white-collar families could only hope that there would be another government contract after the missiles were constructed. The fathers (there weren't many female executives then) had no authority to act, only to react.

"Nowadays, I run across the smell of cutting oil or hear a time clock ring and it will take me back," the friend reports. "Sure, life was simpler then, but there's nothing nostalgic about working for and with people who have no direction, no purpose, no esprit. I'll take management with focus, empowered workers, a market-driven line, and by all means a well-guided staff with priorities any time. One other thing. I have to think the lack of mission in that plant had an effect on the quality of the final product. That's kind of scary."

Management *does* know where it wants to go today. Workers are empowered. Line personnel are more responsive than ever to market shifts. What is the best way to ensure that the administrative staff is serving the corporation and those in line positions as effectively as possible?

Staff Oversight: The View Is Great

For mid-size and larger corporations, I like a staff overseer— the title can be chief administrative officer, or vice president of corporate services, or whatever fits the organization's structure. This executive should be positioned with a full view of the entire staff operation. From this position, exactly what functions does the overseer lead?

Let's be specific. A modern, mid-size American corporation is supported by these staff services: advertising and public relations, government relations, human resources, insurance, investor relations (if publicly held), legal and other professional services, management information systems, real estate, and transportation, among others. Note that I've excluded finance, primarily because some vice presidents of administration also are the corporations' chief financial officers. Others keep the functions separate.

Our chief administrator has three broad responsibilities:

• To ensure that each staff department has a clear understanding of the corporate vision and how the department helps everyone keep that vision in focus.

• To ensure that each staff department faithfully serves line functions.

• To ensure that each staff department knows and works with all other departments, realizing that their collective will should be an exact reflection of the corporate vision, and therefore is greater than the sum of departmental wills.

Some may ask, "What will the CEO do?" I feel strongly that the chief executive had better be paying attention to the market and to the customers the company serves. There are executives with riveting presence, and there are executives with a sixth sense for where the economy as a whole is headed. But the leaders who best serve their companies these days are, first and foremost, experts on their own products, services, and customers. Having a chief administrator allows the CEO to concentrate on the chief executive's most important contributions to the corporation.

Stated another way, the chief executive officer of a corporation geared for the year 2000 and beyond will be responsible for "a very tightly run company, focused on a single line, or closely related lines, of business with a heavy component of debt and closely held stock, upward of a third of the total shares in the hands of a few top owner-managers," contends Harvey H. Segal in his recent book, *Corporate Makeover.* Saddled with debt and on perpetual display to shareholders who also are peers, do you think the CEO will want to pick who sells or leases the company's fleet of trucks? No, but a chief administrator might want to sit in on the process.

Let's talk with some chief administrators to find out more about their responsibilities. Like me, I think you will be struck by their sense of self-awareness and by the breadth of responsibility from one company to another....

'Don't Call Us Multinational'

The senior vice president of a worldwide corporation ("Don't call us multinational; that makes it sound as if we do well in some countries and not in others") based on the Eastern Seaboard has one overriding concern—the impact of globalization on his company.

"We're moving to a 24-hour, seven-day-a-week operation," he says. "Staff functions must be continuous. My biggest concern at the moment is providing a common database as our people circle the globe."

This senior manager also is in charge of research and development, and he is finding that the globalization challenge affects R&D staff, too. "Everybody here is aiming to reduce development time. We want to make use of every hour, day, and week. A research and development project can't sit idle. I have to find ways to get R&D into the product 24 hours a day."

This manager is involved in issues of critical importance *for which the chief executive officer has no time.* All the CEO may know is that the chief administrative officer is making it work. At the company in question, the administrator points out, staff is very fluid. "We don't think it's in the interest of any company to track any given path. Shake up your staff and let it resettle—it happens consciously or unconsciously here all of the time. Rigid walls? There are none here. It pays not to leave the organization static for too long. New interfaces should develop."

The Virginia-based manager has the authority to use a number of staff and line organizations to form a project focus-team. The leader may or may not have any functional expertise with the project's objectives.

In contrast to this freewheeling approach (dictated in part by the far-flung and rapidly changing nature of the East Coast company's markets), a Midwest vice president and chief administrative officer in an import business sees more rigidity.

"A horizontal staff operation sounds great—very contemporary, very open. But there are a few subjects that just don't pertain to certain departments.

Minimizing Delay

"Don't get me wrong. If—let me think—if we determined that the size and look of a specific package should change, we would, of course, rely on our advertising and marketing people. And we'd talk to inventory control and—transportation? Of course. But we wouldn't arbitrarily drag, say, human resources into the decision-making process. My job is to minimize delay by deciding who can contribute, then focusing every contributing staff member on the problem. Ideally, the first time the CEO notices this project, it will be because it has produced increased income."

The chief of administration for a publisher of school and library books goes by an editorial title, but he holds the reins on such departments as acquisitions, art, contracts (legal), editorial, human resources, and systems. The administrator oversees everything from who and how many people to send to a book fair in Italy, to keeping an eye on vendors such as printers, freelance writers, editors, photographers, and illustrators. The "line" operation here is a nationwide group of salespeople supplemented with a cadre of telemarketers.

"We (a small executive group led by the director of marketing) decide what kinds of titles we want, based on feedback from sales and from what other publishers are showing at fairs. The staff can tell me what is available, or it can help me find or formulate something for which there is demand but no title—yet."

The publishing executive points out that he is the one who must furlough staff personnel during times when sales are slack. Normally, this is a seasonal chore, but it had to be done for an extended period during the recent recession. "I was charged by the president with this job, and I worked with human resources so that it was done as gently as these things are ever done around here." And what was the president of the company doing at the time? "He and the head of finance were canvassing banks for money to underwrite the publishing of more titles. That struck us all as the most important thing he could be doing, since without cash, we'd have no catalog and, therefore, no sales in the fall."

Corporate services at a leading Mid-South insurance company are designed to support the company's profit centers: life insurance, group insurance, and investments. The director of corporate services oversees printing, receiving, building services, utilities, and telecommunications. "If properly administered," says the corporate services director, "this alignment allows the profit centers to take services very much for granted."

This woman, who has served the company for 15 years, began her career in the controller's office. She has been corporate services director for a year, following several organizational and structural changes. At various times, she reports, corporate services has been overseen by everyone from the vice president of data processing to the head of human resources. Finally, the company decided to put one person in charge and then eliminate duplication by more thoughtfully assigning responsibility. "But our company is unique within the insurance industry. Among my colleagues, I find that the human resource function, for example, reports to everyone from marketing to data processing."

Up Through The Ranks

Does one need to be a renaissance man or woman to talk management information systems in a morning meeting, followed by point-of-purchase advertising strategy in the afternoon? It can't hurt. Seriously, though, a chief administrative officer is most often a person who knows not only a range of business matters but his or her company, as well. Says a chief executive officer, "Our administrator, who was named by my predecessor, really did start here right out of high school. He has been someone who has accepted every bit of training and education we offered, working his way through the ranks. No, the job he has now isn't a reward for his loyalty. We really needed someone who knew the business. I don't see how an outsider could do it."

Earlier, I pointed out that a few chief administrators also serve as chief financial officers. A former employee of mine, who worked at Krause Milling and at a Fortune 500 NYSE baking company as chief administrative officer, believes finance and the other departments should not be mixed. Wayne F. Caskey, now chief operating officer for a commercial factor in Massachusetts, says people who excel in finance and those who excel in administration draw on different sides of the brain. Finding a person who can deal with two such dissimilar aspects well is exceedingly rare.

The CAO's role differs at least a bit from one company to the next, Caskey points out. "At Krause Milling, three of my five areas of responsibility were performance roles. At Interstate Bakery, I was in more of a supervisory capacity. Both of these positions prepared me very well for the position that followed as group vice president for Universal Foods. There, I had profit-and-loss responsibility for five of the company's seven operating divisions.

"I was nothing but a labor negotiator until the age of 37," says the Yale Law School graduate. "Then, I served as a director of personnel, where I managed 10 or 12 people and learned about a number of things I didn't know—compensation, psychological testing, training, etc. When I signed on with Krause, I brought with me the legal and personnel experience, plus some political activity. I used what I knew, and I learned how to manage such things as public relations, government relations, real estate, and transportation. With each move, my experience broadened."

Caskey's only note of caution involves longevity in the chief administrative position. "In long-range terms, the CAO job would have gotten stale," he says. "It's a collection of functions that is somewhat the same. All of the functions are cost centers, not profit centers. In many companies, the division vice presidents really make or break the organization. Still, for companies of a certain size, having a chief administrative officer is vital."

I feel I was lucky to have come across someone like Wayne with the scope of expertise and personality to administer five diverse departments. Speaking of personality, perhaps personal differences are the reason for the separate strengths of administrators and financiers. Finance at Krause Milling remained completely separate. The chief financial officer and the chief administrative officer reported to the chief executive officer. An organization chart with the CAO under finance would be unnecessarily complex.

Incidentally, you may wonder what happened to Avco. The facility in Richmond, Indiana, closed more than 20 years ago. After a bumpy ride manufacturing short-line farm equipment in Ohio in the 1970s and early 1980s, what was left of the company was purchased by Textron. Today, there are two entities that bear the once-familiar Avco name. Neither manufactures anything; the larger of the two is involved in consumer credit.

K e y   P o i n t s :

○ Knowledge of the final product and a sense of accomplishment are key to an empowered workforce.

○ A lack of mission has a devastating effect on product quality.

○ The goal of a staff overseer is to make sure all departments understand the corporate vision, serve line functions faithfully and work collectively with each other.

○ The chief executive should focus on the markets and customers served.

○ An effective leader must, first and foremost, be an expert on the company's product or service.

Chapter 17

"Never write municipality when city says the same thing."
— Mark Twain

"The most important thing in communication is to hear what isn't being said."
— Peter F. Drucker

I don't have a great deal of patience with quizzes, even though they may be popular. So this chapter on communications will be the only one in the book that poses a question up front and answers the question at the end. The query is, what's wrong with this chapter from the standpoint of a corporate communicator, be he or she the CEO or the vice president of public relations? Don't cheat by skipping to the final paragraph....

There is a common denominator all employers seem to be looking for in the *National Business Employment Weekly*—and everywhere else. It is someone who possesses "superior communications skills" or is "a world-class communicator" or "can communicate with numerous publics, and at all levels of labor and management." Companies don't want just their sales managers to be able to communicate. They expect financiers, researchers, and engineers to express themselves well in writing and on their feet these days, to all kinds of audiences.

Ironically, at a time when we need good communicators most, fewer and fewer executives have the skills needed to receive, interpret, and transmit information. Yes, many of them are comfortable at a keyboard. But there is a big difference between filling in a spreadsheet and writing a document or providing a verbal answer people will readily understand. What can be done to improve internal and external communications?

Here is an example: you are the CEO of a company with numerous sales branches. You point out in a regular report to the conglomerate that owns your firm some persistent, negative numbers at one branch. The conglomerate asks you to look into it. For the sake of example and to promote "management by walking around," you decide to personally visit the apparently troubled sales branch, which we'll say is in Roanoke. You fly to Roanoke, conduct interviews, look over the books, observe the tenor of work, and return to your office. Now that you're ready to dictate your message, what do you say?

First, ask yourself what the conglomerate most wants to know. Amplify your answer and you will have completed the assignment in a concise, businesslike manner. What follow in parentheses are the parent company's most likely questions. The statements after the parentheses comprise your response.

(Is the Roanoke branch still losing money?) Acting upon your request, I find that the Roanoke branch continues to lose money. *(How much money?)* Specifically, the branch lost $43,696, as the result of $154,492 in sales and $198,188 in costs and expenditures during the most recent 30-day sales period.

(Why is it losing money?) There are several reasons for this sustained loss. In order of importance, I believe them to be:

• **Intensified competition.** Our two leading Eastern Seaboard competitors, Frammis and Grommit, have new and automated warehouses in the area. Either can fill orders more quickly than our branch, with a lower error rate and fewer back-ordered parts.

• **Intensified pricing.** To ensure that the investments in their new warehouses are justified, the competitors are cutting prices steeply. Our aging branch, with its modest warehouse, is caught in the middle of a price war.

• **Mature market.** Our products—building supplies—are purchased by contractors on a seasonal basis. Despite inviting new home interest rates, unemployment figures and factory closings in Roanoke indicate that not a lot of ground will be broken by contractors this year.

(What do you plan to do about it?) Within five working days, we will decide how to address ongoing losses. Our options, in order of likelihood, include scaling back our operation, probably on a permanent basis; cutting prices and adding direct marketers for a 90-day trial period; or departing the market altogether.

In less than a typed page, you have anticipated the conglomerate's questions. Brevity isn't the most important thing; it's close to being the *only* thing these days. Within a very tight space, you've also told your inquisitors why you are writing **(acting upon your request),** how current your figures are **(during the most recent 30-day sales period),** and how soon you plan to act **(within five days).** Visionary that you are, you've even previewed your options. You're to be congratulated for leaving the emotion—"They're a great bunch of guys" or "This is the most antiquated group of managers in the organization"—completely out of this succinct report. And all you did was decide what the conglomerate needed to know, and in what order it wanted to know it.

That's a far cry from telling the conglomerate what it wants to *hear.* Equally important, you were prudent enough not to comment on personalities or conduct. Had your findings involved malfeasance or misfeasance, your first contact with a person at the parent company should have been on the telephone or face-to-face. Don't even hint at anything on paper about someone's trustworthiness that you cannot absolutely prove. Happily, that issue only brushes the subject of communication; it's something an experienced manager can handle thoroughly and without any sort of visible furor.

Research has shown that the most successful business letters contain the following:

- The purpose of the report stated in the first paragraph.
- A contract sentence (indicating what major point will be covered) immediately following the stated purpose.
- Simple sentences in subject-verb-object order, and subjects and verbs as close to each other as possible.
- Active verbs.
- Easily understood language.
- Short paragraphs, headings, and lists.

These requirements weren't arrived at idly. A study conducted in 1991 by the U.S. Navy found that mid-level officers, corresponding in civilian life to middle managers, spent 17.2 percent less time reading a short, plain, and direct letter than they spent reading the same information couched in a bureaucratic memo. In dollars and cents, Naval personnel learned they would free up more than $250 million a year in working time if all communications were clear and concise. Adding the time difference of their 358,000 civilian employees, the Navy found it might realize savings of $402.5 million annually!

The Planning-Communications Link

But communications is more than dollars and cents. Mary E. Brevard, director of investor relations for Universal Foods in Milwaukee, Wisconsin, believes strongly that planning and communications must be linked. "There's no point in communicating unless you know why you're doing it," she says. "Too many companies just decide to produce a newsletter or write a news release without knowing what purpose it plays, how it fits in with the goals of the company. Here, we don't do anything unless it meets a strategic objective."

Before joining Universal Foods in 1993, Brevard was with the Gehl Company, a diversified manufacturer of farm and construction equipment. She was drawn to that company by new management that appreciated the strategic importance of communications and wanted to make planning an integral part of the communications process. Her job was to serve as a facilitator, linking any of several publics with managers who spoke for the company. "Our strategic objective internally was to use managers and supervisors as good front-line communicators between the company, our people, and other publics. We wanted to institutionalize this as part of the way we do business."

Unfortunately, the economy in 1990 and 1991 prevented Brevard from fully implementing the company's communications strategies. "We had to put out a lot of fires," she says. The managers had some, but not all, of the training they needed to speak with confidence about the company and to coach employees. More important, she says, a corporate goal of keeping all employees completely informed had not been fully implemented. But the strategy of Brevard's department may have changed along the way.

"The role of communications in rough times is to maintain confidence in the company and its actions," she says. "That's true for employees, for shareholders, for the media and for the public. We have to be timely, and we're finding that memos or newsletters can't take the place of face-to-face meetings between managers and people."

Incidentally, Brevard previously performed marketing/public relations functions for a pair of finance-related service companies. "There is little difference between communications for a service company and for a manufacturer. In both cases you are dealing with intangibles," she says.

A Manager's Audiences

Today's managers must address several audiences. They are, in order of importance:

- The people who buy the company's products.
- The people who work for the company.
- The people who work with the company.
- The people who own some or all of the company.
- The people who make up the business and financial community.
- The people.

Let's take a brief look at each group....

Buyers, and potential buyers, of the company's products must know the features and benefits of your product or service, how it might be superior to the competition, whether any special precautions need to be taken, and whether (and if) anything precipitous might occur. It is incumbent upon you to pass along all of the news that could affect customers in a timely and forthright manner, and in the venue easiest for them to use. Why else, for example, does an owner's manual contain information on maintenance? You would never formulate maintenance requirements in a news release, hoping all owners would read and heed the release.

Any short-term gain realized in sitting on negative product information will be lost when it is revealed that your organization did not provide full disclosure to its customers. The chances of your being found out are virtually certain. Even if the information remains buried, you will be perceived by your own people as an untrustworthy organization, and morale will suffer. Always take the high road by communicating honestly, quickly, and clearly. Tell customers what they want and need to know, and make the information easy to find.

Employees need clear, concise information, too. Without it, how can you expect them to respond to your company's strategic goals? Beyond teaching them how to do the best job possible, it's wise to dispense with outmoded "us-and-them" thinking of management versus labor and to keep them fully informed about the company's sales, earnings, and fiscal well-being. They may have read that a significant shareholder recently sold a large block of stock, that the company is restructuring, or that the long-term outlook for your industry is clouded. Answer their questions: "How will this affect me and my family?" "How will it affect my job?" They owe you their best effort; you owe them honesty.

My nomination for the most neglected people in the communications equation are suppliers. Reliable ones today are diligent enough to tell you immediately of a deadline missed or of a price incorrectly quoted, but do you make the effort to teach them all they need to know about your business? There are things no worthwhile supplier should have to learn from the business section of the local newspaper. Don't assume that all managers who deal with suppliers have mastered the art of communications. And don't assume you've done your job by adding all suppliers to the public-relations mailing list.

Investor relations, says Mary Brevard, are very predictable in terms of Securities and Exchange Commission requirements, but can be chaotic in terms of how the market will react. "There is a gray area between what is required disclosure and what is important to keep people from being surprised. A good investor-relations person must balance the letter of the federal requirements with the company's communications strategy."

The needs of investors and the needs of the business and financial community are similar but not identical. Shareholders generally are satisfied with a shorter-range picture, whereas banks, brokers, debt holders, and bondholders want to be given an honest appraisal of the company's long-range plans. If your firm plans well, and if those plans are communicated well, this can influence the company's bottom line for years to come.

What does the public want and need to know? "Will you continue to be a part of our community?" "If so, for how long?" "Will you be hiring high school graduates this year?" "Will you recall workers who were laid off?" Ed Menninger, formerly a public relations manager with Sears, Roebuck and Co. in Chicago, and now the vice president of a public relations firm in New York City, believes companies that keep the public in the dark are doing themselves a disservice. Sears, which had 17 million credit-card holders and tremendous customer loyalty in 1970, could have done more to fulfill its public-interest responsibilities.

"The reaction among some executives was 'Why tell them?' My reaction was, 'Why not?' Give easy access to those who are interested, and interest those who visit your stores," he says.

The CEO As Communicator

A reporter for a prominent business magazine has her own thoughts about communications. "Not all CEOs are good communicators. I attribute that in part to the fact that leaders surface in all departments. There was a trend for a while to make financial people the heads of companies. With some exceptions, these guys—and they did all seem to be guys—weren't equipped to be grilled by a reporter, or to stand up to an irate shareholder. In defense of some of them, they schooled themselves. I can think of several caterpillars who became butterflies once they realized what was required.

"What makes a CEO a good communicator? That's a tough one. In the old days, it was willingness to lay down the law to everybody," she says. "That isn't effective anymore. Here's the best I can do: a skilled communicator can immediately read his audience. He knows a flock of reporters and the annual meeting of shareholders want to know different things. He delivers the information each group wants to know in the manner easiest for each group to absorb. The signals he picks up from the press may be that they are looking for forthrightness, intelligence, and good nature, in that order. Shareholders may want precision, patience, and a willingness to hear them out."

Today, the reporter continues, there are fewer excuses for the inability of the CEO to communicate well. "Most large corporations and numerous consultants offer their top people wonderful training in crisis management, shareholder relations, press relations, and more. The people who go through such training are ready when the time comes."

Speaking of readiness, have you by now concluded what's wrong with this article? Had we followed our own advice, the opening paragraph would have contained the information we most wanted to convey: **There must be a strong link between a communications program and corporate planning and**

strategy for that communications program to succeed. Mary Brevard could not have articulated it better.

Study the speeches, articles, and news releases of others in positions of authority. Are they forthcoming with what is most important, or do they bury it? And if the important aspects are buried, is it because the speaker or writer does not know the audience, or is he or she trying to de-emphasize information the executive would just as soon not pass along? Analyzing your words, analyzing the words of other business leaders, and getting to know your audiences will make you a better communicator.

Key Points:

○ Everyone—top executives, accountants, researchers and engineers—must communicate effectively in writing and on their feet.

○ Brevity is the most important characteristic of good business communicating.

○ For a communications program to meet strategic objectives, there must be a strong link between planning and communications.

○ Today's managers must address several audiences:
  • the people who buy the company's products;
  • those who work for the company;
  • those who work with the company;
  • the shareholders;
  • the investment and business community.

○ Always take the high road. Communicate honestly, quickly, and clearly.

○ Skilled communicators can read their audiences and deliver information they want to know in a manner they can understand.

Chapter 18

"The salvation of American industry will be found on the factory floor."

—Malcolm Baldrige

No less a person than Malcolm Baldrige, former secretary of commerce and a recognized authority on quality, made that observation. His message is reinforced by *Business Week,* which recently delivered this opinion: "U.S. producers can compete more effectively with their foreign rivals by making an ironclad commitment to manufacturing."

There are two basic components in the manufacturing profitability equation: people and equipment. While the latter is receiving increased attention, companies have been neglecting the people component, especially the abilities and training of those most responsible for managing the entire manufacturing process. Part of the problem is attitude. With all the glamour, pizzazz, and perks attached to financial management or sales and marketing or mergers and acquisitions, the manufacturing manager has become the low person on the corporate totem pole.

Fewer and fewer chief executive officers are chosen from the operations sector. Fewer and fewer CEOs—especially in smaller, closely held companies—have hands-on, production-line experience. Candidates for master's degrees in business administration shoot for the opportunity to don the executive uniform and manage from the corporate suite, or make big bucks fast in investment banking or consulting. There are few mentors to extol the advantages or describe the excitement of learning a business on the manufacturing floor.

Why is it important to know manufacturing? Because, according to Anthony P. Carnevale, the American Society for Training and Development's chief economist and vice president for public affairs, a revolution has taken place there. In the 1970s, "though American managers continued to work well with technical elites to develop innovations, they fell short in all other areas.

"The failure stems, at least in part, from top-down management styles and the hierarchical structures that support them. Those traditions are no longer consistent with the realities of modern production and service delivery," Carnevale says.

"In the modern workplace, the manager is challenged to adjust to a new workplace where people are more autonomous and managers have less direct control over performance. The culprit who stole managerial control is technology. Technology has conferred autonomy on skilled workers by taking over repetitive tasks and allowing the combination of many jobs into fewer jobs that combine skilled workers with more machinery. Armed with technology and skill, they are far less subject to managerial control than their predecessors."

I don't know about you, but I find Carnevale's words an irresistible invitation to work on the line and learn what *really* is going on in contemporary manufacturing.

An example of his contentions can be found in one of Milwaukee's quieter companies, which does most of its manufacturing out of state. At this firm, a young and aggressive human resources manager was put in charge of a large plant. He had none of the traditional manufacturing skills or experiences and was a history major in college.

Wages were out of sight at the plant due to an incentive system gone wild. Productivity was low, and morale was terrible. But the manager went after the situation with enthusiasm and creativity, learning what really took place in the manufacturing process. After three years he had turned it around, based on his increased understanding of production. Until recently, he ran a $100-million division, including the plant to which he was originally assigned. Some of the most successful companies—and managers—I have known have been those where trainees were turned loose with A-to-Z responsibilities for a single project or operation.

CEOs in these companies know that you can't learn to run the whole business unless you have mastered the ability to make the individual parts work. They want to see young people on the shop floor with their sleeves rolled up, learning about machine tools, assembly, scheduling, and shipping. It's irreplaceable experience in training for the top.

Robert Lear, a senior consultant with Krause Consultants, Ltd., and executive-in-residence at the Columbia University School of Business in New York City, not only teaches but also regularly counsels students. He accepted the university position following a distinguished career as a chief executive for two companies listed on the New York Stock Exchange. Lear consistently urges young people to take courses in operations. He recognizes the value of manufacturing experience in human relations, in productivity through the skillful melding of people and equipment, and in seeing myriad components come together to meet complex schedules. Aren't these the attributes required of every leader of a corporation?

Snobbery, Training, And Recruitment

There is a subtle kind of snobbery prevalent in many companies. It begins with training and recruitment.

How many human resources people can identify management candidates who come from the shop floor? What kinds of programs do companies have that will give shop supervisors—and they're getting younger and younger every year—the opportunity to acquire the training that will enable them to relate their experience and responsibilities on the floor to the entire corporate structure and understand how different functions contribute to profit generation?

These people may aspire to management positions, but we aren't encouraging them to do so. And, even if they don't harbor these ambitions, how much greater will their contributions be if they understand how they can affect an income statement, the components of a balance sheet—and, ultimately, their personal success?

In too many cases, companies go outside to hire managers who, never having faced the challenge of delivering an order on time, don't have the slightest idea of the frustration involved in coping with antiquated equipment, or the satisfaction of solving a complex production problem. With little realization of the creative challenge inherent in the manufacturing process, is it any wonder that they often underestimate the contribution the veteran shop worker can make and, in their ignorance, generate controversy instead of cooperation?

My point is that it's high time the leaders of our companies begin to examine their attitudes toward manufacturing. What kind of people are running our plants? What resources, training, and development programs have we put at their disposal? How are we using their experience and knowledge?

How do we view industrial engineering, quality control, scheduling? Isn't it time we awarded these specialties the professional status enjoyed by the design engineer, financial manager, or marketing executive? Are they not equally important to the ultimate success of our organizations?

I'm not advocating the overthrow of the corporate structure. I am campaigning instead for an adjustment in values that will help us unite our corporate resources so that our companies run as smoothly and productively as the best manufacturing equipment.

Once you are committed to teaching executives production, where do you begin? I would tell you to steer clear of the yellow pages and of the many direct-mail offers and find out instead if there is an American Society for Training and Development (ASTD) member on your staff. If there is, and he or she probably will be connected somehow to the human resource function, sit down and explain your aims. Chances are, this person will have some experience and would enjoy putting together a logical program that benefits people, products, and place of business.

If there is no one on staff who can direct training and development, you should turn to a national search firm. Chief training officers are difficult to find because training has become such a growth area. In fact, the ASTD notes the following facts and figures to show the current commitment to executive training. Executives receive an average of 36.3 hours of training annually, with 70 percent of the larger U.S. companies having some ongoing effort. Although upper-level executives make up only 0.75 percent of the total employee population, they receive about 12 percent of the total training budget. Yet if that budget does not include production work, I feel someone is missing the boat.

But back to our search for the ideal trainer. Be prepared for months of scrutiny before landing your perfect person. Meanwhile, ask human resources to screen vendors who offer training media customized to the needs of your business. If you're in electronics and a vendor has a training program put together for the paper industry, it can be tailored to suit your business, or at least serve as a stopgap until the search firm finds training's Mr. or Ms. Right.

Advice From An Expert

Recently, I had the privilege of talking with Steve Merman. He is a training and development executive with Amoco in Chicago, and is active in the American Society for Training and Development (ASTD). While your challenges and those of Amoco may differ in scale, I think you will find his perceptions most interesting....

First of all, he says, "Amoco is a technical organization, so there are lots of scientists and engineers and chemists. They get promoted into jobs that may require an entirely different set of skills than the ones they possess.

"The motivation behind executive education here is to take someone who is technically anchored in his or her career and convert that person to an executive manager. We try to answer these questions: What are the skills and competencies needed to run the business? What has to be done with these people so that they understand the basic principles of accounting, marketing, operations, managing people, empowering people, and getting results from people in this day and age?

"If the company plays its game on a global basis, you need to make this person into a global manager, a person who uses global resources to impact global markets. He or she should receive cultural training, learn how to deal with business leaders from other countries, learn the art of negotiation, be taught a foreign language, and learn how to step into a culture and develop business relations.

"Whether the company is global or not, it will pay you to school these managers in strategic thinking, in how to manage and deal with change and changing markets," Merman says. "A lot of executive development these days also covers leadership training. It's hard but necessary to teach a technical manager to lead the entire unit, to take a hands-off approach, and to be more of a visionary. These people tend to rely on the familiar, on how they've always done it. As a trainer, I have to intervene in their lives, reframe their thinking, and redesign who they are so they can act appropriately in their new position."

The very best trainers, Merman points out, are the former chemists or engineers or other technical people in his organization who have gotten a really good grasp of what the company is trying to teach its future managers. By the same token, I would think that there is at least one potential trainer in your company—and that manager has had at least some production experience. He or she also has a heightened ability to relate to people, to understand the needs of others.

"That person knows, for example, that empowerment is trust," Merman continues. "He or she trusts lower management because the lower management people are closest to the customer and really are most critical to the business. That's a mind-set that is really difficult to undertake."

Their Task And Yours

Amoco is developing global managers who have a technical background. You are taking staff people, exposing them to line functions, and making them world-class managers. Neither job is easy; both require the kind of analysis a person like Merman brings to the task.

Here are several additional points to consider when working with a trainer/developer in formulating a regimen for your executives:

• Tell all the executives in the program what you hope they will learn by spending time in the various production departments. Find out if there are areas where a participant has little or no knowledge or understanding.

• Every budding executive has a finite amount of time, so slant an individual's program toward specific areas of expertise. An accountant might wisely spend time thoroughly learning hands-on inventory control, for example. Inventory is visual proof of where finances reside, whether it is efficiently managed, and if it is kept to a minimum while maintaining productivity of the line. A member of the legal department working in shipping and receiving might quickly discern the effectiveness of the owner's manuals and consumer-warning decals for the firm's various products.

• Make sure every executive in the program has at least a bit of experience throughout the production area. Later, when budgets are being formulated and aired, there will be empathy and understanding where there once may have been apathy and ignorance of the problems and opportunities related to each budget item.

• The most common method of delivering executive training is by way of the seminar. Yet Steve Merman tells us that classroom training is on the decline as creative corporations and training providers inside and outside the company find more effective ways to teach. Can you come up with ways to tell what production training is teaching your people?

• Ensure that each "graduate" has an exit interview. Tell your training director that you want to sit in on the session. Have the candidate honestly evaluate the program based on whether there is an improved understanding of what makes the corporation tick. There will be heightened appreciation of the necessity for manual labor and of the processes needed to add value to a piece of inventory in order to create a salable product.

• Consider how production work blends with the most common goal of executive training: building leaders. Individual development usually focuses on leadership, communication, motivation, and strategic planning. Are your executives applying leadership training to the production area? How does it show?

Forty percent of American competitive improvement since 1929 has come from capital investments, while the other 60 percent has come from the effective application of those investments, according to a labor economist. With this in mind, can you afford not to provide your key people with the best possible training? A portion of that training should be spent on the line.

How important is training, really? One answer comes from John M. Plant, president of Andritz Sprout-Bauer, a Pennsylvania company that manufactures equipment for paper producers and a variety of machinery used in other process industries such as grain processing. Prior to this assignment, Plant was president of the Cleaver-Brooks Division of Aqua-Chem, a Milwaukee-based company that manufactures packaged boilers that are sold worldwide.

"I am of the opinion that the CEO's chief priority is development of people. Career development should never stop. It should be pursued by focusing on continuous improvement and by studying and understanding mistakes."

At Cleaver-Brooks, Plant had numerous managers who did one thing very well. Within a couple of years, he had reduced the number of these salaried people from 225 to 150 by training one person to do at least three things very well. "There was," he says, "a tremendous need to manage the transition from old to new. There were many people who had knowledge and wanted out. They had the desire to pass that knowledge on. I tried to replace two or three people with one strong person, well versed in several areas. To do this, we needed a career plan for each individual.

Focus On Development

"All this was unwieldy to learn, but the people learning represented fairly good talent. We focused on their development. They needed to know how their work would impact the organization. On a scale of 1 to 10, we reached about 5. Everyone now realizes that career development never stops, that it's a part of the overall process, and that there's a direct connection between training, the company's broad strategic issues, and success. Before, we were careful when it came to sharing our strategies. But for career development to reach its full potential, the company must be forthcoming with its employees. It's a leap of faith we had to make."

As ASTD points out, the success of executive training is subjectively measured, in part because executive performance is rarely subject to formalized performance review. Where formal evaluation is conducted, the most common practice is for the executive or the executive's superior to evaluate the transfer of training to daily activities. Neither in-house trainers nor consultants routinely provide follow-up, so finding out if the time was well spent will be up to you.

Key Points:

○ To be successful in their positions, managers need knowledge of manufacturing and operations and how the components of a business work together.

○ Many companies underestimate the abilities of shop personnel who may become excellent managers. Today's worker is armed with technology and personnel skills.

○ Company leaders must utilize the knowledge and experience of their people and recognize the value of promoting those running the plants.

○ Use resources such as the American Society for Training and Development or national search firms to find training officers.

○ The best trainers have some production experience, can relate to others and recognize that empowerment equals trust.

○ The CEO's chief priority is people development.

Section III:
Planning

Chapter 19

"A plan is only a plan that is good intentions unless it degenerates into work."

— Peter Drucker

The cornerstone of my business as a consultant is strategic planning. Twenty or more times a year, I conduct a carefully formatted series of meetings with organizations large or small, private or public, profit or nonprofit, to help each lay the groundwork for the future. Strategic planning can sound inhibiting or vague or clotted with flow charts and printouts. There is nothing complex about it, as the following chronology indicates....

My first step is to meet individually with company executives for 60-minute interviews. I tell all participants at the start that I intend to use all information they provide, but that I will not reveal sources. We talk about their responsibilities, about the organization, and its relative position in its particular industry. The interview is inclusive—my goal is to cover every conceivable thing, from manufacturing costs to market structure to competition and back again.

Following the interview sessions, I arrange a two-and-one-half day meeting off-site with executives chosen by the chief executive officer as the strategic planning committee. The agenda looks at where the company is today, where it wants to go, and how it will get there. The days are full, with 20 hours of intense discussions and dinner together each of the two evenings.

As the moderator, I set the tone and the ground rules for this look into the future. I tell the group that the playing field is level—all team members are equal, and each must present all comments in a direct and forthright manner. In effect, each person should act and think as a chief executive officer responsible for the entire business. Participants who are condescending or address the boss when they should be speaking to the group (or are late returning after a break) are fined. Fines also are levied if anyone goes off on a tangent not in the interest of the assemblage. With luck, the first person who suffers a fine will be the CEO! At the end of the process, the group decides what to do with the fine money.

The initial step down the planning path is to develop a mission statement. This can be done efficiently by using journalism's five W's and an H: who, what, when, where, why, and how. Once the participants decide who they are, what products or services they offer, where the company operates geographically, why it requires certain results, and how it expects to achieve its goals, the mission statement emerges. We take the time to reduce the statement to three sentences or less, fine-tuning the words so that each person understands what each one means.

Introspection

The next step is especially intriguing. Our path winds into and throughout the organization as we search for all of the things affecting the company that the executives can control. We make a list of strengths and weaknesses, prioritizing the key strengths and most critical weaknesses. Usually, weaknesses outnumber strengths. Significantly, internal communications is almost always on the weakness list. Other weaknesses often encountered include teamwork, systems, scheduling, training, individual development, and organization structure. As you may suspect, most companies feel that their people are bedrock strengths.

We then address the factors over which the company has no control. If the inward look was rewarding, this outward look is more difficult and can be frightening. Competition, here and abroad, most certainly is out of the group's control. Other factors evaluated are market characteristics, technologies, the economy, societal changes, and government regulations.

Immediately after writing down these stampeding phenomena, I ask the group to focus on competition. Major competitors are reviewed in terms of opportunities for the company and threats to it. The planning team is told to think about niches in which there is little or no competition. What, I ask, can you do better or less expensively or more efficiently than they?

As you may have noticed, we're assembling quite a lot of information. But we haven't yet reached planning's critical mass... I next ask the group to review the company's financial performance over the last five years. They are encouraged to look for trends: Is the profit margin headed up or down? Are inventories consistently kept at just-in-time minimums, or are they excessive? What about debt— has there been a tendency to borrow more or less, and what is the impact of interest rates on the bottom line? Have capital expenditures been appropriate and performed as planned? What are the key performance ratios that should be tracked? The company's chief financial officer leads this discussion, answering the more technical questions and explaining why variances occur. Key trends that emerge are recorded.

The final step in assessing where the company is today is to identify four or five key issues that have developed during the discussions. All must be addressed in the plan.

The balance of the retreat is devoted to determining where the company should go and how and when its objectives will be achieved. A first step is to ask the group to create a vision of where it wants the company to be six years from today. How big, how profitable will it be? How will the company be organized? Six years is long enough to entail a bit of risk but not so far away that it's irrelevant conjecture.

The team then prepares a list of overall assumptions so that all planning is done within the same environment. Market size, interest rates, inflation, and the impact of competition are among the factors that serve as guidelines. The group then sets policies, or screens, through which the programs in the plan must pass. The maximum ratio of debt to equity, minimum return on payback capital expenditures, position in any market, and maximum investment in a new venture are among the policy statements that could emerge. The policies are for planning purposes, and should not be confused with the employee policy manual.

Setting Objectives

The group then sets *tentative* objectives for the next three years. Three years is half way to the vision, and in most cases objectives will cover each of the next three years. The objectives must be measurable and subject to a "yes-no" answer on attainment. Objectives often include specific targets for sales and profitability for each year.

Objectives should be challenging; people do better with appropriate challenge. At the same time, they must be realistic and attainable—success breeds success, and failure breeds failure. As we all know, a pattern of failure is demotivating. An objective must also be acceptable; you must be willing to pay the price—in terms of people as well as any dollar investment. Finally, the objectives should be compatible, or a priority established. Long-term objectives two or three years out can be set at a level that cannot be reached by the current organization at its present level of knowledge and skill. One-year objectives must be set within the current capabilities of the organization.

We then identify programs that must be implemented to achieve objectives. These programs may involve sales or marketing, communications, cost control, the new-product development process, market or customer diversification, organization structure, and information management. The programs are assigned to individuals or teams, with one person in charge.

The group then breaks for four to six weeks, during which time the programs are developed. A program consists of specific action plans to be initiated. For each action plan, there is a brief description, and the incremental revenue and/or expense expected as a result of the action program. Assumptions used to come up with the figures for the economic analysis are listed. Personnel implications, if any, also are shown. Finally, a chart records the major steps required to complete the action plan, who is to do each, and by when.

The team then comes together for a daylong session to begin the review process. Reviews often are written in pencil, symbolic of change. The program review occurs in an informal atmosphere, with those who prepared it encouraging questions and hoping for new and expanded concepts. I take detailed minutes to record all the ideas and areas for further analysis or investigation. Discussion of a single program the first time through can range from one to four hours, depending on its complexity and scope. Three or four single-day meetings, two or three weeks apart, are required before the team reaches a consensus on each program or decides to eliminate a program as not feasible or appropriate at that time.

At the final session, I ask the group to go over all material developed. Special emphasis is placed on the objectives, which may be changed based on the team's belief that the objectives can be achieved if the agreed-upon programs are implemented.

We also step back and identify the strategies, critical success, or driving factors that overlay and focus the plan's thrust. Financials for the three years also are prepared to determine the cash flow implications of the plan and how the company will "look" on its balance sheet and income statement. The group often is surprised at what it created.

Finally, a 30- to 40-page summary is submitted to the board of directors. This document gives directors an overview they won't get elsewhere. It tells how collective time will be spent, and it details the company's direction. It's also indispensable for putting together the annual operating plan. A complete stranger should be able to take the current plan of operation and the strategic plan, and create a framework for the coming fiscal year.

Questions And Answers

You may have a number of questions at this point. Let me try to anticipate them....

Q. Will this work for any company?

A. The strategic plan is only as good as the group is candid and focused. A company with a great deal of conflict or with severe operating problems will have a shorter-term focus. Its key strategy is to clean up its act before taking on any major new initiatives. Others need sound priority-setting to identify one or two new areas to take on. All must then rally behind the program and accomplish the goals on schedule.

Q. How do I know that planning is right for my company?

A. You probably are already planning mentally. The methods I've described round up those creative thoughts. I tell clients that any size company should plan, and that a workable strategy will emerge if you follow the above steps. Here's some added good news: the plan will be effective the first year, twice as effective the second year, and another 50 percent better by the third year.

Q. You mean we go through this process every year?

A. Why, does the possibility of being fined frighten you? Seriously, you should stick to this format, because it works. And you should take time for an annual planning session to update, refine, and extend the plan.

Q. How do we decide if we need a long-range plan?

A. You're asking a believer why you should believe, but here's your answer. Frequently, I acquire clients in the wake of a major glitch in their business. It may be sudden loss of market share or the introduction by a competitor of a world-class product. Or, it may be the feeling among the executives that they are merely reacting, and they want to grasp the offensive. If there is underlying disquiet, planning can result in a solution. In smaller, emerging companies, a good plan is most critical, since the margin for error is a good deal smaller than it is for a Fortune 500 company.

Q. Whom should I recruit for the planning team?

A. The CEO must be on the team, along with your direct reports and perhaps one or two others whose judgment and experience you value. Bringing these people together and asking for their help in planning will increase their commitment to the company and to you, the CEO. A planning team of 8 to 10 members is ideal, though we've worked with groups of from 3 to 20.

Q. What's in it for me?

A. If you're the CEO, the good and the bad that has been flying below your radar will pop into view. The process will force discussions of today's problems and issues, and it will raise unsettling questions about markets, competition, and your ability to respond.

Q. For this I'm paying a facilitator?

A. You bet! A good one will be certain that the key issues facing the company are presented in a constructive and reassuring way, and the road map to solution identified. You'll also find out who your best critical thinkers really are. I've seen it happen many times. A consultant not only brings experience to the process, but also knowledge through exposure to other clients.

Q. Where do I begin?

A. Perhaps with your peers. Talk to counterparts in other companies, then read current material about the planning process, and examine the resources available. Talk to potential consultants.

Q. I'm concerned—we'll never be able to boil down our mission statement to three sentences or less.

A. An excellent observation. In fact, you've hit upon one of the most difficult aspects of the planning process. If you don't know what matters most to your company, you won't be able to construct much of a mission statement. But if you have your priorities straight, the mission statement will all but write itself, at least after a couple of hours of discussion.

Q. What happens after the plan has been accepted?

A. To achieve your objectives, you and your associates must immediately begin managing the business in the context of your new plan. Business as before won't cut it. Formalizing strategic planning will be among the most exhilarating, exciting, and challenging experiences of your business career. Not only that, but a good plan will add immeasurably to the zest with which your managers view their work. It can unite and energize your organization.

Q. How will the rank and file get in step?

A. You will recall that communications frequently is listed as a company weakness. A sound strategic plan will teach you to communicate with all levels of employees and managers. Your communications will be key as you will want the entire organization to understand the direction the company is taking and rally behind it.

Q. You make the strategic plan sound as if it's bulletproof.

A. At the risk of repeating myself, it's only as sound as the commitment you and your managers have to implementation of the plan. Without such a commitment, your planning will have been solely an intellectual exercise and, in my judgment, a waste of time.

Q. How do you handle such sensitive issues as financial disclosure if you haven't shared the numbers before?

A. The question comes up in privately held companies. The CEO/owner often is afraid such disclosure will be used by employees to take advantage of the company... to demand more pay. Wrong! Without knowledge, estimates of your profits are usually much inflated. With knowledge comes a greater understanding of the business and commitment to its success. I won't take an assignment unless full financial disclosure is made. It shows trust in the group and a willingness to be open to change. Both are essential for a good plan.

Q. What about ownership succession, especially if there are many uncertainties, including timing?

A. It probably is an issue on everyone's mind, and it should be discussed. No commitments are necessary. You may want to lay out the options you are considering. Ask the group for ideas. Promise to keep them informed as your thought process develops.

Q. What if I am using the planning process as part of my program to sell the company?

A. Here again, sale can be mentioned as one of the succession options. I would be very reluctant to position the company with the planning team as one you want to sell immediately. Usually, it takes a long time for such a transaction to occur. Any thoughtful buyer will want to see appropriate attention paid to the future rather than "dressing up" the present at the expense of tomorrow. The smart buyer will see right through such a strategy. You will be well served to do your planning the right way, and let the sale possibility move on a parallel track.

Bon Voyage

If you are successful in selling the business, we'll look for you to take your gains and quickly visit your friendly travel agency to book a trip to a secluded island in the South Seas. Of course, even early retirement requires a bit of planning....

Key Points:

○ Strategic planning looks at where the company is today, where it wants to go and how it will get there.

○ A mission statement should answer the five W's and an H: who, what, when, where, why and how.

○ Examine internal issues, environmental factors and financial performance and identify key issues to address in the plan.

○ Next, create a vision for the future and set tentative objectives to move towards that vision.

○ Objectives may include specific targets for sales and profitability by year. They should be measurable, challenging, realistic and attainable.

○ Programs should contain specific action plans to achieve the objectives.

○ The final step is to identify critical success factors that overlay the plan.

○ A strategic plan is only as good as the group producing it is candid and focused on plan implementation.

○ Any size company should plan.

Chapter 20

Once you've completed your strategic plan, you're home free, right? The answer is a definite maybe. Stated another way, it's an unqualified perhaps. In all seriousness, once your strategic plan is in hand, you need to think about it in producing an annual operating plan. The best annual plans flow logically from the long-range strategies, are highly specific, and may incorporate several new short-term needs that have arisen. An annual plan outlines how you will run the business in the period immediately ahead while you position the organization to respond to its strategic initiatives.

The difference between a long-range and a short-range plan is not the length of time required to carry the plan out. It is instead the length of time the plan will have an effect on the business. Long-range and short-range plans are mutually dependent. Unless the short-range plan is integrated into a single, unified plan of action, misdirection and wasted efforts will be the most obvious results.

What is involved in formulating your operating plan? If you are on a calendar year and your strategic plan is completed by the end of August, let it cool off for 60 days or so. That will leave you another 60 days, from November 1 to December 31, to put together the operating or business plan for the coming year.

The initial step is to develop a revenue projection for the year ahead. This projection should closely resemble projections for the first year of your strategic plan, though projections may vary one way or the other by several percent, based on activity and events between completion of the strategic plan and the present. Interest rates may change, key customers could increase or decrease levels of activity, competition can grow or wither away—there should be evident, logical reasons for any significant difference.

There is no single best way to project revenues by month. If your company sells small quantities of high-cost products, you may choose to forecast by identifying customers and prospects by name. This isn't practical if you sell millions of 89-cent widgets to thousands of different customers. Here you may want to classify information by market segment, dealer or distributor, product type, or a combination.

Being Objective

Once you've projected revenues, you need to collect month-by-month expense plans from your department heads. Admonish your managers not to look at last year's figures, because you won't settle for more of the same. Rather, you should insist on fresh thinking, based not on last year's actuals but on next year's objectives. Obviously, the sales projections will drive the expenses in manufacturing and to a certain extent in other departments as well.

Remind your people to include their expense plans supporting the successful execution of the strategies in the plan. Tell them, too, to formulate their numbers with an eye on the industry, on the economy, and on late-breaking opportunities that may arise. People so busy that they simply tack on 5 percent to last year's numbers are not responding to the process. Such an approach is unacceptable, and anyone who has participated in the planning should know it.

The projections in the operating plan should have a 90 percent guarantee from the management team, assuming no major change in key assumptions occurs. You are spending dollars based on the plan, and should be completely committed to achieving its profit projections. That imperative should not yield a low-ball, conservative plan. Make it realistic and attainable. A conservative document results in a holdback or slowing down of new initiatives that are critical to a company's future. Spend time to plan it right, and then make it happen!

The same planning team that produced the strategic plan should review the operating plan together. It should challenge and critique based on what it wants the company to accomplish both today and in the future. The planning team will discover, among other things, that the sales manager's projections are usually low, while salespeople in the field come up with numbers that are characteristically high. Does optimism grow in proportion to the distance from the home office?

A friend in the Fox River Valley who is in charge of a network of district managers likes to tell how he and his company got the DMs to more accurately provide numbers for the coming year. "At first, we just returned their information with a 'not good enough!' scrawled across it. That was a mistake—

several guys thought we wanted more optimistic forecasts, when in fact we wanted a more thorough approach.

"Then, a few years ago, at our industry's major show, we sat down all of the District Managers and found out few of them understood the importance of the numbers they were providing," he says. "The sales manager told them, 'You can control whether your dealers get the amount and kind of inventory they need, when they need it. All you have to do is give us accurate forecasts.'"

A seminar followed, and it was of benefit to the company and its district managers alike. Today, this company sends each DM a fill-in-the-blanks form with a personalized note crammed with statistics on everything from housing starts to rates of employment in each territory. By asking their dealers a few questions and getting 15 minutes worth of help from a local reference librarian, district managers now are providing forecasts that are worthwhile documents. To maintain some enthusiasm for the task, the company gives the most accurate among them a sizable prize, such as a fishing boat or a golf cart, at the industry's big show each year.

Nailing Down The Numbers

Following the initial review of the operating plan, the planning team should finalize sales figures, then decide on the expense budget. For the sake of accuracy, the planners must take into account product requirements and the company's financial goals. If this is their first operating plan, my experience indicates that the numbers will be too optimistic.

It's impossible to overstate the importance of a team effort. If managers really want the company to evolve into the entity envisioned in the strategic plan, the operating plan must be the product of every planning member. Stated differently, the operating plan is what you intend to do and how you intend to do it in the next 12 months. In contrast, the strategic plan positions the company for that year and the years immediately ahead.

The operating plan will be very helpful in planning the crewing levels in departments whose activity is indirectly related to volume. Knowing of a possible layoff or, even better, a need for more people, months in advance, makes managing such changes a lot easier. You also gain valuable lead time in capacity planning.

From the operating plan you should identify the key goals that must be accomplished in the years ahead. Provide your directors with these three or four goals. Such disclosure will put pressure on you to succeed, but it will also give board members points of reference from which they can make decisions based on what really matters to the company. If you and your managers operate day-to-day and still focus on achieving the goals, your next year will be satisfying, and the company will be positioning itself for the future as developed in the strategic plan.

You should keep score during the year by presenting your financial reports against the plan, both for the month and the year to date. Have your computer spreadsheet show Actual, Plan, Variance, and Last Year. While important, the monthly figures can show big variances from the plan. They should be investigated, but timing of purchases and shipments can cause big swings in any one month. The year-to-date numbers should fall in very close to the plan, especially as the months pass. The sales results should be reviewed carefully to identify any new trends in the market or competitive activity that could have a long-term impact on your business.

A Typical Plan

My preference is to write an operating plan in narrative fashion. Sure, you'll include the necessary financial schedules. But numbers alone don't tell the story. Try to capture the spirit and excitement of what you plan to do in the year ahead. The news may not always be good, but it's helpful to put into words why problems are expected. And for any newcomers or outsiders, including your board, banker, and accountant, the narrative approach is easier to understand.

Let's take a look at an actual operating plan produced for one of my clients. The document is 22 pages of narrative text, with financial schedules appended. Here's a glance at the table of contents:

- Summary
- Financial performance
- Sales and marketing
- Operations
- Capital expenditures
- Personnel
- Linkage to strategic plan
- Goals for the fiscal year
- Opportunities and threats
- Conclusion

Right away, you may have noticed that the plan starts with a summary and ends with a conclusion. Are we being redundant? No. The two-page summary states sales goals and indicates what planners believe the gross and net margins will be. The heart of this summary is a set of four challenges the company must take on if sales and margins are to be reached. "The plan assumes reasonable success in each of these four areas," according to the summary. Other information includes mention of capital expenditures and what will influence them, plus personnel needs. The summary wisely concludes on a positive note: "A new confidence exists at [company] that it can manage change, introduce new products that sell and keep the business in control. All are key in the year ahead as the company establishes a new plateau from which to grow."

Buoyed by the summary, let's examine financial performance. A part of the narrative, these two pages cover everything from after-tax profits to overhead expenses to depreciation to payments on a long-term loan to net worth at year's end. This section concludes with the notation that "sales forecasts were trimmed... and all expenses underwent an even more rigorous review than normal." Such a statement makes the reader realize that there is nothing arbitrary or blue-sky about the totals in this section.

Sales and marketing opens with the contention that the company can and will reach new heights in gross sales. Such success, the plan indicates, is predicated on the introduction of two new products and on continued acceptance of products already in the marketplace. These new initiatives are "less formidable than they appear" because "initial customer reaction to the [new product] has been very positive and all target accounts have placed orders." The remainder of the three-page sales plan points to trends in the various markets served, and notes that the sales and marketing organization is being restructured to better address these changing markets.

Operations indicates that "it will be a busy year for our group" by detailing the start-up of the company's new overseas plant. Foreign costs and wages are recounted, activity and production levels are targeted, suppliers are sized up, and quality is addressed. Operations has as its primary goal the cost-effective presence of the overseas operation, hence the notation on the activity level in the year to come.

Capital expenditures are listed by departments: administration, sales, engineering, and production. The narrative notes that the largest single purchase will be a state-of-the-art, computerized, quality test system, and that tooling for new products accounts for more than half of production's total capital expense plan. The personnel page reports that a drafter and an engineering technician will be hired and shows targeted dates for bringing each on board. Their compensation is incorporated in engineering expenses. By the way, a precise operating plan will always tell how many and what kinds of new employees will be needed and when they are to begin work.

"This operating plan tracks the objectives and programs developed in the strategic plan completed in July of this year." So begins the section on linkage. It goes on to account for the differences in sales and profits between the two documents, and it tells which other strategic plan numbers will be easily met or exceeded and which will offer challenge. "The planning committee will meet each month to review performance against the targets in the operating plan and the major initiatives of the strategic plan. All recognize the importance of maintaining focus on the strategies in the plan and following through on their implementation throughout the year."

The company's eight goals have deadlines and involve everything from after-tax profit figures to the number of units each product line will sell during the coming 12 months. Threats to a positive year number eight in all, while opportunities total five. But, the plan notes, "on balance, the opportunities are more likely to occur than are the threats." As you may have guessed, opportunities are generated from the firm's new products, and threats include domestic and offshore competition.

The conclusion states that the company is at a stage where it can professionally take advantage of identified opportunities. Increased market share and better name recognition will result in growth in volume and profitability as the company attempts to position itself as "clearly the industry leader." Only 16 lines long, the conclusion reminds the reader once again of the connection between the operating plan and the strategic plan by positioning the company.

'See Attached'

Following the narrative are several projections: an income statement, a balance sheet, and a cash flow summary for the most recent fiscal year, plus projected production, engineering, overseas sales, and administration expenses. Finally, personnel requirements are detailed, and there's a summary of anticipated capital expenditures.

Key Points:

○ The best operating plans flow logically from long-range strategies, are highly specific, and incorporate short-term needs as they arise.

○ An annual operating plan outlines how you will run the business in the period immediately ahead while you position the organization for the future.

○ The first step is to develop revenue projections for the coming year. Projections should have a 90 percent guarantee from the management team.

○ The strategic planning team should challenge and critique the operating plan based on key goals for the year.

○ Keep score during the year by comparing financial results against plan, both monthly and year-to-date.

○ Your operating plan should capture the spirit and excitement of what you plan to accomplish in the year ahead. Linkage to the strategic plan is key.

Chapter 21

Planning for the Nonprofit
Corporation

What ever happened to leisure time? If you're approaching middle age, you probably recall widespread concern in the '50s and '60s that many people would soon have too little to do. As workweeks declined to 40 or fewer hours, and as computer terminals were added to desks in many offices, concern grew. Where *would* we spend the time created by flexible work schedules, three-day holiday weekends, leaves and sabbaticals, word-processing programs, spreadsheets and instantaneous projections?

Such concern turned out to be woefully optimistic and premature. As business has become increasingly intense, as markets have appeared and evaporated almost overnight, the only answer seems to be round-the-clock attention, flexibility, and imagination. Today, Americans have more responsibility and less time than their parents did.

For Dr. Gilbert K. Boese, president of the Zoological Society of Milwaukee County, leisure time—or lack of it in the 1990s—is of critical concern. Besides affecting attendance at Milwaukee's world-class, 100-year-old zoo, dwindling leisure time could mean that the not-for-profit society will have a smaller pool of valued volunteers. If a busy executive has only a few hours free each week, he or she is more likely to spend those hours with family and friends than in community service. Boese looked to strategic planning for answers to a number of the society's most pressing questions.

The society's president asked me to assist with the strategic plan. I soon learned that planning for not-for-profit entities (which can include everything from alumni associations to churches, colleges, fund-raising groups, hospitals, and trade associations) calls for a different approach than for, say, a retail chain or a capital-goods manufacturer. Obviously, the organization chart is very different. Groups such as Boese's have a small number of employees who are dedicated, skilled, and probably underpaid based on their competence and professional training. They must work with a large number of directors who are major rainmakers in the community and sit on the unpaid board out of a sense of public responsibility.

Unlike directors who serve for-profit endeavors, the board of a not-for-profit group doesn't spend a lot of time educating itself prior to each meeting. Board members of the Zoological Society are highly placed and highly regarded members of major corporations and concerned private citizens. They are asked at society board meetings to deal with issues unlike any they may encounter in their full-time positions. Here's where the society's paid people are key: employees provide board members with brief, to-the-point oral and written assessments of issues that affect the association's well-being.

Directors Held In Awe

The trouble is, staff members are often in awe of major corporate figures. This awe is created by the fact that a board member may be capable of raising hundreds of thousands of dollars for the society with a single telephone call. In this and many other not-for-profit groups, employees are beholden to such consummate fund-raisers.

"The original intent was to set a series of fiscal goals, then to implement plans and modify them as needed," Boese says. "Not planning makes operation of the society much more awkward between the volunteer board of directors and paid staff. Planning cemented the relationship between our high-level volunteer contributors and employees. The process also gave directors a better understanding of employee roles and provided them with valuable insights into how the society functioned."

A plan was put together that forced directors and staff to discover a real appreciation for the others' commitment to the overall success of the society. It wasn't always easy—occasionally, I failed to get a quorum of the board. I constantly had to remind myself that I could not ask directors to take on the kind of workload normally assigned to for-profit, corporate directors. Yet their standing and wide-ranging intelligence dictated that I make the most of their input. Staff members and I discovered that, among other things, directors can be great salespeople for the society.

The plan reflected the uniqueness of nonprofits. It's much easier to facilitate change, take risks, and come up with new ideas than in corporate boardrooms. Planning gave everyone involved a purpose and a sense of direction; it was a good tool, too, for individual development. Staff members exceeded everyone's expectations, including their own.

"We're in transition," Boese says. "We are a support organization that is transforming into a nonprofit partnership with the county." That implies an increasingly important role for the society. An example of a more formal partnership already exists in Milwaukee. The Milwaukee Public Museum, also a source of local pride, is making the transition to a free-standing, not-for-profit organization with a fixed level of support from Milwaukee County for a number of years.

Among the exciting changes that went into the plan was a new direction for the society's auxiliary board. Before planning began, auxiliary board members organized and ran fund-raising events (only the board of directors sets policy). But the auxiliary's broad membership base and amount of energy and time let us make better use of them. As a result of planning, they developed new ideas for fund-raising, addressed seasonality concerns, prepared a strategy to attract new members, established a new charter, and outlined an education program for their members. Auxiliary members appreciate recognition of their contribution and the chance to undertake new initiatives to support the society. So do directors and paid staff.

Boese points out that such enthusiasm is immeasurably valuable today. "Institutions across the country have had to take a new look at their missions. At the University of California-San Diego, for example, the entire anthropology department, which included tenured professors, was dissolved. The Smithsonian Institution is pondering major layoffs, because it's so dependent on volunteers and the number of volunteers is dwindling. We needed a plan that would keep our not-for-profit organization viable to the year 2000 and beyond."

A very different kind of nonprofit, equally concerned with its future, is the National Funeral Directors Association. The 18,000-member association recently completed a long-range planning study conducted by an outside firm. Because NFDA is a federation, a priority of the planning process was to ensure that the national organization and the 50 state organizations not duplicate services. There were several other good reasons to formulate a plan, says Robert E. Harden, the group's executive director.

"We went outside for planning assistance because the last thing we wanted to do was throw something together by the staff for rubber-stamping by our board. A consultant brings expertise and neutrality to planning. The consultant we retained showed us that we were going in too many directions, and that we were ineffective in most of them. He helped us identify a strong direction while keeping in mind the needs of the membership."

With the NFDA for five years, Harden, and the elected, 16-member national board of practicing funeral directors, have an almost "back-to-basics" long-range priority. "We want the consumer perception of the practicing funeral director to be what he really is—a businessperson who probably has a family, is a part of his community, is sensitive to people's needs, and is enjoyable to work with." That thread will run through the organization's leadership presence, government relations, and education, ensuring that grass-roots members will continue to need and support their national association.

Implementing a long-range plan necessitated raising dues for another client, the Wisconsin Association of Manufacturers & Commerce, reports President Jim Haney. "Once the membership saw the plan we intended to follow, they were very receptive" to the dues hike. The statewide, Madison-based organization is on its second four-year plan, which Haney says is less dynamic and refines the mission of the initial plan. "The great thing about a strategic plan for a nonprofit is that it focuses and simplifies," he says.

A Great Mind

Fortunately, one of the most wide-ranging minds of the 20th century has addressed the importance of not-for-profits in a book on their management. Peter F. Drucker has been teaching and writing about business longer than many of us have been alive. An immigrant to the United States in 1939, the Austrian native says that "nonprofit institutions are central to American society and are indeed its most distinguishing feature."

Drucker points out in his 1990 book, *Managing the Nonprofit Organization,* that the not-for-profit sector represents 2 to 3 percent of the gross national product. With eight million employees and 80 million volunteers, "it is central to the quality of life in America, central to citizenship, and indeed carries the values of American society and of the American tradition."

Until recently, modern management principles weren't consistently applied to not-for-profit institutions. Drucker says that hospitals formerly saw themselves only as places to treat the sick, and the Boy Scouts saw themselves only as a youth group. But all such organizations do something very different than for-profit operations. Their "product" is a changed human being—a cured patient, a young person growing into a self-respecting adult, or at the Milwaukee County Zoo, a visitor with a better understanding of animals and their relationship to humans and the environment.

Yet not-for-profit institutions and trade associations can't be their most productive without professional management. A critical aspect of nonprofit management is planning. Thoughtful planning can convert unfeeling, minor donors into involved contributors. Planning also can foster among its volunteers the feeling that their participation makes them part of an institution vital to the community. In our alienated world, the nonprofits offer us a wonderful trade—for our time and effort, they make us feel we belong. Such a feeling is priceless.

The first step in putting together a long-range plan is definition of the mission. In the case of the Zoological Society of Milwaukee County, the mission is to continue its priorities to educate people about animals and the environment, and conserve wildlife and endangered species. It carries out this mission, in part, by helping to underwrite, maintain, and improve the zoo. Before Gil Boese can ask for monetary or other assistance for the zoo, he must ensure that his board and his employees understand the mission and channel their energies into its support. Only when everyone takes the mission to heart will the society be ready to seek more widespread support.

Much more than in for-profit entities, the leader of a not-for-profit organization such as Robert E. Harden is seen by the public as standing for that organization. Drucker also says that the very best managers are constantly reviewing their organizations' priorities and passing those priorities along to everyone associated with the organizations. An effective leader makes every member feel like a leader, making decisions that will have a positive influence on the organization for some time to come. "Everyone," Drucker says, "focuses himself or herself. Everyone raises the vision, the competence and the performance of his or her organization."

Toward Performance

"Strategy converts a nonprofit institution's mission and objectives into performance," according to Drucker. Yet, he adds, many not-for-profits tend to slight strategy. Strategy involves knowing the market. That means getting an accurate picture of who enjoys the zoo, and then trying to get a higher percentage of those who might enjoy it to make regular visits. In other words, strategy involves finding out who the customer is or should be or might be, and integrating the customer and the mission. Strategies also are needed, Drucker continues, to help the organization improve and innovate. The third reason for strategies is that they help build a donor constituency.

"Strategy begins with the mission," he stresses. "It leads to a work plan. It ends with the right tools—a kit, say for volunteers, which tells them who to call on, what to say, and how much money to get. Without that kit, there is no strategy." In other words, not-for-profits must train employees and volunteers to use the strategies. The Zoological Society expanded its commitment to raise funds for the zoo and to play a role in conservation in the state, nation, and world. Today the society funds select conservation projects outside the United States. The plan helped focus that commitment. "Strategy," Drucker says, "commits the nonprofit executive and the organization to action."

Drucker points out that a major difference between for-profit and not-for-profit operations is the relatively narrow scope of the former. Performance here is judged by the bottom line. But there is no bottom line in an organization such as the society. How, then, are results to be measured? Results come in either immediate or long-range doses. The immediate result of a promotional effort for new members at the Zoological Society might be a 10 percent increase in members this year. A long-range result might involve a capital campaign such as the one just completed that will create a "Zoo for All Seasons." The society raised $13 million; Milwaukee County contributed $12 million. To round up results for a not-for-profit organization, look at key performance areas and ask, "Are we doing what we are supposed to be doing here? Does the need for what we are doing remain? Do the results justify our work in that area?"

When To Say No

All the top not-for-profit entities, be they hospitals or schools or religious organizations, know when to say no. They decide internally that "this is not what we do best. Let someone do it who does it better." Boese's Zoological Society may decide that direct mail is an efficient way to generate new members. It then must decide whether to do it itself or hire the job out. Colleges and universities have used student volunteers to raise funds via telephone. But many institutions have turned to an Iowa-based firm for telemarketing because the Iowans have state-of-the-art equipment, trained callers, and thorough follow-up. This allows the schools to tend to their mission—producing intelligent, capable, and productive young adults.

In contrast to business, not-for-profit organizations are dependent on volunteers or rank-and-file members. Yet such organizations could learn a great deal from well-run corporations, where managing people is a real priority. Nothing hurts a not-for-profit more than poor use of a volunteer's time. And if a salaried person is misused or underused, that's even more unfortunate. As if the executive director does not have enough to do, he or she should work to develop both volunteers and staff.

The best organizations make employees, volunteers, and members all feel indispensable. This is a more complex relationship than it sounds, since there is little control over who as an individual may volunteer or qualify for membership. A percentage of volunteers in any organization does so because they believe in the cause but also because they are lonely. "When it works," Drucker states, "these volunteers can do a great deal in the organization—and the organization, by giving them a community, gives even more back to them." But if some volunteers cannot get along with others, they must be culled from the organization. A point to be addressed in any strategic or operational plan is recruiting and screening of volunteers.

The board, Drucker says, is both the tool of the not-for-profit chief executive and the chief executive's conscience. For this relationship to grow and prosper, the executive must develop a clear work plan for the board. Being completely candid at all board meetings and paying attention to every board member is a must. Playing to one or two friends, the author says, will soon result in the dismissal of even the most talented leader. The effective executive takes responsibility for making it easy for the board and for employees to do their work.

Finally, the not-for-profit executives need to think about their own development. Many of the movers and shakers who sit on the board are expert at knowing when to ask for more responsibility, to delegate responsibility, to expand the scope of the business, or to depart the present position. Drucker reminds us that self-development is action, the result of asking oneself the right questions. Among the best ways to find answers is to assess your position relative to the planning to which the organization is committed.

As you can tell by now, running a not-for-profit organization is at least as difficult as running a business. You may not have to deal with OSHA or the NLRB on a steady basis, but the subtleties and shadings involved in managing people is a constant challenge. The best way to manage this challenge is with effective strategic and operational planning.

Key Points:

○ Strategic planning for not-for-profit organizations calls for a different approach than for-profit businesses.

○ The planning team should be made up of both paid staff members and volunteer directors. Each group plays a key role in educating the other.

○ The environment of a nonprofit organization makes it easier to facilitate change, take risks, and develop new ideas.

○ A strategic plan should help a nonprofit focus and simplify.

○ Sound, professional management can help not-for-profit institutions and trade associations achieve their most productive levels.

○ The first steps in developing a strategic plan are to assess the organization today, determine how it should be positioned for the future, and develop the programs to accomplish that future.

○ Nonprofits are dependent on volunteers. The most effective leaders make every employee, volunteer and member feel invaluable.

○ A not-for-profit organization is judged by key performance areas, not the bottom line.

Chapter 22

Ford, Gimbel, Chanel, Jobs, Kroc, Rubenstein, Walton. Business history is studded with the names of entrepreneurs and inventors who "went into business for themselves."

Many of the most successful started at a time when the field for innovators and innovations was wide open. The current failure rate of new businesses (only about 20 percent make it beyond the two-year mark) reaffirms that it's the rare entrepreneur who succeeds today like the legends did.

Success in today's super-competitive markets, jammed with new products and services, requires not only an unusual idea but a well-researched working plan. Many an otherwise sound concept goes down the drain because the entrepreneur simply isn't prepared to tough it out and has not done any homework. If you're ready, if you have the 1-in-10,000 successful idea, give yourself the leverage of a good plan.

To work for you, your startup plan will require more candor and creativity than anything else you may compose in your entire career. For openers, you probably won't have a track record. Assumptions in the plan will be based on secondary research. Almost all of its components will be untested. But you have to begin somewhere, and without a reasonable plan, even if the documentation is tenuous, the odds are against you.

Acquiring financing and help as you chart your course through the shoals and whirlpools of a new venture will depend on your plan—its depth and vitality. If you haven't done any writing since your last exam in high school, consider hiring a business-oriented freelancer. Just be prepared to spend time with the writer and don't be afraid to ask for a rewrite if the plan fails to express all of your wants and needs.

Where do you begin? With yourself. I call this the mirror test. Look yourself in the eye and ask, "What exactly do I bring to this business? Is my concept really original? Is this, in truth, a new product or an innovative service? Do I have the specialized market and technological knowledge I'll need? How about the other functional skills? Can I line up a good team? What of my patience, optimism, realism? Am I ready to work harder than I ever did before? Will my family give me emotional support?"

If you have passed the critical mirror test, you're ready to put pencil to paper. This assumes, of course, that you have taken the time to put pertinent information together in a fact sheet—specifications, raw materials, definition of purpose and use—and you've applied for patents, copyrights, and trademarks, if appropriate. As part of your fact sheet, submit to the discipline of what Theodore Levitt now calls the "competitive distinction." Is your product real or cosmetic? Does it matter?

Do-it-yourself market research is next. Start with documented facts: market size, growth rates for consumer or industrial products, user profile and demographics in a retail or service business. Reliable sources for such input include trade and merchant associations, the U.S. Department of Commerce, and the Small Business Administration. I find the annual *Thomas Register of American Manufacturers* of value, too. A word of caution: if you're in a crowded, high-growth market such as computer software, it may pay to explore industry reporting services that sell their data.

Do some comparison shopping. What do competitive products look like? Who's marketing them? Check the packaging—how are they presented to the potential buyer? Can you compete with the muscle already in the marketplace? How is the market changing? Research the competition thoroughly. Read the annual reports and 10Ks of publicly held companies and the Dun & Bradstreet reports of others.

If you don't already, subscribe to the trade or special-interest magazines dealing with your product, and fill out all the "bingo cards" for competitors' product literature. Attend trade shows if you can. Dates and places are available through magazines and associations.

Research may be easier if the competition is local—friends of the owners, neighborhood merchants, the local credit bureau, customers, relatives, and former employees can provide you with information. This is also the time to research distribution systems, the vital links between production and end users. Especially if yours is a revolutionary product or concept, you must identify an effective structure: one in which the people will understand and recognize the potential of your product and can visualize the profitability in getting it into the right retail outlets or to users willing to pay for the product's unique qualities.

The Second Step

Ready for step two? That's the planning needed to take your product to market. First, should you test-market? If so, where and for how long? How will you document results? What is the rollout plan for territorial expansion? What role does your own sales group play? Do you have the experienced people who can make it happen? This will be a critical timetable, and, inevitably, it will take longer than you expect. What volume will you need to sustain you until the break-even point is reached? What market share will you aim for in each territory?

Don't expect to put your competitors out of business or push them off the shelves. Acceptance takes time. Even Procter & Gamble, with its muscle and market savvy, has its share of failures, spending years in testing, refining, and retesting products. This is also the time to plan for an ongoing product-development program to stay ahead of the competition and to lower costs.

There are other marketing considerations. Try, for example, to anticipate competitive response. You won't be the first or last to go head-to-head with well-established, entrenched companies. After all, Apple succeeded against IBM. If you're cutting into attractive, profitable volume, expect competitors to attack with a vengeance. Your market research will have disclosed other businesses the competition may have scuttled. Analyze similar situations. Visualize competitive actions and prepare strategies to respond.

Your plan should include packaging, product design, warranty terms, and service strategies. And if you haven't written them, back up and put credit terms at the top of the list. In a startup situation, a hefty discount for cash, at least in the first six months, may be better than an extra 3 to 4 percent of margin. In fact, solving cash-flow problems will allow you to solve many other startup complexities.

How will you promote your new venture? Weigh advertising against public relations. Your user profile and distribution will help to determine which way you go and how you will budget. Don't overlook the buyer/distributor visibility of trade shows. This brings us to the whole question of outside experts in advertising, public relations, packaging, interior design for retail establishments, logos, accounts, and management. Your time probably will be spent in bringing your business to fruition, and it may be cost-efficient to go outside for specialized talent. Above all, pick people with experience that qualifies them to handle your business. Don't turn important tasks over to relatives or someone's kid earning a degree in fine arts.

Research fees and track records as you would any other component of your plan. Examine any consultant as thoroughly as you would a prime distributor.

How Much Should It Cost?

Now, let's talk pricing strategy. Your market research and anticipation of competitive response will be helpful in establishing the best pricing levels. A key question is sensitivity of product class to price. Caviar and canned corn respond differently. Do low price and high volume go together? Which price segment is growing fastest? Where should your product fit? How do your planned distribution channels and their markup requirements compare with your need for a reasonable return? The answers to these questions will enable you to prepare monthly unit and dollar sales forecasts for your first 12 months, and quarterly for the two years that follow.

Now you've reached an important juncture in your plan. Part one will have been completed and, in the process, will have enhanced your understanding of the market. It will be packed with facts to gladden your lender's heart. You should have a tough-minded, realistic confidence in the strategies and numbers you will watch and live by in the months to come. Now that you've developed a market strategy, let's think about putting together a thoroughly documented startup plan....

Typically, entrepreneurs are so enthused once their marketing strategy is defined that they rush out and start renting production or retail space. Restrain yourselves, please. There is more, equally important, planning to be done.

The first relates to product design. Engineers, in particular, become so enamored with technology and all the innovative bells and whistles they can incorporate in a product that they lose sight of its purpose. Design features constructed around the basic concept must respond to market needs—needs that have been affirmed in your initial market research. It's very tough to create market demand with your first-born product.

Make sure the design will live up to your promises. The more technically complex the product, the greater the need for a final design that is simple and foolproof. Your financial success depends on customer acceptance, and that will be based on performance and reliability. Aesthetics are important, especially in consumer products. People want to buy attractive, graphically interesting products with tactile appeal. Status adds to sales of certain products. There's prestige in purchasing something innovative, reliable, and of superior quality—as in Volvo automobiles, Godiva chocolates, and Steuben crystal.

As you write the engineering section of your plan, keep your eye on customer acceptance and its relationship to financial success. Focus on functionality, test procedures and results, component availability, and ease of repair. Emphasize innovative technical advances that constitute "competitive differentiation." But continue to back up the technical thrust with demonstrations of reliability, cost control, and innovation. It's better to be second in the market with a high-performance product than first with one that is problem-ridden.

Spend Your Money Well

Now you're ready to think production or delivery of a service to a customer. What will it take to get it together? Plan carefully and creatively. You can blow a lot of money assembling an oversize showplace structure with new machinery and an untrained work force. This facility may not work—or work only very expensively.

Look for cost-efficient escapes. Explore subcontracting both the manufacture of major components and assembly of the finished product. There are many operations that have the infrastructure and experience to do the job at a lower cost and, certainly, at lower risk. Did you know, for example, that STP actually is a marketing company? The Florida-based firm's automotive additives are made by various chemical companies. Ford Motor Company is subbing out more and more work, evolving into an assembler, distributor, and marketer, with less emphasis on traditional manufacturing. Both operations some time ago realized what they did best and subcontracted everything else.

Should you subcontract, make sure your specifications are fully developed. Insist on ironclad confidentiality agreements. Additionally, be sure that highly qualified individuals will represent your interests by inspecting production, monitoring methods, and controlling quality procedures in subcontractors' plants. Subcontracting will enable you to use a supplier's purchasing experience, reputation, and credit rating. With common components or materials, you can use their inventories, too.

There is no law that says you have to do everything yourself. In fact, the best way is to find others who will perform functional activities at their incremental cost. That leaves you free to concentrate on getting the product distributed and sold. Retail or service businesses may require less commitment to fixed assets but, even so, these startups warrant the same initial research into comparative costs of the most effective way to reach target markets.

Your plan should point you to the cheapest way to get the job done while you are learning to shortcut the production process, reduce manufacturing costs, and exert superior quality control. If there is no viable alternative to in-house manufacturing, consider the strategy of employing experienced craftsworkers who have done it all before.

Thoughtfully articulate a comprehensive system of internal checks and balances. Examine every aspect of your new business for the relatively small number of key result areas that will spell the difference between success and failure. Each will deserve analysis and follow-up at short intervals. This may mean every shift, every week, or at the close of each day's business.

Don't set up control procedures to respond to accounting requirements. A monthly financial statement is an important historical document, but it won't help you take immediate, corrective action in key result areas. Spend your time and effort getting control mechanisms in place. The critical functions that you must control to stay on top of business may include cash management, new orders, receivables, inventory, work in progress, daily manufacturing costs, personnel head count, reject rates, market share, inventory turnover, and call frequencies on key customers. The list goes on. Just be sure to define and establish controls *before* you start, not after.

Your business—whether manufacturing, financial services, or retail—won't succeed without good people. Plan to start with a small, experienced crew that will work hard and smart, and will respond to the excitement of sharing in a success. There is enormous untapped potential in retired people in all vocations and professions. They can bring enthusiasm and ingenuity to a startup situation. Knowledge of the market and competition and contacts will be especially important if yours is a direct-sales force.

Include in your plan biographical information on all key individuals who will be part of the business. Consider the contribution that an independent board can make, and scout around for good directors.

Financial Arrangements

A startup plan is an assembly of a number of critical components, interdependent and all essential to a successful venture. Your financial strategy is not the least of these. What arrangements have you made with partners on compensation and dividends? How will you reward a hard-working employee group? A clear understanding of these arrangements will be reassuring to the entire organization, as well as to outside investors.

A friend of ours started a wonderful business in Florida about 10 years ago, but his zeal for growth caused him to overlook some of the basics of compensation. Terry Higgs has a firm in Delray Beach that creates the lovely and complex waterfalls seen in larger hotels and shopping centers. Higgs became so intent on getting new business that he turned over the shop to a talented but thin-skinned minority shareholder. This shareholder worked long hours seeing to it that molds were made and orders shipped. All the time he was steaming because there was nothing on paper about any kind of stock dividend or sharing of profits. When he abruptly wanted out, it put the company in a temporary spin—and taught Higgs a lesson.

"If I'd spent less time making sales calls and more time with [the minority shareholder/manager], I might have suspected the discontent," he says. "The only thing that saved me was that my brother is an engineer. I called him and begged him to quit a good job as a plant manager in Louisiana to run my shop. This time around, I spelled out the compensation package in great detail."

In other fiscal matters, it may seem strange not to have discussed the need for detailed, in-depth pro-forma profit-and-loss statements and balance sheets until now. They are integral to any startup plan. However, they will be the result of the planning process that has been described. Your market, competitive position, distribution system, marketing costs, manufacturing, engineering, and quality control—the strategies underlying your approach to the business—will dictate how your pro-forma profit-and-loss statement comes together.

You will be surprised at the initial results, probably unpleasantly. That should not be alarming because you will go back and start phasing out noncritical activities. Not everything has to start on day one. If manufacturing costs appear to be out of line and gross margin is inadequate, evaluate the design for frills that can be eliminated.

Keep in mind that your gross margin should reflect your product's uniqueness. If you don't get it at the start, it's tough to achieve later. Aim for a gross margin at the top quartile of your industry. Remember that you will be starting with low volume and high overhead, so you should expect losses for a certain period.

The financial analysis must include a balance sheet and will require assumptions for inventories and receivables. Test them to be sure they are realistic and attainable. Meanwhile, you must decide how much capital you will need. The figure may hinge on how much debt you are willing to assume. The final element in your written plan is a definition of the fallback positions available if your initial financial projections do not materialize on schedule.

Complex Plan, Complex Business

As you can see, writing a startup plan is no snap. Its complexity correlates to the complexity of your business, and its depth to the availability of information and your own related experience. Don't rush the process. It's pivotal to your immediate success and the precursor of the strategic, operating, and financial plans you will write as your business grows. When you think it's complete, put it aside for a few days, and then go back to it with a fresh mind. You'll be amazed at the ideas that will emerge as you look at it critically in retrospect. Read it as if you were an independent investor considering a piece of the action. If it weren't your idea, would you invest? Is it a viable, potentially successful business?

If your response is a resounding "yes!"—you're ready to put your plan into action. As you proceed, stick to its goals and constraints. Don't fall prey to management by impulse, discarding all your thought and work. Constant review, reassessment, and testing of assumptions will result in a stronger plan as you proceed, and a healthier, more profitable business as you progress.

A client of mine, Fred Wojcik, acquired a mail-order firm in 1989. In five short years, he has experienced virtually every startup asset and liability known—and he is now turning a profit. His company, Cheyenne Outfitters, sells, as he says, more than western wear. "We sell a lifestyle. I'm a baby boomer, and we all grew up in blue jeans. Put a woman in a blouse and jeans in a corral and she looks western; put her in a mall wearing Docksiders, and she takes on an entirely different look. We decided to go after that crossover market."

Wojcik's firm once was a retail operation that dabbled in mail order. It was acquired and staffed by a larger firm that projected $25 million in annual sales and offered the operation to Wojcik because sales were only $7 million. Fred made several key decisions:

• He became personally involved, taking over the marketing aspect and spending large amounts of time in Wyoming, even though home base was Wisconsin.

• He developed a correlation among Cheyenne Outfitters' marketing, merchandising, and catalog presentation, resulting in a well thought out direct-mail marketing program.

• He found financial backing, and, when his financiers in Minnesota and Wisconsin pulled out after a year, he sold some assets and minimized inventory to become self-financing.

• He was committed to hiring good people, but only if he needed them. Consequently, designers and copywriters are employees, while photographers, color separators, and printers are not.

• Part of his strategy is based on the company's constantly improving ability to estimate its needs. Fashion is a seasonal, "what you order is what you get and no more" kind of business, so estimating needs is critical.

• Simultaneously, Cheyenne Outfitters is cautiously expanding its customer base to become more than a brief fad.

It's safe to say that Fred Wojcik has compacted at least a decade's worth of experience into the last five years. He is a strong planner, and he had been involved in a number of turnarounds previously, yet nothing else has been as riveting as doing it all for himself. No matter what your business, you'll find that's the case.

Key Points:

○ Only 20 percent of new businesses survive beyond two years. Success requires both a good idea and a well-researched, carefully constructed business plan.

○ Before launching a new business, determine what knowledge, unique skills and personal resources you can contribute.

○ Market research is an essential step. Examine demographics, market size and competition.

○ Plan carefully before taking your product to market. Packaging, design, promotion, service, warranty, and credit terms are considerations. Test market your business concept.

○ Your financial strategy should reflect a clear understanding of arrangements with partners, investors and employees.

○ Planning should lead to the development of a detailed, in-depth pro-forma profit-and-loss statement.

○ Use your startup plan as a guideline which you constantly review, reassess and test to build a stronger, healthier business.

Chapter 23

*A banker is someone who lends you an umbrella when the
sun is out.*

> — Anonymous

We are fascinated with business failure for the same reason
we hit the brakes to stare at a traffic accident—it's painful to
view, but perhaps something can be learned from it. Most of
us learn more when we come upon a business success. It
thrills us to find a principled, diligent person who has
breathed new life into a troubled or backward corporation.

No matter which business periodical is your favorite,
you're apt to read at least one such piece per issue. I wish
there were room here for all of the heroes and heroines who
have pointed businesses in the right direction. Since there
isn't, I'll introduce you to a few I've known in my years as a
consultant. But let me preface their stories with a thought
from a peer....

Financial consultant Michael Devitt frequently reminds
me of the pivotal role banks and bankers play in turnarounds.
Recently, he captured their "Catch-22" nature perfectly:
"Banks do seem most willing to lend when you least need it.
But a good commercial banker will work hard at understanding customers. You have to remember that a lending officer
has up to 50 business customers to monitor. The problem, of
course, is that when you're short, your numbers don't look so
good. Remember, too, that bankers are constantly having to
justify their actions to federal examiners. It isn't easy."

With Mike's admonishment ringing in our ears, let's
proceed.

Autotrol

Jim Schwerdt, retired president of Autotrol in nearby
Glendale, Wisconsin, can thank bankers for that position.
"About 20 years ago, I returned to Milwaukee wanting to start
my own company. My background was in the automotive
aftermarket and military electronics. But in working with
bankers, they kept telling me I was needed at a company

called Autotrol. I began there as vice president of the controls division.

"The division was reporting only $4 million a year in sales. There were a number of problems—we were losing market share, our quality was bad, and our people were untrained and unhappy. It was a classic situation. Two entrepreneurs began the company by making controls, but were focusing on new ventures in wastewater and other areas. They were neglecting the company's existing business as they bought and sold other businesses that didn't relate to controls."

Schwerdt is almost apologetic about the transformation. "It was a classic case. It sounds cliched, but the first step was to define the problem... I asked employees to write job descriptions—what they were doing, what they should be doing, what they wanted to do. Second, I asked everyone in the division where the problems lay and to rank problems by priorities. I was amazed at the accuracy of the people well down in the ranks. They were able to tell me exactly what the problems were.

"I must have asked 100 questions for each statement I made during those first six months. I talked to everybody, even our competitors. You'd be surprised how forthright a competitor will be if you're seeking opinions. At the end of six months, I found that we were in a number of markets we shouldn't be in, and we were developing products that had no chance of success."

Before taking action, Jim produced a written solution for the company's problems. He circulated the document widely within Autotrol because "I felt we had to have everybody buy on as to what the problems were. It got quite personal. People were spending time on products suggested by the president or vice president, and ignoring the best product we had, namely, the business we were in. We were making everything from sewage treatment products to pool equipment. The head of sales was spending four days a week in the office handling orders because we were always late and our quality was poor.

"I'm just a facilitator. I got the people to write the plan by which we would turn the business around. Groups of three or four would work on a portion of the plan, meeting regularly to define and write their area of expertise. I was the critic. 'Why A rather than B or C?' I would ask. They were skillful at defending what they'd written, and their learning curve was very steep.

"After initiating the plan, we found it to be 60 percent complete after the first year, 30 percent more following the second year, and the final 10 percent after the third year. In other words, within two years we were able to correct almost everything that was wrong. We sold one division within the first three months and another three months later. Only 2 of 40 key people left the company, indicating that the talent to turn things around was there all along.

"At that point I began our Chinese fire drill—the company's first tactical plan. I had been places where tactical plans were presented to the board of directors, then shelved. In contrast, we said to ourselves, 'Let's put down what we really think we can do!' I can tell you that our track record against each year's tactical plan since has shown an average deviation of less than 3 percent. That's incredible. The people know what they're doing, they have good rapport, there's no allowance for power plays or office politicking. Before, I'd worked for huge companies, and this straightforward approach was a breath of fresh air."

Jim can measure his success in a number of ways. Here are my favorite statistics: "The turnover in most offices is 10-15 percent a year," Jim notes. "In our office it's 5 percent or less. And in the factory it's almost zero."

Here's additional data: "Forty percent of our sales are outside North America. We were the state's "Small Exporter of the Year" in 1990. Our foreign headquarters is just south of Paris, and we have a plant nearby that includes a distributor and a training and service center. We have the same thing in Japan, near Tokyo, and in Australia. And we have a sales center in Singapore... When I joined, we had one guy in Paris selling out of his apartment. That was our international business!

"We meet with every shop employee in groups of 12 at least twice each year, which totals two meetings a month. There is no agenda, and employees can couch their concerns by saying, 'I have been asked to ask this question.' The first couple of years, such meetings were all complaints. Then we progressed to suggestions. Now it's an informational meeting. They want to know about the competition, the market, new products, strategic planning, how they did last year, whether they're staying ahead of the quality curve, etc."

I was called in a few years after the turnaround to help formulate Autotrol's strategic plan. Jim summed up the company's success this way: "When you haven't exercised all of the opportunities in your current niche, the more you get outside, the more chance you have of not being successful. You have no presence in the market and no knowledge of the market, therefore the risk is much higher. You have to exercise all of the opportunities in your own niche before you look anywhere else."

Company Y

Jim Schwerdt makes it sound easy. Perhaps for him it was. A manufacturer who prefers anonymity, some distance west of here, experienced a turnaround, too. But a series of unrelated events also affected this maker of capital goods. From their story we can learn another lesson....

Company Y had, for decades, been the measure by which conservative management of a privately held corporation was judged. In the mid-1980s it hired an aggressive president and began to expand through acquisitions. The products that came with the acquisitions were brought into Y's existing manufacturing facilities during a time of expansion in its markets. The products that Y had always manufactured also were realizing sales increases. While the new offerings added volume, the cost of bringing them into the corporate mix resulted in lower margins and smaller profits than might otherwise have been generated.

Y was an exciting place to work at that time. New markets were constantly being probed, a lot of money was being invested in consultants, training, market research, and other areas. The average employee hardly noticed that profits were not tracking with sales increases. One day, there was a cash squeeze—Y had been sending new products to dealers at a faster rate than the dealers could sell. The retailers were reluctant to add new products to their existing floor plan, and they were stretching payments to Y for, literally, all they were worth.

The company continued its aggressive stance, making another acquisition and shipping product. The entire situation was exacerbated by the fact that the company chose to go public. The pressure to sustain performance was overwhelming. Then, in 1991, every market in which Y was involved went into the tank. Almost overnight, market demand dropped 50 to 70 percent. Incoming cash slowed even more.

The managers knew they were in trouble. They shut plants for extended periods, and cut overhead by reducing the number of salaried personnel 40 percent. They intended to right-size the corporation at a point where they could break even at the reduced level of retail sales. But to reduce field inventory, they had to offer very generous incentives so that the dealers could sell the products they already had. Fewer shipments meant fewer dollars coming back to the factory. And sluggish sales bankrupted several dealers, on whom Y was counting for payment for products. Yet Y couldn't reduce its marketing expenditures, as it had to compete with price specials to protect market share and maintain image.

As you may suspect, Y had a terrible time securing money from banks, especially since stock value had dropped with the recession. Y has pledged that, when the economy turns around, it will be slow to add nondirect people to the payroll. It also promises to react sooner rather than later to hints that the dealer pipeline is filling up. "You just can't afford to be optimistic," a consultant advised. In business today, a company such as Y can't wait to cut in the hope that conditions it doesn't control will improve. "They've developed a worst-case scenario," a consultant reports. "If they beat it, they'll be heroes."

Company Z

In contrast to Y, Company Z is smaller, privately held, and fiscally very sound, with management that could be described as "thoughtfully aggressive." Yet officials had a run-in with bankers when they attempted to expand the market for a product for which there was growing demand. The firm, which has its share of electronics wizards, offered a consumer product that would retail through Sam's Clubs and other, similar warehouse retailers. Yet when officials met with a banker for what they assumed would be a routine show-and-tell of their well-documented plans for money to underwrite the expansion, the bank turned them down.

The bank looked at Z's figures and noted that the retail products were manufactured by a subsidiary overseas, then shipped here for testing and packaging. Inventories were kept out of the country for periods of 60 to 90 days, so they were not considered assets by the bank. Just as this retail bonanza began, Z won a couple of unrelated major projects that required additional domestic and overseas inventories and a long, slow (though eventually lucrative) pipeline to completion. Used to borrowing up to 80 percent against receivables and 50 percent against U.S. inventory, it was turned down on a short-term line expansion to support the introduction of the new products.

The bank refused to consider a waiver, though Z could show quarter after quarter of solid performance. Despite Z's cutting of personnel in the United States to the bone, the bank in question failed to respond to the legitimate need of a company that could be called at worst financially inconvenienced. Bankers on the Z account were afraid of risk due to their own past mistakes, says an expert in the field. Z's eventual solution was a commercial-credit company such as ITT or General Electric.

Commercial-credit personnel saw that Z was in a potential growth phase, and handed company officers a virtual blank check after looking over financial figures provided by an independent accounting firm. The accounting firm isn't a familiar name; in fact, it has only three offices, all in Illinois. But the firm knows and works hard for Z and strongly supported the company during an IRS audit. The accountants knew what figures mattered to commercial credit and prepared exactly what was needed.

Calling Company Z's experience a turnaround may be stretching the definition a bit. However, the company is now a leading player in a retail market it had never previously cracked. Leadership there simply refused to give up when conventional fiscal doors closed. I suppose the jury is still out on Company Y, too, though I chose them as an example of a boom-bust-back-to-reality sort of turnaround. No matter what stage you're in at the moment, perhaps the best advice is to maintain regular contact with a banker who knows business, preferably yours.

Why Turnarounds Matter

As I write this, we are approaching midterm congressional elections. The economy, of course, continues as a major issue. It has long been my contention that people who turn businesses around are doing more for the country than all of the economics advisors and politicians either party can muster. When the private sector creates jobs, it transcends economics. It stabilizes families, fosters self-respect, and makes the future something to eagerly await rather than to anxiously fear. May you be part of a business turnaround in the course of your career.

Key Points:

○ Good commercial lenders will support a business when they are convinced of its potential and confident in its leadership.

○ Diversification into new areas is a major reason for business failure. Explore new opportunities in your own niche first.

○ Regular contact with a banker who knows business, preferably your business, is important.

○ A business turnaround does more for the American economy than any economic advisor or politician. When the private sector creates jobs, it transcends economics.

Section IV:
Financing the Business

Chapter 24

Next to "hands up!" or perhaps "we're broke," no two words carry more potential fear among some executives than "corporate restructuring." If you're a manager, visions of an unseen giant snatching up, snuffing the life out of, and then discarding your company come eerily to mind. Many mergers, acquisitions, and buyouts have followed the unseen-giant scenario, but that doesn't mean your experience will be an unpleasant one. A good example involves a well-known company whose headquarters I can almost see from my offices in downtown Milwaukee....

Now that brewing is less of a dominant industry in Milwaukee, nothing in the world today means Milwaukee like a Harley-Davidson motorcycle. In 1981, a group of 13 Harley-Davidson managers bought the company from American Machine & Foundry (AMF). Their timing could hardly have been worse: a recession of staggering proportions resulted in unemployment among potential customers, and Harley-Davidson's quality compared with Japanese cycles had become a joke. Dealers attending the annual new-model introduction could point to fasteners that didn't fasten, crankcases that seeped oil, and gas tanks that made noises like a Jamaican band as the bikes sped down the road. To compound matters, federal and state anti-pollution requirements were making it harder for the outdated H-D engines to breathe.

Working with Citicorp as the lead bank among four lenders, the buyout team chipped in every cent it could afford and set to work. Legitimate questions are raised about the ultimate value of a restructuring to the underlying business. I suspect that, when historians look back at the 1980s, it will be tough to determine whether restructuring was consistently good or bad. In the case of Harley-Davidson, however, it was wonderful.

Managers who were involved in the H-D turnaround probably see it as the highlight of their working lives. The leverage (debt service) required that they make prompt, correct decisions and think creatively. Every segment of the company had to pay its way and fit within the structure, or out it went.

There was no room for error or procrastination. Managers worked to overcome a recessionary economy as they dealt successfully with organized labor and sought the help of suppliers as they fought to bring their company up to state of the art. A couple of the buyout principals, with weak stomachs, fell by the wayside.

Yet here are some of the things they accomplished:

• In 1983 Harley-Davidson persuaded the normally free-trade Reagan White House to impose tariffs on Japanese competitors. This allowed H-D breathing room for about four years while it redesigned its products and rethought its place in the market.

• Newly-designed engines and transmissions were oil tight, trouble free, and, best of all, evolved from traditional design.

• The new owners tapped brand loyalty by creating the Harley Owners Group (H.O.G.), which has more than 60,000 motorcycle owner-members who participate in dealer-centered activities all year long.

• They aggressively pursued and even prosecuted people who reproduced copyrighted or trademarked H-D items without authorization or compensation. The buyback team also introduced parts and accessories that were available only through H-D dealers, which caused these lucrative sidelines to soar.

• They won a major award for engineering the problems out of their vehicles. Greatly reduced defects have resulted in fewer warranty claims and in the ability to better control prices.

• They also started a massive program to teach their 700-plus dealers how to sell. Dealerships became well lighted and thoughtfully redesigned, sales personnel welcomed shoppers, and everything the dealer stocked was beautifully displayed and moved quickly.

• When they realized what they were accomplishing, buyback members commissioned a book to tell their story. *Well Made in America* has sold very well!

This unusual collection of engineers, bean counters, motorcycle riders, and administrators was able to turn a tradition-bound company around by emphasizing all the good aspects of that tradition and then working as if the group's fiscal life depended on it—because it did. Running long and lean paid off when company stock was offered on the New York Stock Exchange in 1986. The price skyrocketed, and the firm today has made wise investments and acquisitions and is on solid financial footing. With debt under control, the buy-back team is really making the profit wheels turn.

Lest you think Harley-Davidson's incarnations are happy exceptions to the restructuring rule, consider several other Greater Milwaukee corporations. There is Miller Brewing, a company that learned to flex marketing muscle after being purchased by Philip Morris. I like the Miller example for several reasons, perhaps because it is a textbook case of savvy, professional managers creating success. Don't automatically assume that beer always prospers. There are many companies that have gone out of business, with their brands now brewed by others. Ballantine, Carling, and Falstaff come immediately to mind. In fact, Carling wrote a book about how it planned to become the nation's most popular beer. Unfortunately for Carling, Anheuser-Busch read the book.

Then there is Johnson Controls, a diversified technical manufacturer here in Milwaukee that decided to become a major player in the battery business with the purchase of a neighbor, Globe-Union. Globe-Union manufactures DieHard and other private-label batteries. Others I could mention include Manpower, Inc., here in Milwaukee, and Simplicity in Port Washington, Wisconsin.

Restructuring At The Local Level

Not all restructuring takes place among Fortune 500 corporations. A client and friend, David Kraemer, is the president of Edward Kraemer & Sons. The Plain, Wisconsin, firm is in the bridge-building, aggregate products, landfill, recycling and engineering business, employing about 700 people in a multistate enterprise. Dave turned to me for some assistance when he and his father formed a holding company to buy out an uncle. Dave then bought out his father, meaning that he leveraged the company two different times in the past six years. He is justifiably proud.

"It (leveraging) made me a better manager because I *had* to perform," he says. "I have a son who is a graduate student in the Wharton School of Business at the University of Pennsylvania. They are teaching him at this moment that you should run your business as if you had a crushing load of debt, because it will make you a better manager. I can tell you, I'm a better manager because of it."

Kraemer points out that you can generate cash to cover the debt load by issuing stock, by returning consistently high earnings, or by selling some assets. He raised money with the latter two methods, concentrating on that portion of the business most likely to generate cash and profits and selling less profitable assets that were nevertheless of value. Besides turning to me and to a banker, Kraemer bounced his ideas off an outside board of directors that "gives me hell, which is what I want," he says.

In businesses sensitive to economic swings, Edward Kraemer & Sons realized 40 percent growth in those six years in which the two leveraged buyouts took place. Today, David Kraemer is able to do the things all the rest of us do and more: plan for the future, update equipment, hire qualified people, even take an occasional vacation.

I could list other successes, while a foe of restructuring could come up with an equal number of firms that have suffered at the hands of an acquirer. One reason I'm suggesting you keep an open mind is the caliber of person one finds today in the merger-and-acquisition business. Several years ago, I attended a meeting on the financial restructuring of corporate America. Participants heard from some of the most familiar names in restructuring.

Among the speakers were Henry Kravis of Kohlberg, Kravis, Roberts & Co.; and Joe Perella of First Boston Corporation. The discussion centered on the fantastic increase in the number and value of mergers and acquisitions. Recent figures indicate that 3,602 merger-and-acquisition transactions added up to more than $240 billion a year. These statistics are significant when compared to the $122 billion in merger-and-acquisition transactions that took place five years earlier.

The nature of the merger-and-acquisition players at the meeting I attended was somewhat of a surprise. I had expected them to be very smart and articulate. But I had not thought they would be easy to talk with, pleasant, interested in what we were doing, and genuinely concerned about the ramifications of the transactions with which they are involved.

They spoke of responsibilities to shareholders, employees, and communities. They were critical of some of the practices on Wall Street and the self-serving leadership they see in some organizations. I entered the room expecting to dislike these people, but left feeling quite differently.

Those who engage in financial restructuring should hold more such meetings. Maybe then they would shake off the stigma created by the insider-trading scandal that surfaced in 1986 and still casts a shadow over restructuring to this day. Here is a quick recap of the sad circumstances surrounding that affair...

What Investment Bankers Do

Investment bankers match people who need money with people who have it. They work for and with companies that want a merger or acquisition to take place, arranging financing and evaluating the transaction. They raise money for corporations intent on acquiring, and they develop strategies for corporations who want to avoid being acquired. Investment bankers also underwrite corporate bonds, which are issued to create capital for an acquisition. These bankers work with brokers, with attorneys, and with accountants. Keenly interested are those now stuck with a dirty label—arbitrageurs. These are people who buy stocks in companies that may be taken over, making large profits and at times suffering big losses, depending on what happens with a pending deal.

What happened in the highly publicized scandal was this: arbitrageur Ivan Boesky and investment bankers Dennis Levine, Michael Milken, and Martin Siegel, using inside information combined with less-than-subtle threats to the fiscal well-being of many companies, conspired to make hundreds of millions, some say billions, of dollars illegally. All four men served at least a few months in prison.

Why is this of interest? For several reasons. First, it teaches us all that restructuring is something we should approach with caution, whether buying, selling, or arranging for debt that will let us control our own destiny, but that may limit our operating flexibility for years. Second, there would have been no scandal had there not been insiders willing to leak their knowledge. Third, despite the rap such a scandal gives Wall Street, the economic system is still standing; the Securities and Exchange Commission and federal prosecutors did their jobs. And fourth, I would hope that the investment bankers active today are honest and cautious to a fault.

But what happens if your company is sold and you chafe under the new system? Some managers atrophy, while others find places to put their talents to use. Edmund Fitzgerald, president of Milwaukee's Cutler-Hammer Corporation, first became vice chairman of acquirer Eaton Corporation. He then moved on to become chairman and chief executive officer of Northern Telecom Ltd.

When Aqua-Chem, a Milwaukee company owned by Coca-Cola, was sold, our long-time friend Peter Marshall departed the company for a career in investment banking and consulting with the local office of Kemper Securities Group. Marshall has, in the last 10 years, helped a number of companies restructure. Today he is president of a point-of-purchase display and marketing services company. He has wonderful insight into the process.

"There are three types of restructuring," he says. "They are financial, strategic, and management. Financial restructuring is a restructuring of the corporate balance sheet. Strategic restructuring involves finance, but it also involves rethinking the company's mission and its products. Management restructuring may involve aspects of the first two, and it can result in fresh leadership."

Harley-Davidson, he points out, was a strategic restructure. Management asked what the consumer would pay it to produce, and how the company could add value to the product. The answers resulted in major improvements in quality, so that H-D could ask a premium price for a premium motorcycle. Also, principals realized that there was a depth of loyalty and a mystique about the product that would erode unless quality improved. Armed with these realizations—and coming off a recession—they experienced resounding success.

Three Avenues To Capital

Another way of stating what Dave Kraemer knows, according to Peter Marshall, is this: "Management begins the restructuring process by realizing that there is a need for capital. That capital can be had in three ways: from retained earnings, by borrowing, or by finding investors who want a part of the company's equity. Normally, restructuring requires all three, but allocation among the three sources will depend on where the company is now.

"The ideal scenario is to amortize debt over the life of the assets," he continues. "The debt would mature when you replace assets—five to eight years in many high-use assets. One more thing: You can plan better with long-term rather than short-term debt, though most debt has some kind of floating range. You will pay more for long-term financing, and you have to look at both the interest rates and the terms of the loan."

Marshall, and many others who follow the economy in the Midwest, would prefer that Harley-Davidson was still privately held rather than publicly held. This is because too many publicly held companies, Marshall believes, "are badly run due to how executives are compensated and how boards are put together. A privately held company is playing with its own money. Besides making better fiscal decisions, it has more regard for the employees and the community."

Asked to name someone who knows how to play the restructuring game, Marshall quickly comes up with Ted Turner. "He is a visionary. He was the only one who perceived the value of film libraries. He understood the evolution of the entertainment market. A few years ago, the networks laughed at TNT and CNN. No one is laughing now."

Turner, you may recall, got involved in restructuring by issuing high-yield junk bonds in an attempt to take over the CBS television network. This was, Marshall says, a no-lose situation for Turner. If he had managed to acquire the network, he would have landed a giant corporation that had been badly run. As it turned out, his takeover attempt failed, and he returned the money paid for the bonds. He had been able to raise a large amount of money at no cost or risk to himself.

In contrast to Turner's vision, Marshall points out, there is the case of George Gillett. He acquired numerous television network affiliates in a declining and increasingly fragmented market. As a result of these and other acquisitions, he has been forced into bankruptcy, and his empire has been sold off, usually at distress prices.

There is at least one more restructuring method that a corporation should consider when exploring all avenues. That is the ESOP or employee stock-ownership plan. ESOPs, Marshall says, work like a trust. "ESOPs offer several advantages to the seller, but they are very complex," he warns. "Yet they are treated very well by the tax codes, and offer employees real potential value."

The investment banker/consultant warns that there are wild cards in the restructuring deck. The economy, the direction in which interest rates are headed, and the twin threats of competition and technological obsolescence are four. Another is whether the corporation considering restructuring is in a cyclical business. Marshall says cyclical businesses such as airlines, automobiles, or retailing need not be any more worrisome than any others—if those who manage the businesses provide a cushion of equity for downturns. The fact that many airlines, auto makers and retail chains have had to restructure shows that they failed to provide that fiscal cushion.

Speaking of cycles . . .

"The Midwest has too many cyclical businesses," he says. "But Midwestern companies learned their lessons in the 1981-82 recession. That's why the recession in the early 1990s affected East and West Coast firms much more than those in the Midwest. People here were prepared, whereas firms on both coasts were too thinly capitalized."

Marshall says his interest in restructuring is piqued not by the balance sheet, "which is only a photo of the business at any one point in time," but by the operational side. He finds intelligent operators able to restructure, even if it means acquiring significant debt, and coming out with a stronger, more viable corporation.

As for that unseen giant we talked about at the beginning of this chapter, there are worse things than having the corporate headquarters move from your hometown to New York or Chicago. "Consider the alternative," Marshall says. "It's really being done to save other jobs. There are always winners and losers in this sort of thing."

Key Points:

○ "Corporate restructuring" may not be the nightmare you anticipate. Many merger-and-acquisition players are qualified, concerned and reputable.

○ Approach restructuring with caution—whether buying or selling. Acquiring debt may limit control and operating flexibility for years.

○ There are three types of restructuring: financial, strategic, and management.

○ When restructuring, explore three sources of capital: retained earnings, borrowing, and new investors.

○ ESOPs may be an option. Though complex, they enjoy favored tax treatment and offer substantial employee rewards.

○ Wild cards in the restructuring process include the economy, interest rates, competition, technology and business cycles. They can upset the best-laid plans.

○ Restructuring may result in a stronger, more viable business.

Chapter 25

"Many traditional owner-managers of profitable, closely held corporations are motivated to 'go public.' It is the 'in' thing to do."

Such was the advice offered in the heyday of "go-go" money managers who were looking for a new, hot issue, and of companies that were eager to oblige. Since that paragraph was written in 1970, countless companies have gone public. They have created happy and disgruntled well-to-do underwriters, stockbrokers, and lawyers, along with some happy and unhappy purchasers of Initial Public Offerings (IPOs).

What public ownership has done for managers is highly problematic. The book quoted above, *Why, When and How to Go Public,* has been unused on my business-library shelf for years. In part, that's because some managers now approach public ownership with less zest. Also, I tend to be skeptical about the benefits of "going public," especially without intensive study of its drawbacks and benefits.

There are times, however, when it may be the only course open. I'd like here to provide guidelines to follow in making that decision, and some of the considerations and conditions to observe.

Among the reasons often given for issuing stock are:

• **Estate planning.** Public ownership establishes current and future value for shares of the company. It is one way to provide liquidity for heirs.

• **Diversification.** This reason is somewhat elastic and may stretch from an owner's desire to diversify personal holdings to management's belief that it facilitates the corporation's acquisition program.

• **Capital.** The growing pains of a young, emerging, high-growth company may be satisfied only by an infusion of funds for expansion, for plant and equipment, for working capital, or for research and development. Additions of new equity money may increase leverage, and the company that foresees the need for additional funding in the future may find it opportune to take the plunge to establish recognition in the "market."

• **Prestige and image.** This sometimes translates into an ego trip for owners who want the world to recognize their personal success. It's not valid in my book, but companies have been brought to market for that tenuous reason—usually with somewhat less than happy results for shareholders. But being publicly held can establish and maintain a national image.

Can you stand up to the scrutiny of public ownership? To help you make up your mind, get analysts' reports on some of the most beleaguered public companies. Read carefully the more subjective sections of these reports—especially the ones in your industry.

Also, be sure to read "Heard on the Street," the popular column in *The Wall Street Journal*, and study the treatment of companies in your local newspaper.

Talk to your counterparts in publicly held firms. Ask them if, given the opportunity, they would go "private." Ask them how they feel about that time-honored institution, the annual meeting. How do they feel about shareholder relations?

Unsolicited Advice

Can you stand the "help" you're going to receive from public owners—from individuals and powerful institutions? These suggestions may range from dividend policy, to board membership, to criticism when earnings are off, to the visibility of disclosure requirements, to your own compensation. Will you be able to structure your deal so that you can retain control?

Is it going to serve your interests to have your shares widely held? Do you need national visibility? Will disclosure hurt your competitive position in the marketplace?

Please think very carefully about those new owners. Will you be comfortable if most of your stock is held by your neighbors? Is yours an industry best understood by sophisticated investors—money managers looking for high-growth companies? Get a composite picture of your ideal shareholder family fixed in your mind so that you can communicate it to your underwriters. If it's unrealistic, they'll let you know.

I sincerely believe that you can't approach the going-public process without considering all of these questions thoroughly and thoughtfully. I don't think that public ownership is wrong—but it's not right for every company. The time to find out is before you sign up with an underwriter.

If your company's needs will be met by an offering, and you've decided that you can live with, or that you may even enjoy, sharing ownership, your next move must be to look at the organization. You have to examine its products, markets, and potential as the investing public would.

For openers, are sales at the requisite level of at least $15 million to $20 million? Was net income in the past fiscal year $1 million or more? Do growth rates—historic and potential—meet the requirements of institutional investors and financial analysts? How will proceeds of the underwriting be used? There are no hard-and-fast requirements. Emerging high-tech companies have successfully gone public without a cent of profit, some even without sales. The preceding financial criteria are, however, a good guide to potential acceptance.

Ask yourself how the "market" is going to view your company. Will your management team and board of directors stand up to scrutiny? What is the outlook for your markets? How is your company positioned? How do you stack up against the competition?

Last, timing is a consideration. If your company is a shining star in a troubled industry, or if your performance is likely to deteriorate or wobble in the next year or so—in short, if you have any misgivings—it may be prudent to re-examine financing alternatives as either short-term or permanent solutions.

Picking Your Advisors

Suppose you've come through this preliminary evaluation feeling that it's the right move for you. Who are the people you need to work with you—to evaluate strategies and help bring your offering to fruition? It will take the services of accountants, legal counsel, underwriters, and communications specialists.

If you're going to do it, do it right. Get the best possible people to advise you. Don't take a "yellow pages" approach. Again, talk to your peers and counterparts for their recommendations. Don't settle on any one firm in any one discipline until you have interviewed the principals, staff, and past and current clients. Whatever you do, make your own choice—don't take a package you don't like. One last word—bring plenty of money.

Number one on your list of team players will be legal counsel. This assumes, of course, that you have been using the services of a qualified accounting firm and that your financial statements are in good shape.

For example, you will need to provide a five-year earnings summary and at least three years of audited statements. If you go public in midyear, you will have quarterly reporting requirements. Accountants experienced in serving publicly held companies will help you evaluate investors' acceptance of your financial condition. The services of both accountants and attorneys are essential in filing and clearing the preliminary and final registration statements and other required filings.

Going public is not an assignment to be trusted to the uninitiated. It is a complex legal process, and you will be best served by firms well-grounded in the requirements and filings of the U.S. Securities and Exchange Commission.

The importance of your investment banker cannot be overstated. The considerations in selection are legion. Does the firm understand the industry? What is its track record in managing initial offerings? What is its reputation for providing an aftermarket? How do clients feel about its financial advisory capability? Has the firm you are considering successfully handled companies of similar size and intent? And, what is the status of its research department?

This all sounds like a complicated process, but from my observation, it's one that will pay dividends no matter which way you go. You will be opening your company to the scrutiny and evaluation of several new publics, and these advisors will be working closely with you for months. They will help you determine whether you can live with the new accountability that goes with outside ownership.

The foregoing has been an overview only. A good business library will detail the filing process from start to finish. Do your homework, pick your accountants, attorneys, and investment bankers carefully, and don't forget to conduct a self-examination.

An Inward Look

A number of attitudinal changes will accompany the new role of a chief executive officer who has shared ownership with the public. Disclosure will be an entirely new experience. Running a closely held company, you've reported only to a small group of shareholders or partners, or maybe to no one at all. Your business has, quite literally, been your own, and you've been able to protect all information that you felt was confidential.

Welcome to the goldfish bowl! Beginning with your prospectus, you will be required to report information you've never before made public. This ongoing disclosure process is necessary to enable investment professionals to evaluate your company's stock.

The information is essential for the brokers who will sell the stock to their customers. And it is essential in helping individuals make their investment decisions. As shareholders of other companies, you and I have benefited from these disclosure statements. They're necessary and expected.

Nevertheless, it can be onerous to report, for example, results by "business segment," so that the world knows your gross margins. And, if you've been used to chatting about your business and its prospects, you'll have to be careful about passing on information that constitutes premature or selective disclosure. You and all your managers will have to learn to live within the constraints of being "insiders."

Plan your communications program with the same thought you give to every other operation. How well you communicate is critical to your long-term success as a public company. It affects stock price, analyst coverage, trading volume, and shareholder acceptance. With its importance, you may want to engage the counsel of professionals who specialize in financial communications. Financial public relations is another instance where going public involves expense—and strict adherence to Securities and Exchange Commission rules.

I've seen that it's sometimes very difficult for a manager to maintain objectivity in all situations. Specialists can be of inestimable value here. They can help you meet the information needs of the press, analysts, and shareholders. But their advice is only valid if you give it careful consideration. Perhaps that's a big change for the CEOs of companies that formerly were in private hands—they will have to listen to and heed a much larger circle of people if they take their companies public.

On the plus side, sharing the potential of your company with shareholders can be a wonderful experience. There are few acts more rewarding than standing before an audience that depends on you for income, and telling them that the company has had a good year, that the future looks promising, that you've created jobs and made community contributions, and that you enjoy the mutual trust and dependence public ownership provides.

Public Ownership As Marketing Tool

Many companies look at public ownership as another marketing component. Certainly people with a stake in Chrysler or Ford or General Motors are more likely to buy the respective automaker's products. Others who have successfully used public ownership to advance themselves include Apple with its computers, Mobil Oil with its views on oil exploration regulations, and RJR-Nabisco with its high degree of consumer recognition. Frequently, I look to invest in a company with an enthusiastic CEO who understands and enjoys the public arena, while running a successful business. A friend of mine bought shares in Microsoft after using a Microsoft product and concluding that it was head and shoulders above its competition.

Do public pronouncements appeal to you? Are you sure? Perhaps it's wise here to point out that you may be dealing with smart and powerful blocs of investors who have their own agendas. Recently, we spoke with Kurt N. Schacht, general counsel for the $30-billion State of Wisconsin Investment Board (SWIB). The retirement funds of state, county, and local employees and officials are invested by SWIB, which has 70 employees and is one of America's 10 largest institutional investors.

Schacht notes that a common complaint about shareholders large and small is that they are too concerned with the next quarterly dividend and could not care less about the long term. "Speaking for this board, we truly believe we are a long-term investor. We take that approach, looking at long-term performance rather than short-term gain."

SWIB has what it calls the Investor Responsibility Program. Traditionally, it has consisted of two major responsibilities: exercising its rights as a shareholder and voting proxies as if they were an additional asset, and representing shareholder interests by initiating and supporting shareholder resolutions in the corporate governance area. As a public fund, SWIB must also address many social issues such as investing in tobacco and improving the environment. Future topics may include doing business with Northern Ireland, owning shares in weapons producers, corporate contributions, and equal employment opportunity.

While their goals may be commendable, it's easy to see how this could get out of hand. If shareholders vote for the immediate and unconditional closing of your subsidiary in Ireland, it could result not only in the loss of jobs there, but in a fiscal blow to the company and possible delays in components needed for production. With many of the largest institutional investors such as the powerful California Retirement Plan representing traditional activists (teachers, union members), you may find yourself a lot less freewheeling than you were when privately held.

To be fair to SWIB and others, they insist on many reasonable notions. Schacht points out that his organization seeks to correlate executive compensation with company performance. That's a logical goal, as is the SWIB contention that poison pills may be needed by a company in a particular situation, but that, long term, their existence tends to diminish the value of a company.

Long term also is on the mind of John Evans. He is first vice president and a portfolio and mutual-fund manager for Robert W. Baird and Co., Inc., in Milwaukee. "Compared with 15 years ago," he contends, "it's unmistakable that shareholders and, therefore, management, are more concerned with immediate earnings.

"The Japanese have a point. They tell us that short-term results come at the expense of long-term well-being. Management may be so preoccupied with the short term that there is reluctance to fund research and development or to expand geographically, which can involve a lot of startup money."

Pressure To Perform

The pressure, particularly on mutual-fund managers, can be intense. "If you're an institutional investor and a mutual-fund manager, both of which I am, my investment returns are published in the press, and there is an increasing emphasis on these returns, especially in the mutual-fund category," Evans notes.

He also points out that stock prices these days can be greatly affected by earnings reports, and that management is much more closely connected to stock prices. This is so because, for many chief executive officers, stock options are their principal form of compensation. "The CEO is very much interested in the short term, especially if he or she anticipates retiring in the near future." Evans adds that CEOs—and their boards—would vote "overwhelmingly" to take their companies private if it were possible to do so.

Internally, public ownership and disclosure may complicate some relationships such as negotiating with bargaining units. But with the right kind of communications, it can instill a new sense of responsibility throughout the organization. If workers can become owners—through an employee stock-ownership trust, incentive-oriented stock options or a payroll savers program—they'll gain a new commitment to and enthusiasm for their work.

You can use your company's position as a respected, widely held corporation. Customer recognition, lending relationships, management recruiting, debt financing, the influencing of pertinent legislation—all can be enhanced by being among those well-followed companies with an attractive price-to-earnings ratio.

Making acquisitions for stock is certainly much easier (and less dilutive) if your shares are appropriately priced. Owners of a closely held company may regard your shares as a way to diversify their own portfolios. But, as I indicated, keeping communication lines open is no small task. If you're in it for this kind of leverage, then use it effectively and consistently.

As you may have gathered, I'm ambivalent at best about "going public." Some of that attitude can be attributed to my experience as a director of publicly held corporations. For example, companies can become so attractive that they become ready prey for acquirers. I've seen corporations with outstanding management, with great product lines, making a real contribution to a community, absolutely torn apart through unfriendly and unfavorable tender offers. I've seen countless hours and untold sums devoted to takeover defenses, to seeking partners who would preserve the intrinsic worth of a corporation—and then seen it all lost when the predator succeeds.

More and more, managers and directors are conscious of their responsibility to shareholders. They may be forced into accepting offers that are too good, in the short term, to refuse, but that reduce the economic worth of the corporation in the long run. It has happened to some fine companies here in Milwaukee and in many other towns and cities.

Retaining control over the destiny of an operation that you and your managers have built is among the uppermost considerations you face when deciding whether to go public.

Planning in a public company is bound to have a different focus. Your planning team may have to temper long-term hopes and aspirations by the report for the next quarter or the next year. Major corporate moves such as stock buybacks or the timing of capital investments often are viewed with an eye toward impact on earnings per share.

It takes a strong, effective, creative, and determined chief executive officer to establish, internally and externally, the philosophy that the future value of the business is the number one consideration. How well you articulate those beliefs in times of prosperity and adversity will be a test of your communications skills.

There will be a certain amount of trauma in the public arena. I've watched fine, honest, conscientious executives literally worry themselves sick when a single quarter went bad, when a new product didn't move on schedule, when interest rates or the weather or the economy went against them. There is also the matter of risk. Can you take the chance on new product development when the equity capital of many, not just a few sophisticated owners, is at risk?

If times are tough, batten down the hatches, take the actions necessary to pull your company through without the criticism, unwanted counsel, and notoriety to which a publicly held organization is subject.

Key Points:

○ "Going public" demands a cautious approach and intense study of benefits and drawbacks. Public ownership is not right for every company.

○ Among key reasons for issuing stock to the public are estate planning, desire for diversification, need for capital, and prestige.

○ Don't take a "yellow pages" approach. When going public, seek out the best advisors—accountants, legal counsel, underwriters, investment bankers and communications specialists.

○ Opening your firm to investor scrutiny may be difficult. Managers of a public company are "insiders" and must beware of premature or selective disclosures.

○ Public ownership can be an effective marketing tool. Clear communications are critical and can affect stock price, analyst coverage, trading volume and shareholder acceptance.

○ Be wary of focusing too heavily on short-term results at the expense of long-term development. The future value of the business should be the number one priority.

○ Retaining control over the company you and your associates have built is a major consideration when deciding whether to go public.

○ Often the wisest choice is to "batten down the hatches" and remain private rather than face the risks of going public.

Chapter 26

General Electric is great, while General Motors was terrible. Wal-Mart is everywhere, whereas Sears, Roebuck is nowhere. Closer to home, Miller Brewing parent Philip Morris is stellar, and Kimberly-Clark is extremely competitive.

What we are scrutinizing isn't any kind of brand loyalty or buyer preference, but is instead an intriguing way of evaluating publicly held corporations. The same principles can be applied to investment decisions by private companies. The evaluation is dissimilar to the annual Fortune 500 ranking, which is merely a listing of corporations by their size. This is instead an evaluation of America's 1,000 largest public corporations in an entirely different way—in terms of how much value they have created for their shareholders.

As you can tell by the above comparisons, size has little or nothing to do with the evaluations. In today's environment, big is not necessarily good, given the dismantling, restructuring, and reconfiguring that has gone on in the last 10 years. The evaluation with which we are concerned, called the Performance 1,000, is formulated by the New York City financial-consulting firm of Stern Stewart. The firm measures company performance by market value added, or MVA, during the period 1980-1990. More than just an assessment, MVA is part of a way of running a corporation efficiently—but more about that a bit later.

MVA is a reflection by the stock market on the dollar amount that management will add to the funds that shareholders have provided over the years in the form of paid-in capital and retained earnings, and that creditors have lent to the business. In other words, MVA is the difference between the capitalized market value of a company and its total capital employed.

Stern Stewart believes that the stock market is a very accurate judge of corporate performance. If investors expect a company to earn the rate of return appropriate to the riskiness of the business and its capital structure, MVA should be zero. In other words, the stock should be worth exactly what investors have contributed over the years, plus retained earnings and long-term debt. If investors expect a return to exceed the company's cost of capital, MVA will be positive. But if management has not used its resources effectively, or events have conspired against an industry, the MVA will be negative.

A glance at the Performance 1,000 listing will bear this out. Stern Stewart ranks General Electric first among all corporations because it has, in 10 years, increased its market value added from less than $1 billion to more than $32 billion. In contrast, the worth of General Motors (ranked 1,000th in the survey) in the market-value-added column has decreased by more than $10 billion. Stated another way, for each dollar GE received during the decade of the '80s, it created $32; for each dollar GM received during the same period, it lost $10.

MVA measures how well corporations have created value for shareholders by picking the right investments and managing them smartly. During the 1980s, General Electric under Chairman Jack Welch was transformed from a bloated and bureaucratic giant with dozens of businesses into a modern corporation with 13 lean, competitive divisions, all of which are at or near the top of their respective markets. Whereas GE spent money that produced value, GM spent money (tooling, acquisitions) without tangible financial result.

One of the minor coincidences with the Stern Stewart figures is that America's most-admired corporations, as listed in *Fortune,* also are high up on the Performance 1,000 list. They include, in order, Merck, Rubbermaid, Procter & Gamble, Wal-Mart Stores, Pepsico, Coca-Cola, 3M, Johnson & Johnson, Boeing, Eli Lilly, and Liz Claiborne. Except for Rubbermaid and Liz Claiborne, not one firm was lower than 36th in terms of market value added. Average annual return to investors during the period 1980-1990 exceeded 20 percent. No wonder they're admired!

Stern Stewart does some tinkering with the numbers. Among other things, it warns that figures will be distorted when a company makes a major acquisition. The profits of both companies are included in the calculation on return, but only the capital of the acquirer is considered in arriving at its final figures. For reasons too complex to mention, Stern Stewart does not apply the evaluation to financial companies.

The consultant also factors in something it terms "stake-holder commitment." Another term might be "taking care of our own," or "commitment to our communities." Using Rubbermaid as an example, Stern Stewart points out that the corporation:

- Established a profit-sharing plan for employees in 1944, a progressive move at the time.
- Converted a rundown elementary school to a community arts center in 1984.
- Converted another building for social services agencies in 1989.

Lest you think Rubbermaid internalizes its profits, the company from 1980 to 1989 increased its amount of share-holder value added by $2 billion, and has, in the last five years, introduced more than 1,000 new products.

Wal-Mart, according to Stern Stewart, improved its market value added with its "unstoppable productivity loop." The mass merchandiser began by offering lower prices and better service. The result was more satisfied customers, which created more shoppers and more sales. These in turn hiked efficiency, and cycled merchandise and capital more quickly. The result was a higher return (more market value added and, as explained below, more economic value added), which led to more technology and more growth. These resulted in more efficient methods and more innovation, which brought Wal-Mart right back to lower prices and better service. That's where the loop began.

Economic Value Added

In addition to market value added, the Performance 1,000 measures economic value added, or EVA. This concept can easily be applied to investment decisions by private corporations. Instead of looking at raw earnings, Stern Stewart calculates earnings minus the required return on the capital used to operate the business. EVA is a measure of surplus returns, or profits. Stern Stewart believes that "EVA binds all of a company's major planning and policy issues into a completely integrated financial management framework. No other measure can do that, not even cash flow."

This gets increasingly complicated, because Stern Stewart adjusts some accounts to make comparisons among corporations valid. To neutralize different degrees of leverage, for example, EVA is computed as after-tax profits minus the required return on both equity and debt (cost of capital).

MVA measures the value investors expect a company to create in the future. EVA tells investors whether a company is in the process of creating value. Therefore, increases in EVA should be accompanied by increases in MVA. In its March 1991 issue, *Corporate Finance* magazine cites the example of Wal-Mart, which "rollicked through the Eighties with an average return on capital of 24 percent, versus a cost of capital that Stern Stewart pegs at 13 percent," the article states. Wal-Mart's "EVA rose from $36 million in 1979 to $596 million in 1989. As a result, Wal-Mart's market value added shot from just $320 million to $21 billion by the end of the decade."

As noted above, the size of the business doesn't matter. The issue is quality — how capably the managers employ the capital used in the business. All managers are in the same business, namely, to put capital to its most promising use. Bennett Stewart of Stern Stewart indicates that, "to increase their company's stock price, managers must earn rates of return on capital that exceed the return offered by other equally risky companies that also are hungry for funds."

The Performance 1,000 has been lauded by analysts and academics alike. Says one: "It makes sense to take into account the investment outlays to maintain and generate earnings and the required returns on those outlays." Says another: "Simple measures that look at stock-price performance don't consider the amount of investment that went into generating that stock price. From that perspective, the Performance 1,000 does a much better job than its competitors. It also shows that size can help, but it can hurt as well. A manager has to be careful when he grows a business."

Perhaps predictably, approximately one-third of the companies in the Performance 1,000 displayed substantial EVAs. That is, they earned significantly more than their cost of capital. Another third labored along quite close to their cost of capital, neither enhancing nor detracting from their shareholders' investments. The bottom third earned substantially less than their cost of capital.

This is all food for fiscal thought, but how does a real, live corporation apply Stern Stewart principles? The Manitowoc Company, Inc., some 90 miles north of Milwaukee, is a leading manufacturer of cranes and related products, and of commercial ice machines. The publicly held firm also does ship-repair work. I first learned about the Stern Stewart Performance 1,000, and how companies can apply Stern Stewart principles, while working with The Manitowoc Company to develop a strategic plan. The firm has taken MVA and EVA to heart, with encouraging results.

A New Way To Measure

Bob Friedl, vice president and chief financial officer of the company, sees the program as "a different means of measuring success." Founded in 1902, The Manitowoc Company went public in the 1970s. The company's divisions all are part of mature industries, so Friedl, President Fred Butler, and fellow company officers focus on return on invested capital as Stern Stewart would compute it. Their goals are:

- Maximum profits.
- Reduced invested capital.
- Maximum market share.
- Maximum earnings per share.

Aren't these the goals of everyone in manufacturing, you might ask? "Yes," Friedl says, "but what makes EVA intriguing is that there is a direct link to the shareholder value issue. Other management theories don't make that connection.

"All business units in our company must meet certain criteria. They must meet certain objectives. Each will bring up recommendations on what should be done with excessive assets, or on ways to reduce the size of the investment," Friedl says.

Reducing inventory is one way to cut the company's capital employed. Other ways include improving collections and selling unused or underemployed fixed assets.

Friedl notes that EVA doesn't tell a company what to do with an accumulation of non-operating cash. Rather, Stern

Stewart and such business schools as the University of Chicago study the correlation between earnings per share, return on equity, and the price of company stock. "One of the lowest correlations found was earnings per share," Friedl points out. "There was no meaningful correlation between it and the price of a share of stock. But there is a definite correlation between stock price and EVA."

As an example, Friedl reports that his company in 1992 entered into a $26 million sale/leaseback of its rental fleet of boom-truck cranes and crawler cranes, following an analysis of this investment based on its EVA. "Rental was profitable, but now we have earnings without a higher-cost equity capitalization," he says. "Our cash flow and flexibility have increased. Selling the rental fleet made us leaner, and getting lean will generate cash."

The Manitowoc Company also factors in the status of its individual divisions. The company's ice machines generate a 45-50 percent return on capital, making for phenomenal EVA. Though part of a mature industry, the ice machine business is not as volatile as the company's less profitable crane or marine divisions. Obviously, the firm would prefer to increase market share where the return on capital will be highest.

Once a company such as Manitowoc "leans down," and reaches the point where the cost of increasing market share further becomes prohibitive, what happens? Again, this is not the concern of Stern Stewart. However, The Manitowoc Company officers might opt to look for new markets; search for new products; and evaluate mergers, acquisitions, and capital restructurings. The point is, a corporation that is performing well has the luxury of looking at such options.

Earlier, we mentioned companies operating in or having ties to Wisconsin. Here is an alphabetical list of several companies in the Performance 1,000 and their 1980-1990 rank in the Stern Stewart scheme of things:

Ameritech, 29; Anheuser-Busch, 31; Archer-Daniels-Midland, 73; Banta, 730; Bemis, 338; Briggs & Stratton, 835; Burlington Northern, 980; Cray Research, 516; Dart Group, 789; Deere, 683; Eaton, 485; GTE, 19; General Electric, 1; Georgia-Pacific, 291; Great Northern Nekoosa, 210; Harley-Davidson, 603; Harnischfeger, 695; ITT, 973; Johnson Controls, 619;

Kimberly-Clark, 75; Lands' End, 467; Nucor, 287; Philip Morris, 2; Rockwell International, 340; A.O. Smith, 941; Snap-On Tools, 293; Sundstrand, 777; Tecumseh Products, 855; Tenneco, 76; Universal Foods, 411; and Western Publishing, 599.

Since that survey was conducted, Briggs & Stratton has adopted EVA, and now manages the business to enhance its economic value. Profits have increased dramatically as a result of re-engineering of its manufacturing and the constant focus on economic value added throughout the company. Its stock price has increased dramatically and the company's adherence to the principles of EVA have been widely publicized.

Is the Stern Stewart Performance 1,000 bulletproof? No, and it isn't presented as such. In fact, companies engaged in volatile businesses can perform adequately for a period and then quickly disappear. An example is Midway Airlines, ranked 719th in the 1990 poll. The Chicago-based carrier liquidated assets in the spring of 1992.

On an industry-by-industry, market-value-added analysis completed in 1990, Stern Stewart foresaw that pharmaceuticals added the most value for shareholders, while cars and trucks added the least. Oil and gas, telephones, and retailers also served shareholders well, whereas steel, aerospace, airlines, and paper neither added nor subtracted a great deal from their value.

Which industry a business is in can have a powerful effect on its well-being. All of the pharmaceutical companies in the Performance 1,000 rank near the top because, as a group, they outperformed all other industries in the 10 years being surveyed. In contrast, Chrysler, Ford, and General Motors rank 998th, 999th, and 1,000th, in part because their industry continues to lose ground to imports, and because automobile sales are the first things to go soft when a recession hits.

Challenging The Conventional

An aspect of the Performance 1,000 I like is the way it challenges conventional wisdom and forces creative initiatives. The 1980s were said to be terrible times for retailers, many of whom were over-leveraged. But as a group, led by

Wal-Mart, they performed rather well. Turning in even better performances were beverage companies such as Coca-Cola, Pepsico, and Anheuser-Busch. The latter increased its share of the $15-billion beer market from 30 to 46 percent. The Performance 1,000 ranks Anheuser-Busch 31st overall. Coke and Pepsi are even higher, at 5th and 15th, respectively.

If you are a chief executive or chief financial officer, Stern Stewart's expertise is something you may want to tap. I like its concept very much, because it's a more accurate barometer of how a corporation is being run. And with shareholders looking over corporate shoulders these days, shouldn't the officers who are realizing good return on investment be recognized? The Performance 1,000 is such recognition. As The Manitowoc Company is finding out, it's a sound litmus test for producing good corporate chemistry.

Quoting *Corporate Finance* once again, the magazine concludes that "The Performance 1,000 then is just what managers and investors have been looking for. It provides a framework in which to assess a company's ability to create value for its shareholders. More importantly, this list demystifies the financial decisions of management. A company either does or does not invest capital wisely over time."

Key Points:

○ The stock market is, over time, an accurate judge of corporate performance.

○ Another measurement is the Performance 1000, which rates firms by how much value they create for their shareholders and takes into account return from all capital invested.

○ MVA—Market Value Added—is the difference between capitalized market value of a company and total capital employed.

○ EVA—Economic Value Added—is the difference between earnings and the required return on capital employed in the business.

○ The size of a business doesn't matter. The issue is how capably managers employ the capital used in the business.

○ Though the Performance 1000 is not foolproof, it accurately assesses a firm's ability to create value. It can force creative initiatives and demystify financial decisions.

Chapter 27

The first time I read the sentence, I was half way into the next paragraph before it sunk in. I paused, then read it again—and again: "Recent research has shown that many American firms have abandoned lucrative markets because of poor accounting information rather than an inability to compete."

Can those 23 words, taken from John Leslie Livingstone's *The Portable MBA in Finance and Accounting*, be true? Did America cease manufacturing television sets, cameras, sub-compact cars, tennis shoes, and inexpensive clothing simply because the bean counters spilled the beans in an incomprehensible manner? It's highly likely.

Remember that the United States emerged from World War II as the only industrial nation with its manufacturing base intact. The quantity of goods sold overseas was limited only by the fact that we wanted some of the products to enjoy ourselves. The numbers associated with manufacturing were all but ignored; such information as cost of goods sold or operating expenses was looked on by management as padding to flesh out the optimistic messages in the annual report.

It took an out-of-balance of trade to prod accountants into furnishing information in a form that would help executives make more timely decisions. The modern manufacturing firm in the global marketplace must either be the low-cost producer of a product, or must make a product that is unique and in sufficient demand to justify a premium price. To compete, American executives have to manage not only their production and distribution systems but their costing systems as well.

Cost accounting has been around since laborers greatly outnumbered machines. To find out how much it cost to produce a product, the most important figure once was the total created by adding together all wages. Today, machines in an automated plant cost many times more than wages and salaries. What's needed is a new way to assess the company's fiscal position. One way is the introduction of an activity-based cost system.

Tailoring On-hand Information

Jerry Doyle, head of Gerard A. Doyle & Co., Milwaukee, is a consultant in the areas of management information systems and business planning, primarily for health-care facilities. A software consultant, too, he points out that the figures needed to establish an activity-based cost system for a given company usually are already at hand. Part of his service is to tailor an information system that will collect necessary data and present it in such a way that his client—the business owner—can make sound, timely fiscal decisions.

"Even the smallest businesses already have accounting systems in place," he says. "The activity-based system is one way of measuring the indirect costs in a company. There are ways of quantifying and reporting indirect costs so that decisions can be made on whether a service or a product is profitable."

The indirect costs that must be considered include how people spend their time. That covers the chief executive officer, engineers, sales personnel, and more. Their collective time must be accounted for and judged on whether their service or product is profitable. Can their costs be managed, and do they add value to the company's product or service? If not, out they must go.

"You probably don't want to impose a mechanical system that requires employees to report on their whereabouts every 15 minutes of the day. A better method is to conduct interviews that cover the many ways in which people spend their time. Even salespeople, for example, spend some time in support activities. Do these activities add value? Value is added if the customer is willing to pay for it."

There is no computer program written that will take a company completely through the procedure, Doyle says. On the other hand, you need not even employ a computer in order to come up with relevant answers. "Interviewing for productivity is an art, not a science. You have to know whom to interview, what to ask, how to find the cost drivers... It's different than filling out a time sheet, which most people resent. They learn to figure out what's wanted rather than what's needed. An occasional, intelligent interview works—your employees will tell you the truth."

A consultant can help the CEO formulate an activity-based interview process. This is infinitely superior to the standard-cost approach, because costing only measures material and direct labor, whereas an activity-based interview will reveal indirect costs. "Standard cost systems lack meaning," Doyle says. "Business wanted something better. I apply activity-based cost systems to the health-care industry. It works equally well whether products or services are involved. In fact, a service business can have many more indirect costs, and you can greatly improve the profits of a service business by eliminating the non-value-added activities."

Crawl Before You Walk

Another Milwaukee-based financial consultant, Michael Devitt of Devitt Consulting Group, Ltd., feels that the kind of system used is less important than getting your hands on the correct figures and convincing the boss of their importance. "Most entrepreneurs are people who know how to make it or how to sell it, so they aren't interested in the financials. I take their financial statements and put them into a spreadsheet format.

"Normally, they know this month's results and year-to-date. I show them results for every month. This month-by-month presentation will help them spot trends. I also do comparative formats. On the left side of the spreadsheet are current-month figures and figures for the year-to-date. They are followed by 'the budget' or 'the plan' and a variance column. Then come the same month last year and the current year-to-date versus year-to-date last year. Between the monthly spreadsheet and the comparative format, an entrepreneur can tell if changes are occurring."

Devitt, who also advises firms on computer-systems acquisitions, estimates that only 25 percent of those who run small corporations have any sort of business plan written down. "That doesn't mean there is no plan," he says. "It's just that owners are carrying the plan around in their minds." Recently, I asked Mike to take a look at the financials of a local manufacturer. The company had retained me to assist it with strategic and operational planning, but it was in much more dire and immediate need of someone to go over its figures. Here's what Devitt found out:

"Their CPA had taken numbers furnished him by an internal person who had guessed at all of the figures! There was nothing to back up the numbers associated with inventory or anything else. What had happened was, the company had been sold to a larger firm, then bought back. An assistant was the only person left in internal accounting and her boss either failed to pass on the procedures or they had been lost. The outside accounting firm is partly to blame, because they just weren't as watchful as they should have been."

This happens much more often, in otherwise solid firms, than we might guess. Devitt recently went to the aid of an area manufacturing firm that had, for a number of years, been run by a woman. "Mom really knew the business, but she died suddenly and the kids had no training. No financial training, no management training, nothing. The mother had run things for five years without writing anything down. The kids were dependent on the internal accountant but the company changed computer systems and found itself in financial trouble. The children came to me and said, 'The bank says we have to use you.' The company now has its first written budget."

Devitt notes that one of the first places he looks for trouble is under inventory. If figures are overstated month after month but the inventory isn't there at the end of the year, clouds form on the fiscal horizon. If your business lacks a talented, in-house accountant, you may want to purchase a turnkey system that requires only plugging in and a bit of orientation before an employee can begin feeding numbers into it. The most common financial planning tool in such a system is the electronic spreadsheet.

Spreadsheets let business people view the impact of prospective decisions and policies on the bottom line. With capital always dear, it's wiser to use a model before embarking on a major change of direction. Contemporary software speaks English and has numerous menus that help the person at the keyboard enter the right figures in the right places. Projections are a snap, too, since electronic spreadsheets are configured to make instant changes in whole sets of figures.

Pro Forma

Entrepreneurs who seek money from a bank often rely on spreadsheets for their pro forma income statements. A pro forma statement uses a set of assumptions and projections to assist the bank in determining the firm's line of credit. Spreadsheets also are vital for checking budget alternatives. Should you buy or lease a piece of capital equipment? Should you borrow for the purchase? Will the increased productivity realized offset the expenditure? If so, when? What about depreciation and the impact of taxes? Spreadsheets make for informed choices and an improved bottom line.

Most of all, a spreadsheet or similar financial program will give a business owner the speed he or she requires to make meaningful decisions. Some figures are needed only occasionally. Items such as depreciation really don't change much and therefore don't need to be readily at hand. But items such as receivables are important and should be updated as often as the boss looks at the computer screen or ledger. Other figures that should be immediately at hand include sales, cost of goods sold, gross profit, operating expenses, and net profit. Credit and collection information may or may not be an issue with the owner, who probably is acutely aware of who pays promptly and who does not.

Going Horizontal

Activity-based cost systems are easy to spot—whereas cost accounting involves a vertical column of numbers, activity-based costs frequently are linear. This is known as process-flow mapping: companies want to show that costs are the result of activities such as design, production, and support of the firm's products. Showing how work and money flow makes it easier to understand and manage resources.

Traditional volume-based cost systems meant that high-volume items subsidized low-volume business. That's because high-volume items generate more labor hours and therefore are burdened with more of the overhead pool. Only after overhead is broken down by activity and traced accordingly do real costs come into focus. Volume has proven to be an inaccurate method of figuring overhead.

If by now you're convinced that an activity-based costing system (or some sort of financial presentation) will give you a more accurate picture of your business, what can you do? Doyle and Devitt both like people who talk to their peers. They note that there are many trustworthy and aggressive outside accounting firms that will be as tenacious as you like in presenting timely financial matters. If you want to improve internally, too, here are six steps recommended by Livingstone's *The Portable MBA* for creation of a new system:

1. Make sure your firm's cost-accounting problems stem from lack of an activity-based costing system and not from other factors. Your first clue may come from marketing. "We cannot compete given our high costs." This could be caused by three factors: your technology is substandard, your operations are inefficient, or your cost-accounting information system is obsolete. Ensure that neither of the first two factors is the real culprit.

2. Envision your operation as a continuum, from the design stage through customer support. Develop process-flow charts for each stage: design, production, distribution, support, etc. Identify the activities that are the cause of resource consumption.

3. Trace the functional costs, as reported in the general ledger, to the activities identified by the process maps. Don't be surprised—some activities draw from many different function areas. Setup, for example, may draw from material handling, indirect labor, and tooling. It helps to think of the manufacturing process in a linear format (row totals), rather than in a functional format (column totals).

4. Divide the total cost for each activity by an appropriate measure of that activity to develop a costing rate. An appropriate measure is one that remains constant over the life of the activity. For example, if all setups are pretty much the same, the appropriate measure would be the number of setups. But if they vary, it makes sense to measure them by time consumed (cost per minute of setup), or by complexity (simple, average, difficult).

5. Using these costing rates, follow the costs of your operation to the appropriate level: order, product line, facility, or customer. Note that not all costs can be traced to the unit level. But it is not always necessary to trace costs to the unit. Decisions may be made based on the order level.

6. Facility costs will cause the most problems. Some accountants feel that a cost-versus-price model is sufficient. They argue that one can price the products so that the margin (price less direct costs) covers the facility costs plus the desired profit. If you feel that total costs must be calculated, then allocate the facility costs to the units.

Thinking Logically

This may be a marked change in the way your organization processes information. It should be introduced gradually and expanded as the logic of an activity-based system is seen by your managers.

We may never return to the day when U.S. business and industry were head and shoulders above all other industrial powers combined. But if we are to compete globally now and into the 21st century, we will have to keep scrupulous, timely track of our financials. A trustworthy accounting firm is invaluable for the work that is to come.

Key Points:

○ Managing costing systems is as important as managing production and distribution.

○ Standard costing measures only material and direct labor.

○ An activity-based system also measures indirect costs, including how people spend their time.

○ All businesses should prepare monthly financial budgets and manage by an annual plan.

○ Spreadsheets let business owners play "what-if" games and provide a fast, helpful tool to decision-making.

○ Activity-based costing may dramatically change the way your organization processes information. Introduce and expand it gradually.

○ Scrupulous, timely tracking of financial performance is essential for business success.

Section V:

Governance

Chapter 28

Whenever I see the word family alongside the word business, I'm reminded of a prominent Ohio clan. Living almost palatially just outside Columbus, they had been in the grain business for more than 50 years, and it had paid off handsomely. They owned elevators that stretched as far as Chicago, plus dozens of over-the-road trucks and a series of contracts with major cereal and baking companies. Everything was in full bloom—until the founder and patriarch suddenly died.

Overnight, the late farmer's three daughters squared off. These middle-aged pillars of their communities broke into the father's office in the middle of the night, they created phony codicils to his will and they spread more rumor and innuendo about the business and about each other than can be found in the average supermarket tabloid. One had another arrested. Once the jailbird's attorney bailed her out, she sued. There was a countersuit. Sons-in-law ran into each other at a football game and came to blows. I later learned that their collective bickering resulted in the sale of the business for far less than its fair-market value.

Before you think, "We're different, we're a close-knit family," consider what money—and the fear of not getting one's fair or inherited share—can do to the best and most reasonable among us. The prospect of a cash windfall (or of losing that windfall) can cause family members to act unpredictably. One of the most famous examples of a family implosion involves the Binghams of Louisville. Reams of words have been written about the way in which these otherwise intelligent people succumbed to intergenerational and intragenerational wrangling, and the consequent decline of the Bingham newspaper empire. Many other companies are sold when family members want to use their share of company ownership in other ways. Local examples include Allen-Bradley, Harley-Davidson, and Schlitz.

"Family business is an oxymoron," says David Tolan of Tolan Schueller & Associates, Ltd., a Milwaukee insurance executive and a resource for people who intend that their businesses remain family-owned. "Think of all of the characteristics of families—they are nurturing, there's equality, no one's accountable, it's a right-brain enterprise. In contrast, business has to deal with discrimination and fault-finding; it demands accountability; that's all from the left brain.

A Trio Of Systems

"The problem with family businesses is that you are dealing with three distinctive systems: the ownership system, the management system, and the family system. It's been said that no family business ever required a job description or an annual review of a family member. In non-family enterprises, things are simpler. You decide how close Harry adhered to the business plan, and if he didn't adhere, he is fired. Integrated circuitry makes a family business run. When things go wrong, it may be dealing with the ownership system rather than the management system. And ownership may have nothing to do with the company's future prosperity."

Tolan points out in all seriousness that family businesses have been known to compensate the mentally defective to the tune of seven figures annually, and that such foibles are exactly why families in business get the bad rap they don't necessarily deserve. To counteract this reputation for putting heart ahead of mind, he says, family businesses in the '90s have become obsessed with smooth transitions from current to future management. The first step in such a procedure is to set goals and objectives by asking the right questions.

Upon taking over the reins of a family business, the new boss should first of all decide on a successor and how the succession will occur. I can hear people out there saying, "Get real. Sitting in the president's chair for the first time, the last thing you're thinking about is your successor." Unfortunately, that's usually the case, particularly if something precipitous such as a death or a buyout has occurred and yesterday's shirt-tail relative is today's president. Smart managers, however, won't be able to get succession out of their heads until they have dealt with it.

Here is an example. I've known John since we sat down together for the first time as members of the board of a company here in the Midwest. At the time, John had been president of his family's furniture-manufacturing business for three years. He had worked there as an adult for a decade. The business, which now employs 75, was started by several people, one of whom was John's great uncle. His grandfather reorganized the operation in 1935, and John grew up working summers in the factory. He earned a business degree from a prestigious university, worked in banking, and spent three years in the military before returning to his hometown and signing on with what was by then his father's company.

"I returned to [name of firm] in 1969, which was somewhat premature. But there was a buyout and they needed someone like me. Since becoming the chief executive in 1976, I think I've done a lot of things right. We just celebrated our 100th year with a three-day open house, so the community appreciates and understands what we're trying to do here. I've successfully raised money, which is always tough for a privately held firm, and I've served on a board that is in part made up of relatives with minority shares in the business. I even believe I react well to the unexpected—a good example is that an OSHA inspector just walked out of here. And I've grown to understand and deal successfully with a union on one hand, and the industry in which we compete, here and abroad, on the other. But I'm 49 years old, and I just keep putting off a formal plan of succession."

Solid Management

John is modest—he really is an exceptional manager. He has caused the business to grow and prosper. He has acquired insurance in the event that he is unable to perform. And he has turned, as needed, to the best minds he can find outside the company for specialized advice while practicing a very open style of management. But he will admit that there's no contingency in the event of his sudden death or disabling. "In the short run, we could continue," he says with a sigh. "But in the long run we would have to bring someone in because we're pretty lean here, and everybody's job is very well defined. I'm both president and treasurer. We have a sales manager, a plant manager, an industrial engineer, and four or five foremen. The succession thing won't go away until I solve it."

A prominent attorney who specializes in advice to family-run businesses points out that John's firm could be run by one of the minority shareholders. "Stock in the company creates a host of factors that are different from businesses that are owned and operated by different people. You're potentially qualified because you're in the family. This is a whole different system of choosing leadership. It isn't divorced from a merit-based system, but it's not exclusively a merit-based system, either.

"People who have never been employed by a family business don't realize that subjective promotions lead to other differences. A family-operated business usually has a reputation of taking care of the family and its employees. The principals of the company subscribe to a slightly different set of values than are found in the typical publicly held corporation. There's often a feeling of extreme benevolence toward employees, there's the contention that there are fewer pressures on a family business and that you'll be more equitably treated there than in a non-family operation."

The most expeditious way to deal with succession, says the attorney, is to find the so-called man in between. "Generations don't always line up precisely, so hiring an interim manager is a common device. But the idea of a family owning a business and committing to an outside manager long term, and becoming passive shareholders—you get the worst of all worlds when you do that. I rarely see that last very long. Yet an interim manager, compensated well and with a carefully drawn contract, can be a wonderful immediate solution and a good example for a successor to emulate."

Our attorney friend also feels that an interim manager is a sound choice when looking out for the children's interests. He notes that raising children in the context of a family business can be very difficult, and that it's a far better thing if a child first gains some outside credibility before returning to run the parent's plant. "The person who is handed the business desperately wants fealty and respect from people who report to him or her. It's important to get it. But if the successor has done absolutely nothing, there's a tension that can develop."

The best strategy of all, the attorney adds, is good health. He also notes that there are wise counselors inside and out of the legal profession, and that intergenerational operation of the family business really is driven by tax laws. Bringing in a consultant to resolve succession is a sign of strength rather than weakness. It should be done with the full knowledge of the board, especially if the board includes members of the family, who have stakes in the advice given. Larger family-owned operations may bring in an attorney, an insurance expert, an accountant, a banker, and others to serve as a committee whose aim is to pass the company on into perpetuity.

Opting Out

What happens if a minority shareholder wants fair-market value for his or her stock? By the time the family is in its third generation of ownership, there will be otherwise rational men and women who demand liquidity. It's often said that there is no one more powerless than a minority shareholder, but that's true only if the minority shareholder isn't a director, or consistently fails to show up and speak at the annual meeting. Shareholders with no other ties to the company want dividends that may compare favorably to the interest rates of long-term bonds. Why, they wonder, should we hold this stock, invested in a company that may be miles from our home, when it pays little or no dividend? There is no easy answer to this question, as many families have learned.

No two founders and no two businesses are alike. Yet there are some threads common to all businesses that we should examine. Founders often are portrayed as people whose many flaws somehow add up to success. They work too many hours, perform menial tasks others could do, fret about their enterprises 24 hours a day, fail to share problems with people who could offer solutions, and wonder why their children don't want to take over some day. Perhaps their biggest delusion is assuming the kids want the business. Often parents don't even bother to ask the kids whether they're interested in taking over.

Cliches surround the family, too. The kids are shiftless, they take for granted what their parent has accomplished, the spouse is a silently suffering servant, etc. The children may act dismayed or bored when their entrepreneurial parent talks of succession or retirement. But before any succession moves are made, it's imperative that the family be brought into the equation. If I were in charge here, I'd round up everyone and hold an informal retreat. I always envision doing this on a nice boat on Lake Michigan (there's no escaping involvement, and there is no telephone). The founder has backup material in order to answer all questions and there are no distractions. He or she should avoid being maudlin about death or succession and instead stress that the family is all in the same boat here because the boss needs their advice.

A Rewarding Day

Properly conducted, you may return to shore feeling better about your business and your family than ever before. That's because your day on the boat really is an opportunity for all the family to share their dreams. The founder shouldn't insist that the children's ambitions be cast in stone. Rather, the kids are along so that the founder will get a sense of how they see themselves relative to the family business. The founder also should point out who among the employees should be taken care of as part of the plan of succession. It's not out of line to think about changing titles and forms of compensation to insulate key employees against an unpredictable and unhappy future.

The following day, the founder may want to hold a similar meeting with key employees. If there are shareholders outside the immediate family or the business, they should be told what the leader is thinking. Whether the founder is meeting with the kids, trusted employees, or succession advisors, anyone with a financial or family connection should be apprised of what's on the boss's mind. In a sufficiently wide and diverse circle, the founder may learn more about a talented nephew or others who would be prime long-term succession candidates. At the very least, he or she will have caused everyone to ponder individual and company futures.

At some point down the road, the owner may want to issue stock. The purpose, of course, is to pass on a percentage of business ownership to family members. This is a move that requires the assistance of a tax expert and perhaps others inside and outside the company. What are the differences, for example, between leaving specific portions of stock to specific family members and leaving a lump of shares to all of the children in the same generation? Depending on what the children decide to do with their lives, how much stock and the way it is received could have ramifications for the firm in the future. Equal stock distribution may not always be in the best interests of the majority of people involved.

Rules For Survival

Leon A. Danco, a nationally known expert on the family-owned business, indicates that there are five requirements for the survival of a family-owned business beyond the present generation. Writing in his book *Inside the Family Business* the Cleveland-based author lists the following:

1. The selection and support of competent advisors.
2. The contribution and discipline of committed outside directors.
3. The energies of dedicated and informed managers.
4. The acceptance of responsibility by competent successors.
5. The education, training, and accommodation of the family.

When you stop to think about it, the founder, the founder's child, and the founder's grandchild all must adhere to these rules during their separate tenures. And of the five criteria, only number five is of no consequence to a non-family enterprise. But survival anywhere, to anyone, is fundamental.

Let's hope our friend John, whom we met earlier and who is 49 years of age, presents himself with a solid plan of succession before he blows out the candles on his 50th birthday cake.

Key Points:

○ The money and power involved in family-owned businesses may divide even a closely-knit family.

○ A family-owned business must deal with three distinct systems: ownership, management and family.

○ Making a smooth transition from current to future management is an overriding issue. Begin by setting goals for both business and family. Ask the tough questions.

○ Succession should be one of the first decisions of a new leader.

○ A well-compensated, professional interim manager who can train may be a good solution when a firm is "between generations."

○ A child should gain experience outside the family business before joining it.

○ Problems arise when business owners assume their children want to join the firm without ever asking them.

○ Candid communication among family members and employees is essential for a smooth transition.

○ The survival of a family-owned business beyond the present generation depends on several key players: competent advisors, committed directors, dedicated managers, responsible successors, and educated family members.

Chapter 29

"A strong board makes a first-class management even stronger... A professional board makes management even more professional... An optimum relationship between board and management creates an almost unbelievable dynamic...."

—Kenneth Dayton

I agree wholeheartedly with this philosophy, expressed by Kenneth Dayton, past president of the Dayton Hudson Corp., writing in the *Harvard Business Review.* It is a superb assessment of the value of the independent professional board.

Outside directors of publicly held corporations are universally accepted as shareholder representatives and constitute a powerful force in corporate life. Can privately held companies also benefit from a board comprising a majority of outside directors? I am certain they can.

The outside director brings a different perspective and experience base to the boardroom. A wealth of knowledge in functional areas such as marketing, finance, human relations, operations, or planning is available. An independent board can help managers make decisions that might otherwise be influenced by personal feelings.

For example: Should the long-term but no longer effective manager be replaced, or are there alternatives? Should relationships with a lender be improved or changed? Where should cutbacks in operations first occur? How effective is the research-and-development program and its oversight? The independent view and knowledge of alternatives can be most helpful in answering these questions. Outside directors can be supportive counselors—and perhaps just as often should be emphatic critics. Whether the company is large or small, there is no room for—and no value in—a rubber-stamp board.

Board Recruitment

How do you go about finding qualified people who are really interested in working with the privately held company? There are many experienced executives, educators, researchers, engineers, or scientists who would welcome the opportunity. Directorships expand their horizons. The benefits cut both ways.

Some of the selection techniques that have been successfully used include these suggestions:

• Search out top officers in larger companies—or in companies you have long admired—with functional skills you would like represented on your board. Think of the human relations, marketing, or financial vice presidents. The boardroom is no longer a male stronghold—don't overlook a growing bank of talented and qualified female executives. You may also want at least one person on your board whose profile closely resembles the typical buyer of your product or service.

• Consider faculty members in the school of business of a nearby college. While educators may not have business experience, many have a large store of knowledge about industry, and many serve as management consultants. They can bring a refreshing perspective or new outlook to the boardroom.

• Look beyond your immediate area for well-qualified executives. With the speed of air travel, a director can serve effectively from any location. It can be worth the price of a plane ticket to get the right person.

• Consider using executive recruiters. Some specialize in director searches. Their results often are excellent.

Should you try to find board members who align perfectly with such committees as audit, compensation, and nominating? Robert W. Lear, former CEO of F. & M. Schaefer and an executive-in-residence at Columbia Business School, offers this advice: "Set down an outline of what you would like your board to be in total. You need people of different ages so that the majority of the board won't retire at once, and different talents—marketing, finance, perhaps an academic, or someone who knows research and development. Once your board is constituted, pick someone who may have previously served on an audit committee to head your audit committee, for example. Or, if that isn't possible, hand audit committee responsibility to someone who has come up through the ranks of control or finance."

Who besides the board should attend the meetings? Assuming you are chief executive officer and chair of the board, you should invite the president, the chief operating officer (they may be one and the same), your own legal counsel, the head of investor relations and the company secretary. The latter takes the minutes and is therefore present for all meetings. Everyone else, from the vice president of marketing to the head of manufacturing, can be scheduled to report various matters to the board as you may deem important. Schedule any special presentations at or near the start of the meeting so that the presenter doesn't have to sit in the hall endlessly and wait to be called.

Several other tips come to mind. Move items around on the agenda from one meeting to the next. Note that each item should have an estimate of the time to be consumed by discussion. I like board meetings that begin either early in the morning or late in the afternoon. Morning meetings should end by noon and afternoon sessions by 7 p.m. This will allow you to schedule a meal at the conclusion of the meeting. To minimize accidents, keep the coffee urn some distance from the table. If the meeting lasts more than two hours, schedule a break. This will endear you to the thirsty and to those who smoke.

Assume you have been able to put together a board of five directors—three independent outsiders, yourself as chief executive officer and your selected successor. How do you maximize the return from the investment in your new board? Before any candidate attends a meeting, spend some one-on-one time acquainting the new director with your understanding of the business, its problems, opportunities, competitors, facilities and industry position. Similar meetings should occur once a year.

Refrain from describing fellow board members—or key people within the company, for that matter. You don't want to cloud your new member's judgment, and getting to know fellow board members by what they bring to the conference table is an enriching experience. Also, do not let any individual discussions replace the deliberations that can properly take place only when all directors are present.

Bob Lear, who also serves my company as a senior consultant, knows a CEO who has this hard-and-fast rule: The board will suggest all new members; the only common qualification for board prospects is that they are not known personally by the chief executive officer. The CEO spends some time with each potential director and has the option to say, "This person and I are going to be instantly incompatible, and therefore I don't want him (or her) to be nominated for a position on the board."

Independence Is All-Important

That doesn't mean board members should not have strong opinions. Quite the contrary! As the chief executive, you need to talk to someone about problems and opportunities and where you are leading the corporation. A director can be a best friend only if he or she is thoroughly backgrounded and willing to be candid with you when you need answers. Your directors owe you candor, and you owe them proper conduct as a chair. That means you consult them if an acquisition or other opportunity suddenly raises its head; consultation is most certainly called for prior to a major capital expenditure.

Bob Lear and I have served on many boards. He says some chairs are downright arrogant. "Frequently, they will take actions without consulting the boards. The usual line at a board meeting runs something like this: 'We have to have approval of this capital project because we've already installed the machinery.' Many CEOs have great confidence in themselves. If they act like this repeatedly, they're probably trying to sneak something past the board and questions should be raised. I go back to them and demand to know why there was no telephone conference prior to the expenditure."

Speaking of conferring, how often should a board meet? Ideally, Bob sees a major corporate board meeting once a month, with five meetings a year the absolute minimum for meaningful action to take place. Five meetings will cover each quarter plus offer a chance to appraise the company's strategic policy. With facsimile machines, telephones and overnight delivery, there is no reason why a majority of directors can't get together on very short notice to help the CEO through a complex problem. "If I don't hear from a CEO between quarterly meetings, I raise hell," Bob says.

A CEO operating a volatile business may want to take this course of action: provide each board member with a summary of news about the industry and the corporation. This can be assembled and sent out every quarter. Such a "scrapbook" makes intriguing reading and will serve as a summary of matters that can be crucial for directorial decision-making.

Back to directors who are new to the board... They should be provided with a complete package of your own reading material—financial statements, employee publications, history, product literature, articles and bylaws and copies of strategic and operational plans. If your plans aren't in writing, discuss your perception of the company's future and how you expect to achieve your goals.

Prepare thoroughly for meetings. Get agendas and other materials to directors 10 days to two weeks before meetings. Change the agenda format occasionally to keep from becoming bogged down in three-hour discussions of financial history. Keep the focus on the future. From time to time, bring in top executives to report on their areas of responsibility. This is good experience for them, and it helps directors evaluate the quality of your organization.

Take directors off site for two or three days every other year to discuss strategies. Professional guidance at such a meeting can help to stimulate total participation and keep the discussion directed toward critical issues. These sessions will bring your own planning into sharper focus and make it more responsive to your board's thinking.

In a privately held company, the outside director is a thoughtful advisor whose purpose is to help the owner-manager. Directors serve at the pleasure of the owners and can be removed at any time. That won't bother committed directors, who fully understand this position. Thoughtful suggestions will be offered in a way that ensures consideration.

Your mission as CEO is to listen. You need not accept any advice without question, but you owe it to responsible people to hear them out fully. Their contentions, carefully considered, are what you are paying for. Bored or ignored directors will soon retire, particularly if two or three board members are long-time friends and the other two or three are strangers. Effective working boards are rarely made up of close friends. Independence and meaningful contributions go hand-in-hand.

Similarly, your banker, attorney, or accountant will be less independent than is desirable. The optimum environment is one in which suggestions, proposals, approval, and disagreement will flourish—productively.

Paying For Advice

Plan to pay for good advice. The days of the $100-a-meeting fee are over. We at Krause Consultants recommend a combination of retainer (about 60 percent of the compensation package) plus additional fees for meetings of the full board and of committees. Depending on company size, director responsibility, and meeting frequency, annual fees of at least $6,000 to $20,000 are appropriate for a small- to mid-sized company. Review directors' fees regularly, on the same schedule as the compensation package for the CEO.

Look at fringe benefits that can be made available to directors. A medical reimbursement plan or unique health-insurance features can provide tax-free remuneration, which makes for a more attractive compensation package. You might also offer the option to defer fees until retirement. Add an imputed interest factor for use of the director's money, or offer stock in place of cash to encourage continuing interest and commitment.

It's easy for owners of a business to fall into a thought process that bases decisions on known or familiar experiences. But can anyone afford to run a business based on the past, however successful? By surrounding yourself with independent directors who have important functional skills, your chances of considering all of the alternatives and arriving at effective solutions are much greater. If you have chosen your board members well, there will be the added advantage of meeting problems head-on in a stimulating, creative environment.

If you run a publicly held company, you may wonder about shareholder pressures and their relationship with selection of board members. Bob Lear says such fears are exaggerated. "Most shareholders are uninformed, passive, or incompetent. The smart ones are the mutual-fund people. If they don't like what you're doing, they sell your stock. Institutional investors frequently make suggestions to add or drop board members, and sometimes a major shareholder will be outspoken."

Lately, there have been pressures on boards to plan further into the future, while shareholders simultaneously demand a lavish quarterly dividend. Lear says the good companies decide on what to pay shareholders long after their plans are made. "Every good American company is very strong in extended planning. The paper companies, for example, have to plan 30 to 40 years out to make sure there are trees to harvest. Hostile raiders, not corporate boards, are the ones who don't look into the future."

Should you therefore involve your board in planning, even if your company is privately held and board members are mere advisors? Yes, by all means. Tap those active minds for all they are worth. An advisor given too much to do will quickly tell you. Meanwhile, get them involved in the planning process. One way to do this is to draft a long-range plan and then give it to the board to dissect. I guarantee you they will come up with answers to questions you didn't ask but should have.

By now you may be thinking, "Krause has given me a lot of esoteric reasons why I should consult with a board, but he hasn't told me how a board can make or break my business." In plain language, a board can keep you legal. If it forces you to be accountable, you will also be honest—not just honest in the eyes of the law, but honest in terms of sizing up your business and making the hard decisions to keep that business in the black.

Beware Of 'Good Buddies'

With that in mind, here is one more piece of advice: choose board members who won't become cronies. Although it happens infrequently, I've heard of boards where the meetings degenerate into reminiscences because several members once worked at the company or they attended the same college or they played golf at the same club. Nothing can waste time like board-member storytelling. It's unfair to those who don't share the same background and it's unjust to you, because you paid these people to help you steer your corporate course, not tell what it's like to be a sailor.

Ideally, board members will bring written or mental notes based on the agenda to each meeting. I can recall sitting in a communications-dependent corporation's meeting of directors more than 10 years ago when a very independent board member asked about the impact and the corporation's response to the breakup of AT&T. The CEO immediately called in a couple of his senior people to explore the potential benefits and liabilities of dealing with multiple telephone companies. In three or four sentences, the free-thinking and independent director had earned his pay.

Key Points:

○ Outside directors are immensely valuable. They bring a different perspective and experience base to both publicly and privately held corporations.

○ Qualified directors may be officers of other companies, faculty members of local colleges, or retired executives.

○ Besides directors, attendees at board meetings should include the president, CEO, legal counsel, and company secretary.

○ Board members owe you candor and you owe them proper conduct as a chairperson. Consult with them before any major capital expenditure or acquisition.

○ Meetings should focus on the company's future. The CEO should prepare thoroughly, providing agendas and other materials to directors well in advance.

○ In an optimum board environment, suggestions, proposals, approval, and disagreement will flourish. The CEO's mission is to listen.

○ Be willing to pay well for good advice. Annual directors fees for small- to mid-sized companies range from $6,000 to $20,000.

○ Boards force you to be accountable and focused on key strategic issues. They help make those hard decisions that keep the business on track and prospering.

Chapter 30

Several years ago, I helped guide a medium-sized, family-run corporation toward long-term planning decisions. They were happy with the conclusions I reached as their consultant, and I assumed I wouldn't hear from them for another year. Less than six months later, the president of the company telephoned, and he was worried.

This aging founder of the company wanted to retire but feared turning over the company to his elder son, as he had concerns over the son's dedication and competence. The only other family members at the company were a nephew, who did not have the organizational skills to take over, and a son half the age of the older brother. Yet, with a bit more seasoning, the younger son seemed to have all of the qualities needed to run the company.

Having learned at an early age that blood is thicker than water, I approached the founder with trepidation after talking to a range of people inside and outside the organization. I suggested that his son, the president, retire; that the nephew be dismissed; and that a professional manager be brought in to train the second son.

Somehow, it all worked. The founder retired and had the forbearance to stay away from the head office; the elder son took early retirement; the nephew was fired; and the professional manager trained the second son to be a competent executive, respected by his people. Today he is the president of a company that is doing well.

In contrast, how do you feel about Roger Penske being offered the presidency of Chrysler Corporation early in 1992? Did you note that Lee Iacocca decided to stay on the board? No wonder Penske turned down the offer! Who wants to be second-guessed by a CEO who is retired only in theory? The excitement of being at the helm of a major automaker was dampened by the shadow of the firm's extroverted former boss looking over Penske's shoulder.

When I read that a retired CEO will stay on the board, it concerns me. If the new chief executive officer is to function to the maximum potential, the board should be an objective forum with free-flowing interchange, not an occasion for the ex-leaders to tell how things were done when they were in charge. For every retired CEO who sits on the board and holds his or her tongue, there are a dozen who are reactionary and counterproductive.

Here's something else to think about. Robert W. Lear, a former CEO himself, an instructor at the Columbia University Business School, and a good friend, notes that the retired chief exec's range and state of information about the company both diminish after the reins are handed over. Writing in the October 1991 issue of *Chief Executive Officer* magazine, Bob says that the real nightmare is having a board with two or three former CEOs thereon! Can you imagine the number of digressions that take place when these battle-scarred veterans get together, in or out of the boardroom?

Lear failed to take his own advice, retiring at the age of 60 from F. & M. Schaefer Co., only to sit on its board. He says he saw the move at the time as an endorsement of the new CEO. But "now, with the wisdom of age, I think that I would have contributed more if I had resigned."

Look at succession this way: there are a number of business issues too important not to be fun, and the question of management succession should top this list.

After all, what can be more important than identifying and grooming a company's future leaders? Who will run the company 10 years from now? Or, who's ready to step up if ill fortune befalls the CEO the day after tomorrow? And, what is more rewarding than encouraging talented people or watching outstanding managers develop? It's a rare company that handles this issue in the thoughtful, logical manner it deserves.

You would think that the chief executive and directors of large, publicly held companies would keep this question at the top of the agenda. Seldom is it so. Witness the watchful unease of financial analysts fretting over the abilities of potential successors, or the well-publicized entrances and contentious exits of certain executives, or a company's scramble to reorganize when fate intervenes.

Passing The Family Baton

But the fun—and the tragedy, too—is more evident in family-owned companies, where the baton is passed to the next generation as a "right" of ownership. Often the anointed candidate must wait until the founder relinquishes leadership.

I'll never forget one company whose president died at the age of 99. At that point, his son, a mere 68, had to take over— ready or not! This new president had learned something while he was waiting in the wings. He very quickly turned the reins over to his son, and the third generation is now effectively leading this upstate New York company.

If there is both a son and son-in-law in the business, things get even more interesting. No matter that the son can't find his way through the plant without a map; he'll always be higher on the organizational chart than the son-in-law, right up to the day he takes over the front office. Now that we are in an era of competent and competitive female executives, it's interesting to speculate on the future of daughters-in-law.

The tension is worse in second- and third-generation families. Competing factions pit one offspring against another. We all know of examples where the fight was never resolved. Ultimately, the company is sold, most likely to the detriment of the community, the family, the employees, and the customers. Unplanned succession can have far-reaching effects.

A good example involves a long-time friend in Kentucky. His father died approximately 25 years ago while he was in the Army, and he returned to the family lumber business immediately after being discharged.

"I'd worked there as a kid, getting splinters every summer in the warehouse, for two bucks an hour," he remembers. "I went to college and then was drafted. Then, the business was just dropped in my lap. I had a marketing degree but no experience. I wish some sort of contingency plan had been in place. Someone should have been appointed to run things while I got experience somewhere.

"Anyway, I played catchup for a couple of years, and my only sister reached adulthood. She wanted to sell everything, and I was 25 or 26, working so many hours I didn't even have time for dates. In fact, the company had St. Louis Cardinals season tickets, and I never saw a game. Not one. So when she proposed to split everything, I said fine.

"We sold the business to responsible people, and all I did was sell real estate part time for a year—there was a recession at the time, and nothing looked very good. I finally bought the [county-seat, twice-weekly newspaper] and found that I'd learned a lot in the lumber business that I could apply at the paper. I'm sure I could as easily have learned a lot at the newspaper that I could have applied at the family store. But it didn't work out that way.

"Sometimes, I wish I'd been able to take an interest in my father's business before it was handed to me. Or that I could have found someone inside or outside the company to run things while I got up to speed."

The former lumber company president and current publisher has been extremely successful in the business he bought. His sales and negotiating abilities keep his presses running day and night. But he'll always wonder if he would have enjoyed himself even more in the family business.

Non-family Employees

Non-family employees are usually tremendously loyal, not only to the company but also to the person who hired or mentored them along the way. That gives them an intense personal stake in the progress of candidates. If their mentor fails, their job security goes out the window. There are assets and liabilities in being anybody's protégé, even when the mentor appears to be a shoo-in to run the company.

On the other hand, employees often want certain family members to win, and can go to unusual—sometimes destructive—lengths to help them. And if it's a question of opposing family candidates, the work force will line up behind favorites. Productivity and profitability take second place to internal intrigue.

There are some good ways to solve the question of leadership succession in a family company. One top manager and a wonderful teacher of business skills developed a hard and fast—and successful—rule for his company. Any employee's child, while in college, was eligible for summer employment. However, after graduation, no employee's child would be hired without earning five years of experience outside the company.

This man had three talented children, and each had to follow his rule. Today, all are happily ensconced as top officers of three different New York Stock Exchange companies. They found that the outside world offered more opportunity and satisfaction than returning to the family fold. The company is now being led by a professional manager, and the owner's descendants are enjoying the rewards of that manager's success as well as their own.

There are a number of effective practices I've observed in family-owned businesses....

First, insist that children have outside work experience before joining the company. It lets individuals learn what business is all about in environments that offer no special family protection. They develop appropriate work habits, recognize the need for accountability and control, and learn the organizational and cultural nuances that make a company work.

They can't achieve this learning experience in a protected environment as the "boss's kid." If these children return to the roost, each brings a track record and new knowledge and experience that benefit the whole company.

Second, family members must know that more is expected of them than other employees. They have to work better, smarter, and harder. Working long hours, developing thoughtful and considerate relationships with fellow workers, cutting off attempts at favoritism from other employees, and demanding more of themselves will generate loyalty and goodwill that become important corporate strengths as they become leaders.

Third, give the family member responsibility just as fast as it can be assimilated. Fellow employees will know that this person will some day be running the company. They won't resent advancement, which is seen as training for the ultimate position, particularly when measurable contributions are being made along the way.

Conversely, if the candidate drops the ball and doesn't perform to expectations, take appropriate action promptly— but not publicly.

Fourth, select only one family member to join the company, and be sure that person is competent and enthusiastic about the business.

When no family member is an appropriate choice (or available), identify a candidate internally or hire a potential successor. Give this person every opportunity to be great. An "outsider," when given the top job, should be rewarded with the incentives of ownership through stock, to be sold back to the company upon retirement, or through some sort of phantom stock.

Finally, provide for a system of transition with the current chief executive officer.

A Smooth Transition

In one of the best examples I know, the transition worked beautifully when a president was appointed at age 31. His career path was clearly defined and accepted by others within the company.

Initially, only two departments were assigned to him. Over the next five years, he was given additional responsibilities, department by department. At the end of his fifth year, everyone reported to him, and the transition to CEO was complete.

If you're young and about to take the helm of a company yourself, consider the following prudent steps:

• Put leadership succession on the agenda of the first board meeting you call. It should remain an agenda item until the question is resolved to the satisfaction of you and the board.

• If the board is reticent about the subject, appoint a small committee of board members to study succession and make recommendations.

• If the subject appears more difficult, touchy, or divisive than you had imagined it would be, consider appointing a third party to make succession recommendations. There are management consultants who have served you well in other areas and may have experience here. They may have worked with a dark horse employee you and the board have overlooked.

• Once there is board consensus on how the succession will unfold, run the protocol past not only the in-house legal department but an independent law office. Nothing can damage a company—from the cash register to the executive suite—more than a fight for control, particularly if it goes public in the courts. Head it off before it happens.

• Put in place mechanisms that will make the agreed-upon rules of succession difficult to undo. Make the rules hinge on principles rather than people, since people can run off with much younger companions or have automobile accidents or just plain drop the ball.

• If yours is a family-owned business, and if you are grooming a non-family president, it's crucial to separate the holdings of the family from the holdings of the company. Failure to do this can wreck both. Don't ever assume family members won't want their share, in cash, at a moment's notice.

Management succession is so critical that it deserves to be on the top of every CEO's agenda. And the time to begin planning for it is the day one becomes chief executive officer.

This is particularly crucial in the family company, as we have seen. The owner is dealing with emotional issues—and with the future of both business and children. Many of us don't stop to ask whether our offspring have made it clear that they really want to join the company.

Whose Decision Is It?

Have we, without asking, made a decision rightfully theirs? Is it fair to demand they devote their lives to the family company when there are other fields open? If they're forced into the business, will they take advantage of a situation and coast? How is it possible to be sure it's a real win-win situation for parents, children, and company? These are all tough questions.

The time to begin working on the answer to succession is as early as possible—in an atmosphere of openness and candor. It means bringing all parties concerned into the discussion—your management team, the children, and any close or extended-family partners. Remember—the likelihood of your business interests and those of your children being identical is comparable to sharing the same hobbies or favorite books or television shows.

The competence of the future head of your business will affect many lives. It goes far beyond family to employees, customers, suppliers, and community. Thoughtful consideration will protect these "stakeholders" and continue the return on the investment built up over the best and most exciting years of your life.

Key Points:

○ Having the retired CEO on the board may hinder objectivity and free-flowing interchange.

○ Identifying and grooming a company's future leaders are key priorities that companies often overlook. Management succession must be at the top of the CEO's agenda.

○ Unplanned succession can have far-reaching and detrimental effects. Put mechanisms in place to make agreed-upon rules of succession hard to undo.

○ Before joining a family company, children should gain outside work experience and knowledge in an environment offering no special family protection.

○ More is expected of family members than other employees. They must work better, smarter, and harder.

○ Give family members responsibility as fast as they can assimilate it. If they don't meet expectations, take action promptly but not publicly.

○ All parties concerned with succession—your management team, children, and close or extended-family partners—should be brought into the discussions as early as possible.

Chapter 31

As the Frenchman said: What comes around, goes around. Only in the century ahead, it will be moving much faster.

There's nothing like sitting in a concert hall and listening to your local symphony perform the great works of the 17th and 18th Centuries with style, vigor and enthusiasm. It's a little more difficult to sit in that same seat and hear the often strange, dissonant melodies associated with "modern music." But if you listen very carefully, it can be interesting.

It's equally interesting to stand behind my son who with his six-year-old daughter is composing a modern "masterpiece" on their home computer. They call upon the strings, the French horn and the percussion instruments, fitting pieces together with procedures and techniques that are difficult to understand. Then they play it back and it all miraculously comes together…for better or worse.

Speaking of computers, I recently was treated to the lyrics of a corporate president who was about to make a decision on the kind of new computing system her growing company would need. To give herself some perspective, she read a computer history that began with the abacus and ended with an invitation to step into the next century.

"You know," she said, "computers weren't really all that capable at first. They could accept and store and retrieve knowledge, but until they were given the ability to use the knowledge they had been fed to solve other problems, they were very limited. But you should see them now. It's tempting to keep waiting to make the purchase, because prices are on a downward spiral. All the while, functions multiply and capacity increases."

This woman, whom I'll call Linda, was giving me the electronic version of a conversation I'd had with her a few years earlier. I had spotted her as a rising star at a seminar—someone whose ability to concentrate let her shut out extraneous matters and reach solutions.

As I recall, I asked her what she liked most about running a corporation so new the reception area still smelled of paint. Did she enjoy being her own boss after working for and learning from others? Did she like evaluating competing options and allocating assets to support her decision? Or did she most enjoy writing plans and then presenting them successfully to her investment banker? Her answer surprised me.

"I like sittin' and thinkin' and schemin'," she told me, clipping each word with a smile. "I've always enjoyed that. And now that I have officers and a board, I like sittin' and thinkin' and schemin' with them even more. It's as if we're all in cahoots. Stated another way, one of our board members compared what we do to the way a dog walks. Have you ever noticed? A dog kind of lopes down the sidewalk, equally ready to go forward, sideways, or at an oblique angle. We're the same way—I try to keep it all flexible so that we're ready to head in any direction at a moment's notice."

Linda may not know it, but she and her people are as prepared for the start of the new century as any of us. She isn't concerned about the product her company currently produces because the firm can switch products faster than anyone a few years ago could have imagined. She also knows that the basic, underlying principles apply, whether the calendar says 1980, 1995 or 2010.

An Eye On Tradition

Those principles rely on proven and tested traditions, including how you treat people, concern for your customers, commitment to quality and dedication to ethical standards. They all come together to deliver a successful result. I don't see these core principles changing one iota as we gear up for the new century. Many of the principles that worked well in the past will continue to work for many, many years. Let's not lose sight of what got us here as we struggle to understand the latest "jingoism" that floats through the business community.

At the same time, tremendous changes are exploding around us, not only in business but also in society as a whole, the political process, religion and family values. These changes challenge many of our philosophical principles. Compare how people think and live today with just 20 or 30 years ago—a very short time in the nation's history and the blink of an eye in the history of civilization.

For those of us in business, it is disturbing to see the confusion and undermining of many basic principles that have been important to us. We are living in a time of change and chaos throughout society. Managing a business through this dichotomy is going to require great skill until the settling in of what will become a new management age. If you thrive on chaos, you will probably do all right during this process.

Don't look for solutions to problems overnight. There will be no revolution. We can expect 15, 20, or even 30 years of confusion before a more consistent pattern begins to emerge. At times, we will all feel trapped and left behind. At other times we'll be very grateful we didn't try to leap ahead too fast.

Many of the old ways of doing things will no longer work. We can see it in the demand for faster "throughput." New technologies permit over 100 inventory turns a year when less than a decade ago a rate of three or four turns was considered good. The information age will make a great difference in how we do business. Let's use information as a tool and not as a substitute for the human touch in our relationships, creativity and entrepreneurship.

Times will be both exciting and frightening. We must be careful not to get too far out front or we may take a wrong fork in the road. At the same time, we will want to keep focused on the big picture, travel worldwide to learn, talk constantly with customers and peers, and carefully screen and categorize the information we are gathering.

As for being out front, the advantages of thoughtful innovation are well covered in an intriguing new book from the Harvard Business School Press. Gary Hamel and C.K. Prahalad have written *Competing for the Future,* subtitled "Breakthrough strategies for seizing control of your industry and creating the markets of tomorrow." They move across a great deal of ground, and among their better observations is this: "For us, top management's primary task is reinventing industries and regenerating strategy…."

Creating The Future

To create the future, say the authors, "a company must 1) change in some fundamental way the rules of engagement in a longstanding industry, 2) redraw the boundary lines between industries, and/or 3) create entirely new industries."

Competing for the Future is chock full of examples of companies that have created—or recreated—their futures. It's wonderful reading. The cautionary note I would offer is to beware of the tendency to veer excessively from one's mission. If, for example, you make muffin pans and research says your customers are females over the age of 40, how much time should be spent envisioning different customers and figuring how to sell them muffin pans? What will it take to peddle a pan to a 17-year-old boy who loves skateboarding and has an annual income of $800 from a part-time job? Unless kids find some faddish use for your product, it will be better to focus on your present market and improve share. Another option is to seek incremental gains among persons who more closely fit the right demographics. Still another is to use your manufacturing, design and marketing skills to develop new products.

As a leader in your organization, you should be seen as strong, exuding confidence and inspiration while staying very close to your people. You can't explain what's happening in calm, analytical terms. Some things defy such descriptions. Still, people will depend on you for guidance and reassurance.

You will want to show your people that the future will be different and that changes are occurring. Support their learning experiences. Communicate with a passion so they understand your thoughts. Listen carefully to theirs.

Today's executives don't insist, "Here's how we should do it." Instead they ask, "How do you think it should be done?" Your acumen is vital in the board room or for your strategic planning meetings, but on the production floor there are workers' thoughts that need airing and voices that long to speak up. They need to be given the chance.

There are many ways of looking at things. Roger Penske, the 57-year-old businessman who has created a vehicular empire in engine manufacturing and truck leasing (which also allows him to make money and have fun in auto racing), is a prime example of a person whose mind has no walls—a forceful executive who is nevertheless willing to listen to the least among his employees. Penske frequently acquires an ill-operated company, listens to what his new employees have to say, and turns, too, to related companies. "Let's pool our thoughts and we'll all make more money," Penske tells such organizations.

For example, he purchased a controlling interest in Detroit Diesel from General Motors a few years ago. This manufacturer of diesel truck engines was in a woeful state— the organization was top-heavy, the unions were stubborn, the products weren't state-of-the-art and market share was headed south. Penske and Mercedes-Benz, a major builder of diesel vehicle engines, got together and M-B now owns a piece of Detroit Diesel. We can expect better engines from both firms, thanks to this meeting of minds. Penske and Mercedes also own Ilmor, an English firm that makes exotic auto racing engines. A discovery today for the race track may show up in a U.S. or German truck tomorrow.

Collaboration need not always depend on the present tense. As this book is going to press, the concept of interactive television is still several years away. Yet major players such as AT&T and Microsoft are experimenting and even pooling their technology to create the hardware and software necessary to make the product a reality. Better to share the future than to be shut out of it. Better a modest slice of a sumptuous pie than watching the competition feast. Others who have joined forces recently with an eye on the future include America's "big three" automakers and the Japanese firms of Matsushita and Sony.

More and more, we see maverick nonconformists providing creativity and innovation in products and services—and making a lot of money along the way. This has been happening for quite some time, as the following anecdote indicates. Leo Burnett, the legendary ad man, was moving between the floors of his agency on an elevator when it stopped at the copywriters' floor. The door opened and in stepped two fellows who were wearing so much leather they looked as if they'd taken the hide off a couch. Their hair was long and braided, one sported a tattoo, the other jangly earrings. The pair got off at the next stop, the elevator continued its trip and Burnett said, to no one in particular, "Well, they'd better be good."

Such people can play an important role. They may know a progressive, growing market like no one else. Your skills and patience in handling these individuals will be tried at times. You may have to throw away the rule book to make the relationship work. That's okay. Such people can really make a difference. Nothing succeeds amid a flock of clones like a renegade.

Continuity of innovative thought keeps the pioneers in an industry out front. How else to explain the problems of Firestone or General Motors or IBM or International Harvester? Lesser lights have taken on these giants and beaten them, not by unfair competition, as the pioneers might have you believe, but by refreshing approaches to the market. Toshiba, for example, was determined to be a major player in the laptop computer market. During the period 1986 through 1990, they offered 31 different models, with seven different types of displays, at prices ranging from $999 to $9,499. Not all models were successes, but failures merely meant the rapid introductions of successors. Is it any wonder that Toshiba, which did not invent the laptop, has an enviable market share? Also, it's refreshing and encouraging to see the comeback of both GM and IBM.

Complicated Lives

There will be more and more clutter in people's lives, with hundreds of television channels and instant communication anywhere in the world—resulting at times in a harried and frenetic pace. Don't let your people become bogged down in the minutiae of procedures or disc-operating systems or new wrinkles to spreadsheets. Turn back to our chapters on leadership and remember how people look up to you. They'll be watching you for signs of uncertainty or even panic. Here's where you will be a stabilizing force, thoughtfully leading while utilizing only the tools that work for you.

One of the great things that will happen is the response you get by having high expectations of your people. The performance of most will surprise and delight you. The talented young people of today have tremendous analytical skills and know how to use data. They need you to make it impact the business in a practical way.

No one will expect you to be an expert on every subject. You will want to stay alert and learn, recognizing that you are on a journey that requires refocusing and changes of course from time to time.

It's going to be a great journey. The world is your market. Your key people will be better trained, with higher expectations for themselves and for you. At times along the way, you're going to get off the road and bounce along on the shoulder. When you do, make those slight course corrections to get back on the highway to success.

As the journey continues, remember that your business, like the road you travel, is built on a firm foundation. Those principles have brought you far. They represent your very essence and are responsible for what you have created. Never lose sight of them.

Good luck and have fun.

Suggested Business Reading

Blanchard, Kenneth and Spencer Johnson, *The One Minute Manager.* New York: William Morrow & Co., 1982.

Covey, Stephen, *Seven Habits of Highly Effective People.* New York: Simon and Schuster, 1990.

Drucker, Peter F., *Management: Tasks-Responsibilities-Practices.* New York: Harper & Row, 1974.

Drucker, Peter F., *Managing in Turbulent Times.* New York: Harper & Row. 1980.

Kanter, Rosabeth Moss, *The Change Masters.* New York: Simon and Schuster, 1983.

Peters, Tom, *Thriving on Chaos.* New York: Alfred A. Knopf, 1987.

Peters, R.T. and R.H. Waterman, *In Search of Excellence.* New York: Harper & Row, 1980.

Porter, Michael, *The Competitive Advantage of Nations.* New York: The Free Press, 1985.

Steiner, George A., *Top Management Planning.* New York: Macmillan & Co., 1969.

Other Worthwhile Reading

Burroughs, Bryan and John Helyar, *Barbarians at the Gate.* New York: Harper & Row, 1990.

Danco, Leon A., *Beyond Survival.* Cleveland: The University Press, 1979.

Dixit, Avinash K. and Barry Nalebuff, *Thinking Strategically.* New York: Norton, 1991.

Drucker, Peter F., *The Unseen Revolution.* New York: Harper & Row, 1976.

Goodman, Stanley J., *How to Manage a Turnaround.* New York: The Free Press. 1982.

Hickman, Craig R. and Michael A. Silva, *Creating Excellence.* New York: New American Library, 1984.

Lear, Robert W., *How to Turn Your MBA into a CEO*. New York: Macmillan, 1987.

Levitt, Theodore, *The Marketing Imagination*. New York: Free Press, 1983.

McCormack, Mark, *What They Don't Teach You at the Harvard Business School*. New York, Bantam Books, 1984.

Naisbitt, John and Patricia Aburdene, *Reinventing the Corporation*. New York: Warner Books, 1985.

Nanns, Burt, *Visionary Leadership*. San Francisco: Jossey Bass, 1992.

Petersen, Donald E. and John Hillkirk, *A Better Idea*. Boston: Houghton-Mifflin, 1991.

Porter, Michael E., *Competitive Strategy*. New York: The Free Press, 1980.

Sloma, Richard, *No Nonsense Management*. New York: Macmillan, 1977.

Suzaki, Hiroshi, *The New Manufacturing Challenge*. New York: The Free Press, 1987.

Thurow, Lester, *Head to Head*. New York: William Morrow and Co., 1992.

Townsend, Robert, *Further Up the Organization*. New York: Albert Knopf, 1984.

Tschohl, John, *Achieving Excellence Through Customer Service*. Englewood Cliffs: Prentice Hall, 1991.

Waterman, Robert Jr., *The Renewal Factor*. New York: Bantam Books, 1987.

Yavitz, Boris and William H. Newman, *Strategy in Action*. New York: The Free Press, 1987.

Zemke, Ron, *The Service Edge,* New York: New American Library, 1989.